THE APOCALYPTIC GOSPEL

Connie,
Thank you for your friendship & support. May the light of the Son illuminate your soul.

THE APOCRYPHILE PRESS
Berkeley, CA
www.apocryphile.org

ISBN: 978-1-944769-17-8

THE APOCALYPTIC GOSPEL

MYSTERY, REVELATION, AND COMMON SENSE

BY JUSTIN MARK STALLER

DEDICATION

This book is dedicated to the church.
May it please my Lord.

THE POEM OF BEDE THE PRIEST

Translated by Edward Marshall

An exile from the busy haunts of men,
Forbidden now to see his country's soil,
He—the Beloved John—to heaven triumphant soars,
And joins the choir around the King enthroned on high.

His sacred eye surveys the world below,
As over its waters pass the fleeting ships.
Babel and Jerusalem, in conflict, join their several hosts
In quick succession: here they turn in flight,
And there the strife renew.

The white-robed soldier of the gentle Lamb
May with his leader gain the realms of joy.
But the scaly Serpent in the dark abyss
Overwhelms—in hunger, flame, and pestilence—
His gathering hordes.

Desiring to unfold this warfare's dread form,
Its art, its numbers, its rewards,
I wandered through the sacred plains,
Where those of old have sown,
Collecting thence some fruits—but few,
So that profuseness will not cause them to loathe the feast,
Nor forbid the weaker guest from attempting too great a preparation.

And now, if these my scanty morsels please thy taste,
Give praise to God, Who reigns above the skies.
Or else accept a friendly heart's intent,
And, armed with pumice, this my verse erase.

From the early eighth-century commentary on John's Apocalypse by Bede, the venerable "Father of the Footnote." This rendering adapted from Edward Marshall, *The Explanation of the Apocalypse* (Oxford: James Parker and Co., 1878), 10. See also Faith Wallis, "The Poem of Bede the Priest," in *Bede: Commentary on Revelation* (Cambridge: Liverpool University Press, 2013), 99.

TABLE OF CONTENTS

ACKNOWLEDGEMENTS

Regarding the production of this work, there are so very many people to acknowledge that I scarcely know where to start. My former employer, Norman, first funded my education in the trades, and then—when it became abundantly obvious that my strengths must lie elsewhere—encouraged me to depart from the field of carpentry and reenter the world of higher education. He has remained an important source of encouragement, and his was the Rosetta Stone comparison you will find buried somewhere in the book below. My wife has been very patient and supportive as I have pursued my goals; Kathryn left her own dream job as an auto mechanic and found employment as an office manager so that I could go back to school. My father, a pastor and professor, was kind enough to look at my first exegetical work on Revelation—filled with half-formed, half-baked theories which I pray never see the light of day—and to gently redirect my attention to a short work called *The Theology of the Book of Revelation*. "Something a little more like this," he said. Good call, Dad.

I am blessed to have been raised by devout parents in an American, Protestant, fundamentalist, evangelical, Pentecostal, holiness church, and I passed through the care of several fine pastors associated with the wider organization who instilled in me a desire to serve the Lord: to do rightly, to love kindness, and to walk humbly with my God. (Thank you, Bill.) Although I have grown apart in many ways from the faith of my childhood, I will be forever grateful for the careful, sincere training and instruction I therein received, and for that family of saints I still claim as my very own. May the Lord bless you and keep you.

For a time I found a digital niche within the Christian Classics Ethereal Library (www.ccel.org), a free online library containing thousands of classic works of Christian literature, collected from out of the centuries and now hosted by Calvin College. I was a very young Christian when I first connected with its open forums, and matured substantially through my contact with saints from all over the world who had come to examine the great works of the Christian past. I was privileged to be involved in several online discussion groups therein hosted, where I was first exposed to the substance of a more catholic faith. An idea or two developed out of those online groups—concerning John's Gospel and also concerning Revelation—have found their respective ways into this book, but some have fallen by the wayside. I would like to thank Robert, Michael, Dan, Maria, Tom, Noshi, Mike, the CCEL staff, and several others for putting up with me, and for increasing my Christian maturity.

Academically, I have been privileged to attend very fine institutions. It was at the University of California, Berkeley that I first submitted an undergraduate honors thesis to Dr. Daniel Boyarin regarding an alternative hermeneutical approach to John's Apocalypse. His encouragement was a godsend, and much of what is herein presented has been developed out of that early academic effort. Subsequently, I was privileged to attend the Graduate Theological Union as I studied the requisite Hebrew and Greek, and several sections of this book contain bits and pieces of papers and posts submitted to the exceptional faculty of the GTU, especially at the Pacific School of Religion, the Dominican School of Philosophy and Theology, and the Jesuit School of Theology. Without the robust and demanding programs of the Union, and without its interdenominational, multicultural atmosphere, this would indeed be a very different book, or no book at all. It is my hope that I will be able to further pursue this work as I continue my doctoral studies in Christian Spirituality at the GTU.

I would like to thank two people especially in connection with the publication of this book. Dr. Jim Lawrence at PSR has been to me a true teacher, friend, and mentor, and provided both practical advice and emotional support as I drafted *The Apocalyptic Gospel*. I am also immensely grateful to Rev. John Mabry at the Apocryphile Press for his good-humored patience as I have continued to tinker with the final draft, as well as for his many valuable insights into the brave new world of publication. The inevitable shortcomings of this volume must, I fear, be laid at my feet, and not theirs.

Finally, I would like to acknowledge and thank the many fine scholars, interpreters, and exegetes that I have relied upon, engaged, or otherwise cited. I have taken painstaking care to give credit where credit is due, and then some. In no particular order, several of these are: David Aune, David Barr, Richard Bauckham, George Beasley-Murray, Daniel Boyarin, Raymond E. Brown, George B. Caird, Adela Yarbro Collins, John J. Collins, Robert D. Daly, Charles H. Dodd, Elisabeth Schüssler Fiorenza, David Frankfurter, Hank Hanegraaff, Philip A. Harland, John Paul Heil, Matthias Reinhard Hoffmann, Richard Horsley, J. Nelson Kraybill, Bryan Kromholtz, James Kugel, Dorothy Lee, Burton L. Mack, Bernard McGinn, John Anthony McGuckin, Bruce M. Metzger, Francis J. Moloney, Candida R. Moss, Elaine Pagels, Frederick G. Smith, Huston Smith, Jonathan Z. Smith, Arthur W. Wainwright, Faith Wallis, William Weinrich, and N. T. Wright. I had to draw the line somewhere. Additional authors may be found in the bibliography. As I hope is obvious, my occasional citation of these authorities does not signal an unconditional endorsement of all their methods or conclusions, neither their endorsement of my various proposals. Thank you all.

All translations of the scriptures, unless otherwise noted, are my own, and are generally based on NA28 and UBS4.

INTRODUCTION

Frederick George Smith (1880-1947) was a devout student of Revelation from a previous generation. His conclusions were very different from mine. But his prefatory notes relate much of what I must say with a grace much greater than my own:

> "In the preparation for this work, I have gleaned historical information from all the general and ecclesiastical histories, encyclopedias, etc., within my reach, and only regret that I had not access to a still greater number. However, knowing that large books are seldom read, I determined in advance not to write an extensive work, but to condense the subject matter as much as possible, and therefore, I have been obliged to omit much valuable material previously gathered. For this reason many lines of prophetic truth penned by others of the sacred writers have been passed over in silence, even though relating to the same events as certain symbolic visions in the Revelation.
>
> I have availed myself of all the helps and the commentaries within my reach in the study of this important subject. However, I have but seldom referred to the opinions of expositors. In most cases their explanations are not based upon any established rule of interpretation, and the definite laws of symbolic language are usually overlooked or disregarded. Ordinary readers of the Revelation have always supposed that the only course for them was to take the opinion of some learned expositor and to believe on his authority; and when they have found that equally learned and judicious men sustained the most opposite views, they have been bewildered amid conflicting opinions and have decided that, when such men were at issue, it was useless for them to investigate. While, therefore, I have made every available use of their opinions, it was only for the purpose of forming my

> own and of enabling myself so to unfold the nature of the symbols that every one might see for himself the propriety of the interpretation given.
>
> The present knowledge that has been attained of this prophetic book is largely the result of the combined efforts of all who have labored to unfold its meaning. No one has had the honor of first understanding all its parts, and very few have failed to contribute something, more or less, to its true interpretation. Therefore I have endeavored as much as possible to gather up the good from the labors of my predecessors and to combine it with the results of my own study and research."
>
> —F. G. Smith, *The Revelation Explained*, 7-8

But I will add a few things. When I began drafting this book, I was determined to keep the footnotes to a minimum. This was a decision born from my own frustration with scholars who would use footnotes to excuse themselves from clarification.[1] But, upon the insistence of my instructors and editors, I have decided to include more-extensive footnotes, especially where men and women much smarter than myself have said things similar or dissimilar to what I suggest—so that you, dear reader, can make your own decisions. Accordingly, I have (in most but not all instances) included actual words written by actual scholars, and not the citation only, so that you can access pertinent information not only eventually, but immediately, if that is your desire. If that is not your desire, do not worry—I have endeavored to write in such a style as makes checking the footnotes unnecessary, for those brave souls willing to take my word for it. But you should probably check the footnotes anyway.

In writing, I have aimed at a broad audience; scholars and specialists were something of an afterthought. My goal is to get through the forest, so I have not stopped to inspect every tree—though one in

1 For further information on the unlikely and provocative thing I just represented as common fact, cf Currant Lee Outhoffprint, in *A Book to Which You Don't Have Access* (Fringe: Merda Press, 1912), 13-798.

particular demands our attention. In this spirit, I have not attempted to exhaust every puzzle, or to resolve every question, or to critique every errant opinion (of which there are many), or to acknowledge every controversy, or to explain every symbol, or to display a mastery of some subject, or to nuance each point, or to sift through and analyze every hermeneutical option. If that is your interest, I highly recommend G. K. Beale's *New International Greek Testament Commentary: The Book of Revelation,* and also David Aune's three volume *Word Commentary* on the same subject, though these are substantially longer and cost a little more. Alternatively, I have condensed about ten years of research—and a lifetime of interest—into what I hope is a short, easy-to-read volume, one that is the beginning, and not the end, of a new exegetical adventure for the whosoever will.

Furthermore—and this is important; I don't want you to waste your time—there are certain things you *will not* find in the following pages. Within, there are no theories about when Christ will return, no thoughts about what to expect at the world's end, no forecasts about the rise of some impending Antichrist or his evil, global machinations, no attempt to induce popular panic for profit. Those kinds of predictive prognostications belong to a different class of exegesis.

What you *will* find in this book is an attempt to look at the book of Revelation with fresh eyes, and to examine its mysteries in light of the evangelical proclamation of a crucified Christ that is front-and-center in the rest of the New Testament. The end result is an analysis that often cuts against the grain of longstanding academic assumptions and conclusions regarding the book of Revelation, the gospels, and the formation of the Christian canon. It also, on occasion, runs contrary to traditions cherished within certain quarters of the church. If this sounds alarming, my advice is to heed my words of warning, which I offer with the utmost sincerity, and to turn back now. Pay no attention to the man behind the curtain.

Finally, this has not been, for me, a mere game or an idle academic question, but a question of identity, and of truth, and of God. I am no mystic, nor preacher, nor priest, nor pastor of souls. But I am a

Christian. I didn't expect it to turn out like that. To do what I have herein done, I had to release many things that were dear and precious to me. And remarkably, some of these returned, and will remain with me forever. I do not expect you to become or remain a Christian based on what I tell you. This is not that kind of book. (Sincerely: make your own decisions.) But if you embrace the faith, now or later, it is my prayer that you will also embrace me as your brother.

1.1 DISCLAIMERS AND WARNINGS

> *And they brought to him children, that he might touch them, but the disciples rebuked them. And seeing this, Jesus was indignant, and said to them, "Permit the children to come to me. Do not hinder them—for of such is the kingdom of God. Amen, I say to you, whosoever does not receive the kingdom of God like a child will not enter therein." And hugging them, he blessed them, laying his hands upon them (Mark 10.13-16).*

If, in your estimation, the book of Revelation is a strange and intimidating text, you are in good company. Revelation is difficult, the occasion of both fascination and frustration for a wide body of Christians. Though many are not quite sure what treatment the book should receive, others are confident that the Revelation of John contains prophecies predicting the cataclysmic end of our world, at some near or distant moment, and the birth of another. If you've ever heard of the *Left Behind* series or read *The Late Great Planet Earth*, you've been exposed to this type of popular interpretation of John's Apocalypse.[1]

Other readers are not so sure that John intended to predict a distant future, given that the book implies a sense of immediate relevance for the first generation of Christians that received its visions (Rev 1.1,

1 Tim LaHaye and Jerry B. Jenkins, *Left Behind: A Novel of the Earth's Last Days* (Carol Stream: Tyndale, 1995); Hal Lindsey, *The Late Great Planet Earth* (Grand Rapids: Zondervan Publishing House, 1970); Stan Campbell and James S. Bell Jr., *The Complete Idiot's Guide to the Book of Revelation* (Indianapolis: Alpha Books, 2002), 276-290, 5374-5396/6636 (ebook locations).

2.16, 3.11, 22.6-7, 12, 20). In a valiant effort, biblical scholarship has, in recent decades, been therefore appropriately eager to resurrect the "real" meaning of John's Revelation by exposing the social and historical situation in which the book was originally published. If, for example, you've ever heard a scholar assert that Revelation is really about the notorious Roman emperors Nero or Domitian,[2] or that it refers in part to the volcanic eruption of Mt. Vesuvius and the destruction of Pompeii in 79 CE,[3] you've been exposed to this school of thought.

A few interpret Revelation as a story with no secret or hidden meaning at all. Rather, they read it as an entirely allegorical vision, having no significant historical referent.[4] While at least this approach recognizes the presence of allegory in the Apocalypse, it neglects the precedent of Daniel, a book with a noteworthy presence in the Revelator's work, containing apocalyptic visions that require knowledge of, and sympathy towards, certain historical events from any would-be interpreter.[5] John's Revelation of course contains symbolic stories that explore the conflict between good and evil, and yet both books—Daniel and Revelation—belong to similar categories of literature, depicting what might be called "historical" events in prophetic, allegorical language.[6] In both books, readers must supply for themselves the historical pieces of the puzzle, or risk misunderstanding the text.

---

2 i.e., "John's contemporaries would have known that here he refers to an emperor, and some probably would have guessed the emperor Nero, who reigned from 54 to 68 C.E. and was rumored to have been killed by his own sword, although many believed that he had survived." Elaine Pagels, *Revelations: Visions, Prophecy, & Politics in the Book of Revelation* (New York: Viking, 2012), 32.

3 "As we noted, his vision of a great mountain exploding reflects the eruption of Vesuvius in 79 C.E. The dragon's seven heads suggests the emperors of the Julio-Claudian dynasty, as "the number of the beast" may allude to the hidden name of Nero." Pagels, *Revelations*, 33.

4 "The Idealist view, which is often closely allied with the Preterist school, considers Revelation to be only a symbolic picture of the enduring struggle between good and evil, and between Christianity and paganism. It holds that its symbols cannot be identified as historic events either in the past or in the future; they are simply trends or ideals." Merril C. Tenney, *New Testament Survey*, ed. Walter M. Dunnett (Grand Rapids: InterVarsity Press, 1953-1961), 386.

5 cf Daniel 7-12, Revelation 4-22

6 ""HISTORICAL" APOCALYSE (Apokalypse bezüglich der Geschichte). A subgenre of apocalypse characterized by the lack of an otherworldly journey and the inclusion of an *ex eventu*

The aim of this book is to offer up, for your consideration, a specific historical narrative as the primary referent of Revelation's obscure images and cataclysmic events.

As with all strong medicine, a warning is in order: if you are unprepared, decoding John's Apocalypse may do you more harm than good. It was written to be difficult on purpose, as a safeguard against premature deployment. Once you begin to unearth the Mystery so carefully encrypted in this vault of the Christian religion, it may become difficult to escape its power. Knowledge thus acquired may prove disruptive to the practical continuity of your faith. Consult with appropriate specialists if further complications arise.

Furthermore, the book of Revelation is puzzle literature,[7] and one of its great rewards is the satisfaction of dawning comprehension, as strange things become unstrange, as the problematic pieces begin to fall into place. In this sense, reading Revelation is like undertaking a series of exercises; you might benefit from watching someone else demonstrate, but the real benefits are in the doing, not the watching. If you like puzzles, and prefer to solve them on your own power,

---

prophecy of history. The most typical form of revelation is the symbolic dream vision. The content typically includes an *ex eventu* prediction of the course of history, often divided into a set number of periods (periodization), followed by eschatological woes and upheavals which are signs of the end, judgment, and salvation. Apocalyptic eschatology, even in the "historical" apocalypses, typically involves the resurrection of the dead. The "historical" apocalypses are usually related to an historical crisis, e.g., the persecution of the Maccabean era or the fall of Jerusalem. Cf. Daniel 7-12; 1 Enoch 83-90; 4 Ezra; 2 Baruch." John J. Collins, *Daniel: With an Introduction to Apocalyptic Literature*, eds. Rolf Knierim and Gene M. Tucker (Grand Rapids: William B. Eerdmans Publishing Company, 1984), 1879/2057.

Note: Unless we qualify John's "in the spirit" account as a "symbolic dream vision," Revelation does include otherworldly journeys, contrary to the criteria which Collins doth propose, and so he might object to the classification of Revelation as an "historical" apocalypse. On the other hand Collins also acknowledges that it is impossible to neatly group most apocalypses based on so-called common characteristics, John J. Collins, *The Apocalyptic Imagination: An Introduction to Jewish Apocalyptic Literature* (Grand Rapids: William B. Eerdmans Publishing Company, 1998), 6-11.

7 Recent scholarship is starting to pick up on this frequency: "Mystery had become a special *topos* in apocalyptic discourse by the first century." Vernon K. Robbins, "The Intertexture of Apocalyptic Discourse in the Gospel of Mark," in *The Intertexture of Apocalyptic Discourse in the New Testament*, ed. Duane F. Watson (Atlanta: Society of Biblical Literature, 2002), 29. He may have in mind the complex "mystery" fixation represented in the Dead Sea Scrolls.

reading further may interrupt the maturing of your own faculties, and may undermine the natural course of your spiritual development. A supplemental regimen is advised.

1.2 A BOOK OF MYSTERIES

There are several moments throughout the New Testament, and also the Old, where biblical authors and characters intentionally choose to obscure what they really mean. Typically the logic behind this way of speaking is simple enough—one avoids saying the wrong thing to the wrong audience, or even the right thing at the wrong time. Parables, riddles, and mysteries are a convenient way to hide truth in plain sight, to spread your message at the right frequency, so that the right audience picks up your signals, while the wrong audience does not. The book of Revelation is one such message: broadcasted to many, fully received by a few. This is the way Revelation seems designed and intended to function.

Many find this notion unsettling, especially if they envision the Christian gospel as something that is always plainspoken in style and universal in scope.[8] While it is true that the gospel may be universal in scope, it is necessary to remember also that its earliest preachers—men like Jesus, Paul, and John—used parables and mysteries when they were appropriate to the audience and occasion. These were not always plain-speaking men.

Jesus, for example, is depicted in the gospels as frequently addressing the general public in parables, explaining his symbolic stories only to full-time students, those who had qualified for further training and were—under his careful supervision—learning to bait, hook, and reel in an audience (Mark 1.18). Perhaps the best example of this comes early in our earliest canonical gospel,[9] in a passage containing the par-

---

8 "Many suppose that this understanding of parable as dark mystery contradicts the purpose of Jesus' open, simple stories. F. Grant, who argues that Jesus' parables "were a device to aid his hearers' understanding, not prevent it," refers to [the gospel of] Mark's theory [of parables] as "perverse."" Bernard Brandon Scott, *Hear Then the Parable: A Commentary on the Parables of Jesus* (Minneapolis: Fortress, 1989), 22.

9 I assume Markan priority throughout, though some still argue that Matthew came first. Cf E. P. Sanders and M. Davies, *Studying the Synoptic Gospels* (London: SCM – Philadelphia: Trinity Press International, 1989), 51-119.

able of the Sower and the Seed (Mark 4.1-20). In this passage, Jesus tells of a sower who casts seeds on the ground, and describes the various conditions that prevent most of those seeds from growing up and bearing fruit. When his disciples privately express confusion over the meaning of this story, Jesus says to them, "Do you not understand this parable? How will you understand all parables?"(Mark 4.13).

The story of the Sower and the Seed helps explain a primary function of evangelical parables, and alerts the reader (or listener) to a special mode of interpretation that is fundamental to the evangelical genre. Throughout the gospels, Jesus is the sower, spreading his prophetic word throughout the land of Israel. His parables, his "mysteries of the kingdom," his hard sayings, are seeds which take root in the minds and hearts and souls of his listeners—some more successfully than others. There are, of course, people predisposed to reject his message without adequate consideration (Mark 4.4, 15). And some who listen are nevertheless shallow, not having the necessary depth to sustain growth (Mark 4.5, 16). Others are impeded by mundane circumstance, and don't give his doctrine the attention it requires (Mark 4.6, 19). An elect few, however, are correctly disposed and they, according to their various gifts and abilities, receive his message and run with it (Mark 4.7, 20).

The beauty of this parable is that it endures beyond the immediate historical situation of Jesus, who was preaching to Jews in Palestine during the first century. It remains relevant to any teacher of the gospel, and demonstrates the need for evangelical speakers—and writers—to choose their words carefully, to use metaphors and other rhetorical devices in order to sift through the chaff in search of the wheat.[10] This is an ideal method for someone in search of an audience that will not merely listen to a story, but which will also appreciate the point. When employing riddles and mysteries in this sense, the gospel preacher is finding out who is who—who gets it, and who does not (Mark 4.24-25).

---

10 "The parable for Mark is a secret bearer of the kingdom, and his Gospel's narrative is a hermeneutical context for the parables. Mark's Gospel not only proclaims the kingdom of God but is also like a parable a bearer of the kingdom." Scott, *Hear Then the Parable*, 55.

Jesus did not invent this way of extracting the right clientele from a mixed audience. Neither was he the first Jewish preacher and teacher to provide his disciples with symbolic puzzles that required their mental and spiritual attention (cf Prov 1.1-7). These facets or modes of biblical communication are in large part the consequence of an increasingly complex and diverse culture that began to emerge during Israel's post-exilic era, as Hellenism and Judaism started to freely intermix.[11]

Written perhaps one hundred years before the birth of Jesus, the Letter of Aristeas gives an account of the way the Hebrew scriptures were first translated into Greek, for the library of a foreign king. In this epistle, the high priest explains the presence of difficult, symbolic puzzles in the Jewish oracles through an analogy.[12] Eleazar teaches that puzzles exist in scripture so that we can mull them over, ponder them, and—like a calf ponderously chewing the cud—become stronger, more mature, transformed:[13]

---

11 "In the course of the Hellenistic period, even Jewish culture had been penetrated by Hellenic influences. The broad geographical dispersion of Jewish communities throughout the Mediterranean empire had accelerated this influence, reflected in later Jewish religious literature such as the Wisdom books, in the Septuagint and in the biblical scholarship of Alexandria, and in the Platonic religious philosophy of Philo. But with Christianity, and particularly with Paul's mission to expand its gospel beyond the confines of Judaism, the Judaic impulse in turn began a countervailing movement that radically transformed the Hellenic contribution to the Christian world view emerging in the later centuries of the classical era. The powerful currents of Greek metaphysics, epistemology, and science, the characteristic Greek attitudes toward myth, religion, philosophy, and personal fulfillment—all were transfigured in the light of the Judaeo-Christian revelation." Richard Tarnas, *The Passion of the Western Mind: Understanding the Ideas That Have Shaped Our World View* (New York: The Random House Publishing Group, 1991), 106.

12 "Eleazer himself, in accounting for the peculiar dietary restrictions of the Jews, explains them either as having a rational basis with the objective of practicing justice or as having symbolic value demanding allegorical interpretation. They aim at truth and serve as a mark of right reason. "Aristeas" has the High Priest speak like a Greek philosopher. The treatise plainly portrays cultivated Jews as comfortable in a Hellenic setting, attuned to Greek customs and modes of thought, and content under the protection of a Hellenistic monarch." Erich S. Gruen, *Heritage and Hellenism: The Reinvention of Jewish Tradition* (Berkeley and Los Angeles: University of California Press, 1998), 215.

13 *Letter of Aristeas*, 152-164, in R. H. Charles, "The Letter of Aristeas," in *Apocrypha and Pseudepigrapha of the Old Testament in English* (Oxford: The Clarendon Press, 1913), http://m.ccel.org/ccel/charles/otpseudepig/aristeas.htm (accessed March 2, 2014);

> He [the lawgiver, Moses] bids men also, when lying down to sleep and rising up again, to meditate upon the works of God, not only in word, but by observing distinctly the change and impression produced upon them, when they are going to sleep, and also their waking, how divine and incomprehensible the change from one of these states to the other is. The excellency of the analogy in regard to discrimination and memory has now been pointed out to you, according to our interpretation of "the cloven hoof and the chewing of the cud" (Letter of Aristeas, 160-161).

Certain passages are difficult and obscure, argues Eleazar, so that we can feast on them, dwelling on them and reviewing them over time, improving both our faculties and our character. Further, many of these puzzles are fully decipherable only to the "initiated," those who are given special knowledge by an insider regarding the spiritual meaning of the literal language.[14] In explaining Jewish dietary restrictions for a non-Jewish audience, Eleazar seems to be revealing a new dimension in them that is not plainly evident. A critic might argue that he is allegorizing scriptures that require no allegory. An apologist might counter that his was a valid way to make old scriptures relevant to a new situation, for an audience that had recently become attracted to the ancient oracles of the Jews, but was not obligated to observe them—an audience of Gentiles.[15] "Sure, the laws of Moses seem bizarre," says Eleazar. "So let me tell you what they really mean. Let me initiate you into the true meanings of the Jewish oracles." For his Gentile audience, the laws of Moses held no legally binding authority, but nevertheless became morally informative. By the contemplation of these allegorized laws, they were transformed.[16]

---

cf Moses Hadas, *Aristeas to Philocrates: Letter of Aristeas* (New York: Harper & Brothers, 1951), 163.

14 *Letter of Aristeas*, 154

15 cf *Letter of Aristeas*, 136-138

16 "The treatise of "Aristeas" is a complex, multilayered, and occasionally entertaining piece of work. In these regards, it exemplifies much of the Jewish literature in Greek that emerged in the Hellenistic period. No single purpose drove its composition. The idea, prevalent in modern scholarship, that it promoted a synthesis between Judaism and Hellenism is inadequate. Eleazer affirms the uniqueness of Jewish practices and principles, Jewish sages

Keeping this in mind, consider the voice of Paul, apostle to the Gentiles, in the New Testament (Rom 11.13, Gal 2.2). Throughout the Pauline writings we can hear this voice speaking about, and in, mysteries (1 Cor 4.1, 13.1-2, 14.1-2, 15.51, Col 1.27, 2.2, 4.3, 2 Thes 2.1-12, 1 Tim 3.8-10, 16). Paul believed himself to be in possession of a hidden wisdom, to which only a few people were fully privy (1 Cor 1.18-3.4). He was careful to "speak wisdom among those who are mature," which is "the wisdom of God in a Mystery, the hidden wisdom which God ordained before the ages" (1 Cor 2.6-7). This wisdom was a gift of the divine spirit, and was the basis for a method of Christian instruction through comparison and analogy, which was above reproach (1 Cor 2.10, 13). Paul even seems to attribute this method directly to Christ (1 Cor 2.16). And, like Jesus, Paul is more than willing to give his audience only as much wisdom as it can handle (1 Cor 3.1-4).

This approach to revelation—this method of carefully, selectively explaining the things of heaven to those upon earth—is something we find also in the Gospel of John (John 3.10-12). Although in John he tells almost nothing resembling a synoptic parable, Jesus is presented as a riddler at every turn. From his first sayings to his farewell discourse (John 1.52, 16.25-26), Jesus barrages his befuddled listeners with cryptic puzzles and enigmas that they cannot understand. Only in hindsight, and with special assistance, do his followers begin to make sense of the briefly apparent, arresting, and brilliant spectacle that is Jesus Christ crucified (John 15.26-27, 16.5-7).

Being also many other things, our New Testament is a sort of developmental record, one that shows us some of the ways in which apocalyptic and eschatological rhetoric was developed and employed among the earliest believers. The canon is the best of their literary first fruits, consciously sorted and gathered by the maturing church, for the benefit of those who would follow.[17]

---

surpass Greek philosophers, and the Torah receives obeisance from the king of Egypt. This narrative, like so many others, implies that Jews are fully at home in the world of Hellenic culture. The use of a fictive Greek as narrator and admirer of Judaism carries that implication clearly enough. But the message is still more pointed: Jews have not only digested Hellenic culture, they have also surmounted it." Gruen, *Heritage and Hellenism*, 220.

17 "The canon cannot be determined wholly by the church's acceptance of the books. Some were widely received, a few were hesitantly accepted by certain churches and not all by

In the Pauline writings we find a charismatic, apostolic ministry actively reinterpreting the whole of Jewish tradition in light of what scholars sometimes call the Christ event, and what the faithful are often inclined to call the resurrection.[18] In Paul we find early evidence that many people expected a sudden and cataclysmic end to the present order of the world. The apostle comfortably fits in with this crowd (1 Cor 9.16-23), but he has seen some things that he keeps to himself (2 Cor 12.1-6).

In the gospels we find a Jesus who tells parables, riddles, and mysteries about himself and Israel (Mark 2.10, 28), frequently in anticipation of his own crucifixion and resurrection (John 12.34), but also in anticipation of Jerusalem's impending destruction (Mark 13, 14.62). In the synoptic tradition especially, the gospels bind together the fate of Jesus and the fate of Israel, as if they are one single figure (Mark 8.31-32, 9.3-13, 13.14-27).

And, late in apostolic Christianity, we have the Revelation.

1.3 A FINAL WARNING

You may discover, upon further inquiry into the signs and symbols of Revelation, that not everything you know or believe about the Christian gospel is as it seems. You may experience some emotional dis-

---

others, and some were not mentioned until a relatively late date, or else their right to be included in the canon was definitely disputed. Local prejudice or individual taste could influence the verdict that had come down from the churches and the writers of antiquity. Notwithstanding this fact, what one person or section of the church rejected another person or section accepted; and it was not true that those who passed judgment were so uncritical as to accept anything that struck their fancy irrespective of its inherent merits. The critique of the ancients was no less fallible than that of modern scholars. On the other hand, they had access to records and traditions that have now perished, and their testimony cannot be set aside simply because it does not belong to the twentieth century. Ecclesiastical assent to canonicity supplies corroborative evidence, though it may not in itself be decisive." Tenney, *New Testament Survey*, 402.

18 e.g., "The hermeneutical pattern for Paul's interpretation of the Hebrew/Jewish scriptures seems to center on a comparative dimension that relates Israel's redemptive history to those who confess Jesus as the Christ. Paul readily actualized these traditions because he believed that the Christ event had altered history as he understood it." B. J. Oropeza, "Echoes of Isaiah in the Rhetoric of Paul: New Exodus, Wisdom, and the Humility of the Cross in Utopian-Apocalyptic Expectations," in *The Intertexture of Apocalyptic Discourse in the New Testament*, ed. Duane F. Watson (Atlanta: Society of Biblical Literature, 2002), 91.

comfort, perhaps even intellectual or spiritual disorientation. These are unavoidable risks, incumbent upon those who would undertake a journey into higher realms and chance a conversation with the spirits.[19] I cannot guarantee that you will return unchanged, or even changed for the better. Proceed with caution.[20]

I have been so careful to warn you—believe it or not—out of a genuine concern for your wellbeing, and not as a thinly veiled effort to arouse your further interest. As a matter of disclosure I must admit that John's Revelation has been instrumental in my own spiritual formation. The challenges for me have been many and difficult, and so they promise to remain. But perhaps this will not be your experience.

My hope is that you will find what I have uncovered by the way to be beneficial, but the power of evaluation is the privilege of the reader, not the author. Perhaps what follows may seem like the desperate efforts of a modern mind trying to redeem an irredeemable error; you may come to believe that I am deluded, heretical, or—God forbid!—irrelevant. Or perhaps what I must say will seem perfectly

---

19 The ever-enigmatic Edward Swedenborg understood this risk: "249. To speak with spirits, however, is at this day seldom given, since it is dangerous;* for then the spirits know that they are with man, which otherwise they do not know; and evil spirits are such that they hold man in deadly hatred and desire nothing more than to destroy him, both soul and body. ... Those who think much on religious subjects, and are so intent upon them as to see them as it were inwardly in themselves, begin also to hear spirits speaking with them; for religious persuasions, whatever they are, when man from himself dwells upon them, and does not modify them by the various things of use in the world, go interiorly and dwell there and occupy the whole spirit of the man, thus entering the spiritual world and affecting spirits there." Emanuel Swedenborg, *Heaven and Its Wonders and Hell: From Things Heard and Seen*, (EBook: Theodore D. Webber, 2012), 1875-1881/8961; "*Man is able to speak with spirits and angels, and the ancients frequently spoke with them. In some earths angels and spirits appear in human form and speak with the inhabitants. But on this earth at this day it is dangerous to speak with the spirits, unless man be in true faith, and led by the Lord." Ibid, 7455/8961.

20 Kugel's admonition also bears repeating: "WARNING: This book is intended for both the specialist and the general reader, those who already have great familiarity with the Bible and those who have never read a page of it. It is my hope that any reader will be able to learn a great deal from it. But there is one group of readers who must be cautioned about its contents. Precisely because this book deals with modern biblical scholarship, many of the things it discusses contradict the accepted teachings of Judaism and Christianity and may thus be disturbing to people of traditional faith." James Kugel, *How to Read the Bible: A Guide to Scripture, Then and Now* (New York, London, Toronto, Sydney: Free Press, 2007), 253/25533.

sensible, and it will be a minor thing for you to agree; maybe it will seem entirely too complex, and it will be a minor thing for you to disagree. Perhaps you have better things to do with your time, things more productive than the close examination of an esoteric text produced almost two thousand years ago for an obscure religious subculture. In any case, I can only cast my words to the wind. May they take root in the right soil and season.

2.1 THE PROPOSAL

Love never ends—whether prophecies, they will be abolished; whether tongues, they will cease; whether knowledge, it will pass away. For we know in part, and in part we prophesy. But when that which is perfect should come, then that which is partial shall pass away. When I was a child, I spoke as a child, I thought like a child, I reasoned like a child. But when I became a man, I did away with the things of childhood. For now we see through a glass, obscurely; but then face to face. Now, I know of a part; but then I will know even as I also have been completely known. And now remain these three things: faith, hope, love—and the greatest of these is love (1 Corinthians 13.8–12).

John's Revelation is an allegory of the New Testament, a metaphor for the gospel. It is an extensive series of parable-like episodes that depict the spiritual reality behind the historical events of the earliest Christian movement (Rev 4-22). Through typologically sympathetic Old Testament symbols and referents, the book of Revelation represents the experiences of Israel, Jesus, and the church as the experiences of a conjoined body, united in God across space and time. This heavenly vision of the gospel is framed as an apocalyptic prophecy,[1] and is presented to the church as a template or guide by

1 "When someone today is referred to as a prophet or is said to prophesy, we think of a soothsayer—someone who foretells the future. This was not the original meaning of the word. "Prophet" comes from the Greek word *prophetes,* in which *pro* means "for" and *phetes* means "to speak." Thus, in its original Greek, a prophet is someone who "speaks for" someone else. This meaning is faithful to the original Hebrew." Huston Smith, *The World's Religions, Revised and Updated* (EBook: HarperCollins, 2003), 5972/8303.

which it may understand its history, present situation, and ultimate destiny (Rev 1-3).

John the Revelator shared a kindred spirit with those Christian preachers who sought to instill in their various audiences a sense of cosmological significance while relating the astounding story of Jesus' life, death, and resurrection. As with the canonical gospels, the Revelation of John accomplishes this, in no small way, by profoundly relying upon the sacred scriptures, appealing to Moses, to the prophets, to the historians, to the poets and their psalms. In this way, the book of Revelation is an apocalyptic gospel, utilizing the oracles of God to illuminate the life of Christ.

2.2 REVELATION AND THE GOSPELS

Speaking broadly, the canonical gospels rely on the Jewish scriptures in two different ways—directly and indirectly. Direct references are easy to identify. The stories of Jesus' birth in Matthew, for example, are punctuated with five citations of Jewish scripture, each from a different book: Isaiah, Micah, Hosea, Jeremiah, and Judges.[2] Matthew's incorporation of these passages into the story of Jesus' life signals an important interpretive project already taking place in the early decades of the church: evangelical writers are harmonizing various Jewish oracles with the life of Jesus, patterning their accounts of Christ on the records and literature of Israel's exodus, establishment, exile, and return. This is an authorial approach that seems to have grown directly out of the evangelical proclamation; Jesus' life unfolds according to the pattern of the scriptures. In the written gospels, this

2 Matt 1.22-23, Isa 7.14; Matt 2.5-6, Mic 5.2; Matt 2.14-15, Hos 11.1; Matt 2.17-18, Jer 3.18; Matt 2.23, Jdg 13.5. Also: "In detecting organization some scholars have found in chs. 3-25 five "books," each ending with a refrain in which it is stated that Jesus had finished his sayings (7:28, 11:1, 13:53, 19:1, 26:1). These five books have been seen to constitute a Christian Pentateuch based on a typology between Christ and Moses... There are real difficulties about this theory, even though it may contain elements of truth. It is important background for the thesis to be mentioned below that the Matthean infancy narrative deliberately patterns the birth of Jesus on the birth of Moses, and that there are five episodes in the infancy narrative centered round the five fulfillment citations." Raymond E. Brown, *The Birth of the Messiah: A Commentary on the Infancy Narratives in the Gospels of Matthew and Luke* (New Haven and London: Yale University Press, 1993), 48.

unfolding often happens explicitly in sequences that, like Matthew's infancy accounts, appeal directly to the ancient oracles as a prophetic confirmation of the gospel.

Other gospel passages often rely on the Jewish scriptures indirectly, engaging the law and the prophets implicitly. Mark does this frequently, and there can be no more dramatic example of this than the scene of Jesus' crucifixion. As he is dying on the cross, Jesus cries out in a language that is strange and unfamiliar to at least some of those standing by. Although Mark translates the phrase for his own audience, he does not identify the words as a direct quote from the first verse of Psalm 22: "My God, my God, why have you forsaken me?" (Mark 15.34).[3]

It is an assumption written into the gospels at nearly every turn: the evangelical audience must engage what we now call the Old Testament to fully appreciate the events and significance of the New Testament. In this instance, a reader or listener who does not know the psalm will not recognize the reference when Mark's Jesus borrows from it to express his agony. But the reader who does recognize the reference may be alerted to the larger influence of the psalm on the entire Markan crucifixion scene. Like Jesus' cry of despair, the soldiers who gamble for Jesus' clothes and the spectators who mock him are key elements in Mark's portrayal of the crucifixion that closely correspond to the experience of righteous suffering voiced in Psalm 22 (Mark 15.24, 29-32, Ps 22.12-16, 18).

While this scene of crucifixion is powerful even to an uninformed audience, and though Mark is still careful to iterate its essential point—"Certainly this man is the Son of God!" (Mark 15.39)—the account is written so that it can only be fully appreciated by an audience that esteems Jewish scripture as both sacred and relevant. The Markan crucifixion, and indeed the entire gospel of Mark, is filled

---

3 "It seems certain that the words are quoted from the beginning of Psalm 22. Arguments to the contrary are not convincing. The words are not quoted from the Hebrew text, but from an Aramaic paraphrase. (For the Aramaic form Eloi, "my God," in Mark, the Hebrew form Eli appears in Matthew. Any attempt to determine the precise pronunciation would have to reckon with the fact that some bystanders thought that Jesus was calling for Elijah to come and help him)." F. F. Bruce, *Hard Sayings of the Bible* (Downers Grove: InverVarsity Press, 1996), 452.

with implicit references to the Jewish oracles of God. These implicit references or allusions add to the theological depth and import of the gospel without openly disrupting the narrative action, while affording students and teachers the opportunity to investigate and elaborate offstage. The gospels' stories of Jesus' ministry are not only an account of his activities, but also rely upon the Jewish oracles, which consequentially function for Christians as a unified witness to the truth of the gospel, as resources which may rightly be consulted in the quest for the evangelical Jesus (cf Rev 19.10).

One difficulty with the gospel as a literary project is that a written rather than oral account is relatively fixed, whereas the living audience is constantly evolving, and not always as expected or desired. Those exposed to a written gospel, immediately or eventually, may not be willing, equipped, or prepared to dive so thoroughly into the Jewish oracles in search of the evangelical point. There is a real, demonstrable risk that a student of the gospel(s) may attempt to resolve or explain the perplexities of a given passage by inadequate measures, and it seems important to note that the literature of the early church did not develop in a vacuum. Even before the gospels were written, there were Christian teachers, preachers, prophets, and apostles who could guide those who cared to connect the dots between New Testament events and Old Testament expectations. Early Christian literature was not always intended to be self-explanatory and open. Rather, it was frequently and intentionally ambiguous, *requiring* dedicated study (discipleship) that was best facilitated by an informed instructor, often as part of a program or process of spiritual development.

But the gospel is not just for the informed or the gifted—the elect are called to open the eyes of the blind, not to leave them alone and in the dark (cf 2 Pet 1.19-21). Another consequence of employing the scriptures discretely while relating the gospel is that even those people who cannot yet appreciate the tale entirely may derive some benefit from its material. A new Christian initiate may hear the Gospel of Mark, for example, and not catch its many latent references to the law, prophets, and psalms. Yet it is still clear from the story that the crucified Christ is the Son of God, while its remaining ambiguities are an open invitation to further pursue the mysteries of heaven. This structuring of the gospel provides an excellent—even ideal—opportunity for the church to step in, to guide the curious into truth, to bring the light of understanding into the darkness.

All of this is pertinent to the formation and function of the canonical gospels, but applies exponentially to the Apocalypse. The book never directly cites scripture in the manner of the Matthaean infancy narratives, never directly asserts that such-and-such New Testament event corresponds to such-and-such Old Testament prophecy.[4] Rather, in the mode of subtler gospel passages, the book of Revelation is a dense maze of indirect, implicit allusions and references to numerous Old Testament passages, many of which can be easily missed, but seem obvious once you spot them.[5] The final product is a trove of Israel's greatest treasures mapped upon the life of Christ, an oracular mystery that tantalizes its audience with a breadcrumb trail of clues and invitations to interpretation (cf Rev 2.7, 11, 17; 13.9-10, 13.16-18). If a reader fails to detect the presence of the Jewish scriptures in Revelation, she or he is unlikely to follow that trail successfully, but—as long as the book remains unredacted and unexpanded by editors just trying to help (Rev 22.18-19)—the pathway remains open for those who have adequate provisions and engage an appropriate guide.

Detached from the Old Testament entirely, and read as a standalone production, the Apocalypse of John does not look very different from other apocalyptic material produced during the same general

4 It was enormously gratifying to discover a very similar introductory comment on Revelation, complete with footnotes pointing to the first two chapters of Matthew, in N. T. Wright, *Revelation for Everyone* (Louisville: Westminster John Knox Press, 2011), 323/6687.

5 "It is clear that John had studied the Old Testament very thoroughly. Of the 404 verses that comprise the 22 chapters of the book of Revelation, 278 verses contain one or more allusions to an Old Testament passage," Bruce M. Metzger, *Breaking the Code: Understanding the Book of Revelation* (Nashville: Abingdon Press, 1993), 13; cf Henry Barclay Swete, *The Apocalypse of John* (New York: The Macmillan Company, 1906), cxxxv-cxlviii; "However, there is some debate as to whether an allusion must be the result of conscious intention. ... Thus estimates of the number of Old Testament allusions in a given book vary enormously. For the book of Revelation, this has ranged from about 250 to well over 1000." Steve Moyise, *The Old Testament in the New: An Introduction* (London and New York: Continuum, 2001), 6.

era.[6] Even a casual look will confirm that at least superficial similarities exist between Revelation and other contemporary works of prophetic and spiritual import. It is by no means unusual to find Jewish prophets and historians borrowing from the works of their predecessors to paint apocalyptic and cataclysmic pictures during the early Christian and even pre-Christian era. As the academy has rigorously noted, apocalyptic works like Daniel and Enoch and 2 Esdras look a lot like John's Apocalypse, and if we were to set certain passages side by side, an untrained or disinterested eye might have trouble distinguishing the one book from the others.[7]

But by a wide margin, Revelation incorporates and alludes to the Old Testament more consistently and clearly than any other ancient literature that I have yet encountered.[8] John the Revelator is not merely

---

6 "Since the last century, the first word of Revelation, *apokalypsis*, has been used to characterize a whole group of Jewish and Christian writings which had flourished between 200 B.C.E. and 300 C.E. Examples of such apocalyptic literature include Daniel in the Common Testament [Hebrew Bible] and 4 Ezra (2 Esdr. 3-14), which belongs to the so-called Apocrypha appended to most English editions of the Bible. Such Jewish apocalyptic writings include, among others, 1 and 2 Enoch, 2 and 3 Baruch, the Apocalypse of Abraham, and some writings from Qumran. In Christian Scriptures, we find not only apocalyptic sections (e.g., the so-called Synoptic apocalypse, Mark 13 par., or 2 Thess 2), but also basic apocalyptic categories and perspectives. Without question, Revelation belongs to this type of ancient literature." Elisabeth Schüssler Fiorenza, *Revelation: Vision of a Just World,* ed. Gerhard Krodel (Minneapolis: Fortress Press, 1991), 391-396/2255.

7 "Biblical scholarship has long distinguished between Old Testament prophecy and the Jewish apocalypses, which include the Old Testament book of Daniel as well as such extra-canonical works as 1 Enoch, 4 Ezra and 2 Baruch. The extent and character of the continuity and the differences between prophecy and apocalyptic are highly debatable. But the distinction means that the relationship between Revelation and the Jewish apocalypses has also been debated." Richard Bauckham, *The Theology of the Book of Revelation* (New York: Cambridge University Press, 1993), 5, cf 5-12.

8 "It should be clear that the images of Revelation are symbols with evocative power inviting imaginative participation in the book's symbolic world. But they do not work merely by painting verbal pictures. Their precise literary composition is always essential to their meaning. In the first place, the astonishingly meticulous composition of the book creates a complex network of literary cross-references, parallels, contrasts, which inform the meaning of the parts and the whole. Naturally, not all of these will be noticed on the first or seventh or seventieth reading. They are one of the ways in which the book is designed to yield its rich store of meaning progressively through intensive study. Secondly, as we have already noticed, Revelation is saturated with verbal allusions to the Old Testament. These are not incidental but essential to the way meaning is conveyed. Without noticing some of the key allusions, little if anything of the meanings of the images will be understood. But like the

doing what other apocalypticists do.[9] His project is more complex, more subversive, more sophisticated, than some exegetes may anticipate.[10] This sophistication may come as a surprise, as many readers of the Bible subscribe—intentionally or unintentionally—to a myth of early Christian simplicity. It is easy to imagine that, as the earliest apostles are portrayed as simple fishermen,[11] so also are the biblical authors themselves simple scribes, unspoiled by critical method.[12] This assumption unifies

literary patterning, John's very precise and subtle use of Old Testament allusions creates a reservoir of meaning which can be progressively tapped. The Old Testament allusions frequently presuppose their Old Testament context and a range of connexions between Old Testament texts which are not made explicit but lie beneath the surface of the text of Revelation." Bauckham, *The Theology of the Book of Revelation*, 18, cf 3-4.

9 "The student of Scripture immediately recognizes that the symbolic imagery used by John is multifaceted and masterful. John does not merely recapitulate the apocalyptic imagery of the prophets and apply them to the current crisis. He reconfigures and expands them to cosmic proportions..." Hank Hanegraaff, *The Apocalypse Code* (Nashville: Thomas Nelson, 2007), 20.

10 By "subversive" I am here referring to the third stage of genre development detected by Alastair Fowler and outlined by Collins in *Apocalyptic Imagination*, who describes the formation of a genre in three steps: (1) development (2) solidification and (3) subversion, or "the secondary use of the form—for example, by ironic inversion." Collins, ibid, 3-4. The primary difference between my own approach to Revelation and most of the academic treatments to which I have been exposed is that, while most scholars seem presently to view Revelation as the height—or even the very definition—of classic stage-two apocalyptic literature, it seems to me to be perhaps an intentionally ironic inversion of an already-established form or recognized convention.

11 e.g., concerning the study of Jesus and the Gospels, Richard Horsley writes, "It is generally simply assumed that Judean literature from around the time of Jesus provides evidence for a common Jewish culture or "Judaism" shared by everyone in the society except the high priests and Herodian rulers. That assumption, however, does not take into account clear differences in social locations. Apocalyptic literature was written by the literate, cultural (although not political-economic) elite. Jesus and his followers, among whom the Synoptic Gospel traditions originated, were illiterate peasants who cultivated their own Israelite traditions in village communities." Richard A. Horsley, "The Kingdom of God and the Renewal of Israel: Synoptic Gospels, Jesus Movements, and Apocalypticism" in *The Encyclopedia of Apocalypticism: The Origins of Apocalypticism and Judaism in Christianity*, ed. John J. Collins (New York: Continuum, 2000), 307.

12 e.g., "Of course, [the gospels] were written by individuals, but these individuals were not "authors" in the modern sense of the term. Modern authors most commonly write for people they don't know, and they seek to be original and creative. But the individuals who wrote the gospels were crystallizing into writing their community's traditions about Jesus as they had developed in the decades since his death." Marcus Borg, *Jesus: Uncovering the Life, Teachings, and Relevance of a Religious Revolutionary* (New York: HarperOne, 2006), 28.

a broad swathe of militant chatroom atheists, traditional churchgoing Christians, and scholars who ought to know better.[13]

But the frequently-seen caricature of the intellectually naïve and scholastically primitive Christian cannot easily withstand investigation.[14] Rhetoric is not a new phenomenon. Human communication is not just a modern exercise. Consider briefly Philo, an Alexandrian Jew exegeting the scriptures contemporaneously with Paul, who identified the formal study of rhetoric as a basic prerequisite for the would-be student of the Jewish oracles.[15] Already in the age of the New Testament, the art of splitting hairs, detecting motives, of entertaining, persuading, and educating an audience was a well-studied and highly regarded discipline across several fields.[16] Of course, not every disciple

---

13 "One of the great gains of the last fifty years of scholarship has been the recognition that Matthew, Mark and Luke—as well as John, Paul and others—were *theologians*. They were not artless chroniclers or transcribers. They thought deeply and creatively about the Jewish scriptures, about Israel's god, about the achievement of this god in completing the story of those scriptures in Jesus, and about the tasks and problems of their own communities as the people of this god, summoned to a life of loyalty to this Jesus." N. T. Wright, *Jesus and the Victory of God* (London: Society for Promoting Christian Knowledge, 1996), 478.

14 "The paradigmatic concerns of the scribes, whether expressed in the interpretation of oracles and omens, in legal rulings, in the hermeneutics of sacred texts or in their other manifold functions, led to the development of complex exegetical techniques devoted to the task of discovering the ever-changing relevance of ancient precedents and archetypes. (These concerns also led, at times, to the fabrication of ancient precedents and archetypes.) These exegetical techniques were international, being diffused throughout scribal centres in the Eastern Mediterranean world. Texts are used and reused, glossed, interpreted and reinterpreted in a continual process of "updating" the materials. [paragraph] This process of "updating" was particularly acute in prophetic oracular and apocalyptic traditions with their ambiguous messages and unfulfilled predictions. The various techniques of interpretations have been well explored for Jewish apocalyptic literature." Jonathan Z. Smith, "Wisdom and Apocalyptic," in *Visionaries and Their Apocalypses*, ed. Paul D. Hanson (London and Philadelphia: Fortress Press, 1983), 109.

15 Philo, *Preliminary Studies* 17-18

16 "Certainly classical rhetoric has been applied to NT argumentative discourse, on the grounds that Hellenistic rhetoric was widely known and used (if perhaps adapted) by numerous first-century audiences, including those that were Jewish and Christian. Even in these cases, however, there have been those who demur, or consider the Aristotelian categories inadequate: how much more doubt might be raised concerning a rhetorical analysis of symbolic, narrative [i.e. apocalyptic] passages which might better be grist for a study in poetics? ... More recently scholars collaborating in a Society of Biblical literature group have been bold enough to investigate the "rhetorical dimensions of apocalyptic discourse." Apocalypses, at least, are not well comprehended as sheer artefacts,

of Christ must therefore, on the authority of Philo, be a classically trained rhetorician. But it is necessary and good to remind ourselves that, though they be ancients, they do not therefore belong to an inherently deficient race. Rarely is anything new under the sun; the field of rhetorical analysis is older than Hegel and Derrida. While not every Christian is a scholar, and while not all Christians are artists, even some early Christians were both.[17]

That the early church could produce a sophisticated, brilliant, and faithful rendering of the evangelical proclamation—one that depicts the gospel of Christ in its cosmological dimensions, revealing Jesus as a sword-bearing warrior from another world, commanding an authority over those spirits which torment sinners, unveiling through a breathtaking act of self-sacrifice a new testament received from the hand of God—should not, therefore, seem so implausible.

It is true that the allegorical range and complexity of Revelation is unprecedented and can be intimidating, that it is vividly different in style, scope, and content when compared to anything in the New Testament corpus. But we find no less a figure than Paul championing allegorical and spiritual instruction as the foundation of the apostolic gospel (2 Cor 3), and as a privilege of evangelical authority (1 Cor 2.12-14). There are moments throughout the New Testament where authors slip into a distinct oracular mode and speak in ambiguities (cf 1 Cor 15.50-54). Some of these ambiguities—such as the parable of

---

since they possess a suasive dimension. So too with shorter vision-reports in the NT. Such passages, framed by narrative, and replete with symbolism, are by no means devoid of rhetorical strategy." Edith M. Humphrey, "A Tale of Two Cities," in *The Reality of Apocalypse: Rhetoric and Politics in the Book of Revelation,* ed. David L. Barr (Atlanta: Society of Biblical Literature, 2006), 113-114.

17 C. H. Dodd was not describing the Revelator or his work, specifically, but rather the "dominant personalities of the Bible," when he wrote, "The emergence of genius in any sphere is an incalculable phenomenon. It appears at various stages of historical development, among primitive communities and in advanced civilizations alike. The forms in which it expresses itself naturally depend on the thought-forms current at the time, but there is something behind the forms which seems to be independent of such limitations... It is of course always possible to be wise after the event, and to point to certain discoverable factors which may have been favourable to this sudden outcrop, but it is difficult to show why these conditions and no others should have had this effect, or why apparently similar conditions at other times have had no such result. [paragraph] This is true of religious genius, in the saint or prophet." C. H. Dodd, *The Authority of the Bible* (Fontana Books, 1960), 35-36.

the Sower and the Seed—are at least partially explained, but others are left open. Consider Mark's strange original ending (Mark 16.8),[18] the enigma of the transfiguration (Mark 9.1-13),[19] or the so-called messianic secret (Mark 1.34, 44).[20] What would the author of Mark have us make of these outstanding, unspoken declarations that more is going on in the story than immediately meets the eye?

While our various traditions offer us solutions to the challenges of scripture, engaging these passages remains for every reader an exercise in reading between the lines.[21] This exercise is tricky business, because it requires us to do something that is always dangerous: we must make assumptions to reach conclusions.

Above I have attempted to lay out some assumptions upon which the proceeding chapters rely, and in conclusion it seems prudent to summarize some of them again, so that there is less chance for misunderstanding in what follows:

First, Revelation is to be interpreted allegorically, but as referring to certain actual events. Its letter is meant to obscure its spirit, to hide its greatest treasures from the unprepared, as a tree shades a sapling from the burning sun without cutting it off from the light. Next,

---

18 "Although some modern editions of Mark include more, the consensus among textual scholars is that there is no good evidence for including in Mark anything after 16:8." Joseph B. Tyson, *The New Testament and Early Christianity* (New York: Macmillan Publishing Company, 1984), 174; Bruce, *Hard Sayings of the Bible,* 560.

19 Bruce, *Hard Sayings of the Bible*, 428-430

20 "Each of the Gospels is designed to proclaim who Jesus is, to present him to the world, so that people will commit themselves to him and become disciples. But within the Gospels, especially in Mark, is the curious phenomenon of Jesus' commanding people not to tell others who he is. If he wishes people to believe, why does he not allow the open confessions of those who really know him? In the case of demonized people, is this not one time that demons were telling the truth? Could this mean that Jesus had doubts about who he was? This is the problem of the so-called messianic secret." Bruce, *Hard Sayings of the Bible*, 406-408.

Note: The use of similar terminology by myself and by Bruce ("so-called") is a happy coincidence; he and I offer conflicting solutions to some of the hard sayings of the synoptics, but his work remains a valuable resource.

21 "Texts permit more than one reading; literary texts permit various readings; no text permits just any reading. Texts control readings, but so do readers. Literary texts especially invite a variety of readings, for they leave much to the imagination. We must imagine scenes, characters, connections; we must infer motives, values, character; we must reconstruct past events, relationships, sequence..." David L. Barr, *Tales of the End: A Narrative Commentary on the Book of Revelation* (Salem, Oregon: Polebridge Press, 2012), 796/6687.

there are two literary bodies that are equally invaluable for those who seek to unlock Revelation's mysteries: the Old and New Testaments. The Old Testament is vital, supplying John with a wealth of images and passages, sources through which he was compelled, as a Jewish Christian, to advance the gospel. The New Testament—including several epistles and especially its gospels—is equally important, because therein is enshrined the apostolic faith, the witness of the saints, and the literature by which the word was spread.[22] Through this body, we know precisely which story had captured the evangelical imagination (cf 1 Cor 2.1-2, 2.6-7).[23]

---

22 "It is not possible that the Gospels can be either more or fewer in number than they are. For, since there are four zones of the world in which we live, and four catholic spirits while the Church is scattered throughout all the world [Rev 7.1], and the "pillar and ground" of the Church is the Gospel and the spirit of life [1 Tim 3.14-16]; it is fitting that she should have four pillars, breathing out immortality on every side, and vivifying men afresh. From which fact, it is evident that the Word, the Artificer of all, He that sitteth upon the cherubim, and contains all things, He who was manifested to men, has given us the Gospel under four aspects, but bound together by one Spirit. As also David says, when entreating His manifestation, "Thou that sittest between the cherubim, shine forth" [Ps. 80.1]. For the cherubim, too, were four-faced, and their faces were images of the dispensation of the Son of God. For it says (Rev 4.7ff], "The first living creature was like a lion," symbolizing His effectual working, His leadership, and royal power; the second was like a calf, signifying sacrificial - sacerdotal order; but "the third had, as it were, the face as of a man,"—an evident description of His advent as a human being; "the fourth was like a flying eagle," pointing out the gift of the Spirit hovering with His wings over the Church. And therefore the Gospels are in accord with these things, among which Christ Jesus is seated." Irenaeus, *Against Heresies* 3.11.8, closely adapted from "Irenæus against Heresies," in *The Apostolic Fathers with Justin Martyr and Irenaeus*, ed. Alexander Roberts, James Donaldson, and A. Cleveland Coxe, vol. 1, The Ante-Nicene Fathers (Buffalo, Christian Literature Company, 1885), 428.

Note: Here, rebutting the gnostic proliferation of apocryphal gospels, Irenaeus creates hermeneutical boundaries for the evangelical gospel(s) by grounding the fourfold tradition in the eschatological context of John's apocalyptic Christ—roughly *two centuries* before the canon would be formally ratified. Following Irenaeus, subsequent patristic exegesis of Revelation is rife with (but is not limited to) kerygmatic-apocalyptic interpretation, which stresses the life of Christ as a primary subject of John's Revelation.

23 This is not to suggest that the Revelator is (necessarily) working with copies of Matthew, Mark, Luke, or John, or a partial record of the Pauline corpus, or a collection of apostolic letters, laid out on a table in front of him, or that he is (necessarily) directly responding to the written synoptic tradition (as we have it now). While intentional New Testament intratextuality is a plausibility in many instances, Christian canonical literature does not appear to be the Revelator's substantive subject of reference. Rather perhaps, John relies on and refers to an established core of narrative theology that developed over decades in the early church, and is therefore variously manifest throughout the New Testament canon.

Finally, the book of Revelation is a portrait of the Christian gospel in all its cosmological glory, written in an apocalyptic mode suitable to translating heavenly realities for an earthly audience (cf John 3.11-13). Revelation illuminates the ultimate causes and consequences of Christ's ministry: his incarnation, his anointing, his transfiguration, his crucifixion, his resurrection. It is a book that explains the flight of Israel, her exodus through wilderness and exile, her life among the nations, the higher reasons for her afflictions and fortunes. It is a book that affirms the election of the saints, the exaltation of the church, the inevitability of human suffering, and the hope of divine vindication. All of this was, and is, and continues to be the Revelation of Jesus Christ.

3.1 THE HEAVENLY HOUSE OF GOD

"Again, the kingdom of the heavens is like a dragnet, cast into the sea, gathering together out of every kind, which, when it was filled, having been drawn to the shore, and having sat down, they gathered the good into vessels, but threw away the worthless. Thus it will be in the consummation of the age: the angels will come out and shall separate the wicked from among the righteous, and cast them into the furnace of fire; there will be wailing and the gnashing of teeth." Jesus said to them, "Have you understood all these things?" They said to Him, "Yes, Lord."

And he said to them, "Thus every scribe discipled in the kingdom of the heavens is like to men a master of a house, who puts out from his treasure things new and old" (Matthew 13.47–52).

If an evangelist may be compared to a fisherman, the book of Revelation is like a wide-cast net, gathering to itself a varied demographic. The book is powerful, both arresting and alarming. It juxtaposes visions of universal judgment, widespread plagues, and unspeakable torments for the wicked against the eternal rewards of the holy saints who inhabit a glittering city and drink from the waters of life. For many readers, these passages are moving, motivating, even compelling. If history is any judge, this book of mysteries has the capacity to captivate audiences of all sorts.[1] But as a book of oracular wisdom, it is not easily accessed. Extensive knowledge of the Jewish scriptures is prerequisite, as is an appreciation for the Christian gospel. The allegorical format of Revelation makes it an ideal resource for evangelists who must speak enigmatically for the benefit of a mixed audience, as an aid to sorting through those who have been called to the feast and those who have been chosen to feed the sheep.

If an evangelist may be compared to a host at a banquet, Revelation is like a storehouse. What we find therein is meant to sustain the church in all its complexity,[2] and should be distributed responsibly by those who have been instructed concerning the kingdom of heaven. The Apocalypse is filled with treasures both New and Old.

3.2 AN APOSTOLIC STRUCTURE

Many of the theological points that the Revelator labors to illustrate are familiar to us through other New Testament sources, those epistles and gospels which preceded John's Apocalypse. The first epistle of Peter, for example, makes prominent use of temple-oriented imagery to describe the church as a divinely appointed house:

> Coming to him as living stone—rejected by men but chosen by God, precious—you also as living stones are being constructed as a spiritual house, a holy priesthood to offer spiritual sacrifices acceptable to God through Jesus Christ. Therefore it is also within scripture: "Behold, I set in Zion a cornerstone elect, precious—and the believer upon him will not be put to shame." Therefore, to you who believe, he is precious. But for the disobedient: "The stone which the builders rejected has become the chief cornerstone," also "a stumbling stone and rock of offense." Being disobedient to the word to which they too were appointed, they stumble. But you are an elect race, a royal

1 John Herrmann and Annewies van den Hoek, "Apocalyptic Themes in the Monumental and Minor Art of Early Christianity," in *Apocalyptic Thought in Early Christianity*, ed. Robert J. Daly (Grand Rapids: Baker Academic, 2009), 33-80.

2 cf Rom 14

> priesthood, a holy nation, a people possessed so that you might display the virtues of the one who called you out of darkness into his marvelous light, you who once were not a people but now are the people of God, you who had not obtained mercy but now have obtained mercy (1 Pet 2.4-10).

This short but powerful section of Peter's epistle is packed with references to the law, the prophets, and the psalms. The apostle paraphrases a passage out of Isaiah, which promises that the house of the Lord will be a place of refuge in the day of judgment (Isa 28.16). He continues with two more paraphrases, one from a passage celebrating an unlikely election and another alluding to a prophecy that God will be "a snare and trap for the inhabitants of Jerusalem" (Ps 118.22, Isa 8.14). The language of election, Peter's talk of a "royal priesthood" and "holy nation," is congruent with what we find in Exodus, wherein God promises Israel that it shall be "a kingdom of priests and a holy nation" (Ex 19.5). The images of light and darkness are evocative of the prophet Isaiah (cf Isa 9.2-3). The apostolic description of the church as "you who once were not a people but now are the people of God" alludes to the prophetic actions and hope of Hosea (Ho 1.9).

The author of this epistle has collected and condensed passages from different books—including the law, the prophets, and the psalms—and has fused them together as part of a single, coherent metaphor describing the church, this spiritual house built by priests operating under the authority of Jesus Christ, this light shining in the darkness, this institution founded on the cornerstone. It is an apostolic vision, woven out of the scriptures and presented to a Christian audience of both Jews and Gentiles who have voluntarily united in one body. It is an important precedent.

3.3 AN APOCALYPTIC VISION

The first sequence of the Revelator's major visions takes place inside the house of God, as the trumpet-like voice of John's apocalyptic guide invites him to ascend through an open door in heaven, transporting him to a spiritual plane (Rev. 4.1). Thereafter John describes a room filled with strange sights, sounds, and inhabitants. Most prominent is a radiant being surrounded by a glistening rainbow (Rev 4.2-3), sitting upon a throne born aloft by four multi-faced, multi-winged, multi-eyed creatures who sing his praises (Rev 4.6b-8). Beneath the throne is a crystal-like sea of glass (Rev 4.6a), and in front of the throne the seven lamp-like spirits continue to burn brightly (Rev 4.5b). Surrounding all of this is a group of twenty-four elders, men dressed in robes and wearing crowns, and they seem to be engaging the four creatures in some kind of call-and-response ritual (Rev 4.4-5).

These are already present, gathered before, around, beneath, and upon the throne as John enters in—and it gets weirder. The one on the throne produces a scroll that has been sealed shut with seven seals, and his agent issues an oracular summons: "Who is worthy to destroy the seals and open the book?" (Rev 5.1-2). No one in the entire cosmos is found qualified to meet the angel's challenge, and the Revelator—who like us must be keenly interested in what that scroll might reveal—despairs (Rev 5.3-4). But then a champion appears: a lion-like lamb with seven eyes and seven horns (Rev 5.6-7); his reputation precedes him (Rev 5.5). When he takes the scroll, the elders change their tune, producing harps and incense appropriate to the ceremonial unveiling of the scroll's mysteries (Rev 5.8-10), and the whole universe—grouped into appropriate choruses—celebrates (Rev 5.11-14).

But as he breaks the seals, terrible things unfold. From his perch in the heavens, the lamb releases catastrophe after catastrophe upon the unfortunate mortals below. As he breaks the first four seals he unleashes agents of war, famine, sickness, and death, and gives them power over a designated portion of the earth (Rev 6.1-8). The breaking of the fifth seal reveals an altar sheltering the souls of slain martyrs who demand retribution, made to wait (Rev 6.9-11). When the sixth seal is broken, the structures of the universe begin to collapse, and the leaders of the world begin to understand that a day of reckoning is at hand (Rev 6.12-17).

The breaking of the final, seventh seal is suspended in preference for the marking of a numbered host (Rev 7.2-8). When these 144,000 saints out of the Jewish tribes are finally catalogued, they are merged with "a great crowd which no one was able to number, of all nations, tribes, people, and tongues" (Rev 7.9). These two groups—the numbered and the innumerable—join the elders, angels, and creatures in their call-and-response chorus of praise (Rev 7.10-12). A nearby elder identifies this joined host as victims of "great tribulation," saints who have "washed and whitened their robes in the blood of the lamb" (Rev 7.13-14). The same elder then describes the rewards which this conjoined host will enjoy, as the flock of the faithful eternally shepherded in peace and safety inside the house of God (Rev 7.15-17).

And then the seventh seal is opened, and after a moment of silence, the final unveiling commences. Seven angels with seven trumpets take their places (Rev 8.1-2). Another angel with a golden censer takes incense mingled with fire and prayers for retribution, and hurls it at the earth with deafening force (Rev 8.3-5). One by one the seven trumpets begin to sound, each signaling some new and abysmal judgment cast down upon the earth from realms high above (Rev 8.7-9.19). Yet, even after total destruction is visited upon a full third of the earth, those who survive remain recalcitrant (Rev 9.20-21).

Subsequently, the Revelator's visions take him out of this heavenly realm (Rev 10.1-8). Though the temple of God remains a locale of interest (Rev 11.1-3, 19, 12.5, 14.1-5, 14-19, 15.1-16.1, 21.1-4), his view expands, as he begins to see an even bigger picture.

3.4 THE JEWISH SCRIPTURES

Without fail, these enigmatic denizens of the heavens can be found inhabiting the scriptures, across a wide range of Old Testament literature. It is almost as if John the Revelator has reverse-engineered the oracles of God, as if he has poured over the scriptures and, with advanced theological and rhetorical apparatus, discerned and related a metaphysical typology responsible for the generation of a lower realm.

While it is tempting to imagine that these visions came organically and naturally to a prophetic charismatic in a meditative or mystical or dream state,[3] the level of scrutiny, study, and dedication required to assemble these references and deliver a cogent, relevant narrative suggests that it is more like the work of a lifetime, the prod-

3 Wright, *Revelation for Everyone,* 7-9; Bauckham, *Theology of the Book of Revelation,* 3-4

uct of a studied genius or collective.[4] The Revelation is the consequence of devout labor, of a thoughtful, careful literary process that is sympathetic to the Jewish scriptures and dedicated to a Christian agenda. Methodologically it is the outgrowth of the same rhetorical and theological procedures evidenced in earlier apostolic writing, such as we find in the first epistle of Peter. As there, we find in Revelation a vision of the heavenly temple woven together out of the Jewish scriptures. Of course, Revelation is somewhat more elaborate, but the literary approach therein is comparably apostolic, as its author merges together countless oracular sources to create a composite image of the divine house.

The one on the throne lifted up by four bizarre creatures is a good place to start.[5] It is an image taken primarily from the opening of Ezekiel, down to the detail of the rainbow that surrounds the being on the throne (Eze 1.4-28). It is, however, distinctly compressed. While the first prophet describes the creatures as each having four different heads, John abbreviates his description by attributing one head to each of the four creatures (Eze 1.10-11a, Rev 4.7). The four Ezekielian creatures are also represented at length as wheels which direct the chariot of God, and these wheels are said to be filled with eyes (Eze 1.16-21, 3.12-13, 10.9-19, 11.22). While the Revelator drops the wheels, he retains the eyeballs (Rev 4.6b).

In order to understand the Revelator's purpose, it is necessary to investigate Ezekiel, which is a major resource throughout the Apocalypse.[6] Ezekiel's visions allegorize the ark of the covenant, the ornate

---

4 It could of course be the product of both dream-state mysticism and careful literary construction, as Barr suggests, but even in his explanation, literal dreams are obligatorily confirmed as primary sources of literary inspiration. Barr, *Tales of the End*, 705-726, 4784, 4884/6687. Certainly the Apocalypse seems to be the result of decades of evangelical development.

5 "The throne image (Rev 4:2-6, 9-10; 5:1, 6-7, 11, 13), occurs again and again like a keynote symbol throughout the whole book (Rev 1:4, 2:13; 3:21; 6:16; 7:9-11, 15, 17; 8:3; 11:16; 12:5; 13:2; 14:3; 16:10, 17; 19:4-5; 20:4, 11-12; 21:5; 22:1, 3)." Fiorenza, *Revelation*, 882/2255.

6 "Indeed, Revelation is a virtual recapitulation of Ezekiel, from the four living creatures (Ezekiel 1//Revelation 4) to the mark on the foreheads of the saints (Ezekiel 9//Revelation 7); from the eating of the scroll (Ezekiel 3//Revelation 10) to the measuring of the temple (Ezekiel 40//Revelation 11); from Gog and Magog (Ezekiel 38//Revelation 20) to the river of the water of life (Ezekiel 47//Revelation 22). And even that but scratches the surface." Hanegraaff, *The Apocalypse Code*, 122.

box which reportedly contained certain important physical remnants of the exodus (Ex 25.16, 2 Chr 5.10, Heb 9.4-5), and was housed inside the holiest of holy places, serving as the seat of God's commanding presence and overshadowed by two golden cherubim (Ex 25.10-22). In Solomon's temple these two guardians were joined by two much larger counterparts (2 Chr 3.10-13). Ezekiel's "rims full of eyes" seem to reference the four golden rings attached to the ark (Ex 25.12-15, cf 23-27), which served as anchor points for the staves by which it was transported from place to place.

Ezekiel's introduction is critical, because it tells us that his vision was received during the brutal aftermath of a major defeat in which Jerusalem was overrun by a superpower, and thousands upon thousands of Jews were transported back to Babylon as slaves (Eze 1.1-3). As Ezekiel opens, the temple cult is in ruins, and even the ark has gone missing, probably destroyed. But Ezekiel's visions idealize and enshrine the temple and its artifacts in text (cf Eze 40), so that something of its spirit survives, untouched by and superior to the foreign powers that had successfully invaded Israel. Like John, Ezekiel relies on the scriptures and structures of a recently vanished past.

Although the images of his theophanic encounter are explicit, Ezekiel's vision is one that is at least partially closed to an audience that does not know about the ark, the cherubim, the temple. The passage requires special knowledge and rewards those who retain that knowledge with insight into the true nature of their religious experience and culture, thus sustaining an active interest in the Mosaic traditions and literature of Israel for a displaced audience. The Revelator's situation is similar to Ezekiel's. It seems very likely that he wrote in the decades following the Roman conquest of Jerusalem in 70 CE, for an audience that relied in part on a temple culture that no longer physically existed.[7] Like Ezekiel, John's literary adaptations extend the

---

7 "After AD 70 the core of Jewish identify shifted from temple to Scripture. Worship of Yahweh now took place in homes and synagogues rather than in the Jerusalem temple. The Torah—the first five books of the Old Testament—provided a steady anchor for a people cast away from their homeland. Rabbis put into writing the vast code of oral tradition—the Mishnah, eventually incorporated in the Talmud—that taught the faith community how to apply the scriptures to daily life. [paragraph] In this way, Diaspora (dispersed/scattered) Judaism could survive without a base in Jerusalem, and Jewish communities remained

legacy of the law and prophets to a changing audience in changing circumstances.

But the Revelator's depiction of God's cosmic vehicle and throne is not constructed out of a truncated Ezekielian theophany alone. The wings of each creature—six, not four as in Ezekiel—as well as a portion of the song they sing, are straight out of Isaiah (Isa 6.1-4, Rev 4.8). These prophetic experiences of Isaiah and Ezekiel are incorporated by the Revelator into his own theophanic account. The same is true of other details that the Revelator has related. The sea of crystal-like glass around the throne also corresponds to Ezekiel, but has roots in older literary traditions and cultic institutions (Rev 4.6, Eze 1.22, Ex 24.9-10, 1 Kgs 7.23-26, 2 Chr 4.2-6). The seven spirits that burn before the throne like lamps reference the menorah, a special candle placed just outside the holiest of holies in the tabernacle, perpetually alight (Ex 25.31-39, 37.17-24, Lev 24.1-4). The Revelator returns to these seven spirits of God throughout his prophecy, representing them as agents conducting rituals of judgment (Rev 8.2-6, 15.1-2, 6-8), but also as angelic heads of the church subject to the authority of the Son of Man (Rev 1.12-13, 20).

3.5 A JEWISH PRIESTHOOD

The twenty-four elders merit special mention, because they are a widely misunderstood group. Many proposals have been made regarding the value of their symbol. In *The Jewish New Testament* David Frankfurter calls them "John's obscure innovation,"[8] and he seems to be voicing a widespread conviction of the academy. Richard Bauckham guesses that maybe they are "the angelic beings who compose the divine council,"[9] while N. T. Wright suggests that they "represent, almost certainly, the

strong in cities across the Mediterranean world. Because Christianity emerged from within Judaism, Christian congregations often formed in close proximity to Jewish synagogues. But while Judaism was largely an ethnic phenomenon, with actual blood ties among its adherents, Christianity quickly jumped the fence to become a faith for all peoples." J. Nelson Kraybill, *Apocalypse and Allegiance: Worship, Politics, and Devotion in the Book of Revelation* (Grand Rapids: Brazos Press, 2010), 3282/4079.

8 David Frankfurter, "The Revelation to John," in *The Jewish Annotated New Testament*, ed. Amy-Jill Levine and Marc Zvi Brettler (New York: Oxford University Press, 2011), 473.

9 Bauckham, *The Theology of the Book of Revelation*, 34

combination of the twelve tribes of Israel and the twelve apostles."[10] Hank Hanegraaff, who is otherwise notably attentive to the presence of the Old Testament in Revelation, proposes that the elders are significant as a "figurative use of the number twelve and its multiples."[11] David Aune agrees with this same generalization, and further speculates that maybe the twenty-four elders are a symbolic counterpoint to Domitian's imperial guard.[12] Steve Gregg catalogues additional proposals that have registered in popular theory which identify the elders as the Jerusalem Sanhedrin, the Royal Priesthood of the Christian church, the first twenty-four ancestors of Christ, and so on.[13]

Perhaps this common confusion is the consequence of academic compartmentalization. Today's students of biblical literature aren't often mathematicians. If we were, perhaps more of us would recognize the Revelator's reference to the Aaronic priesthood, which—in 1 Chronicles 24, no less—is arranged into twenty-four divisions, as the supervision of the Levitical priesthood is given over by King David to the surviving houses of Aaron (1 Chr 24.1-19). Sixteen chief men from one family and eight from another—twenty-four specific men in all, if we struggle bravely through the math—are named by name and chosen to be "governors of the sanctuary, and governors of the house of God" (1 Chr 24.4-6).[14] We further know that this priestly hierarchy was important in the era of the New Testament, even after the destruction of the temple, because the Jewish historian Josephus

---

10 Wright, *Revelation for Everyone,* 44; F. G. Smith, *The Revelation Explained: An Exposition, Text by Text, of the Apocalypse of St. John,* ed. Joel Erickson et all (Grand Junction, 1906), 62.

11 Hanegraaff, *The Apocalypse Code,* 126

12 David Aune, *The Influence of Roman Imperial Court Ceremonial on the Apocalypse of John* (Chicago: Society of Biblical Research, 1983), 104, 106.

13 Steve Gregg, *Revelation, Four Views: A Parallel Commentary* (Nashville: Thomas Nelson, 1997), 86-88.

14 At least one other person might be willing to go out on this limb, but probably with some reluctance: "Perhaps the reader is to think of the twenty-four heavenly beings associated with the zodiac; or **perhaps they symbolize the twenty-four orders of priests who served the Jerusalem temple (1 Chr 24:4-6)**; perhaps they represent the addition of the twelve apostles to the twelve patriarchs of Israel (cf. Rev 21:14), or perhaps, they represent a combination of earth (4) and humanity (6: 4 X 6 = 24). We should probably resist the urge to choose only one meaning, for it is a trait of our author to use multidimensional symbols." Barr, *Tales of the End,* 2334/6687, emphasis added.

polishes his credentials at the opening of his autobiography with an appeal to these twenty-four sacerdotal orders of kingly priests, from which he claims descent.[15]

Once we recognize the elders around the throne as Aaronic priests who are charged with keeping God's house, the fundamentals of the Revelator's scene may begin to fall into place.[16] Most illuminating in this regard is the New Testament epistle to the Hebrews. Its anonymous author describes Jesus as someone who did not intend to usurp the Jewish priesthood, but who was nevertheless elected by God to become "a great high priest who has passed through the heavens" (Heb 4.14-5.20). Parts of Hebrews rely on a critical connection back to an obscure Old Testament character by the name of Melchizedek, who was celebrated as a kingly priest by at least one psalmist (Heb 5.5-10, 6.19-7.10, Gen 14.17-20, Ps 110.4). There is no apparent trace of any similar, explicit Melchizedek connection in Revelation—while the epistle celebrates a venerable priest, the Apocalypse celebrates a venerable lamb—yet the authors work in concert to impress upon their audiences the same point:

> If indeed then perfection were by the Levitical priesthood—for under it the people received the law—what further need was there for a priest to rise according to the order of Melchizedek, and to be called not according to the order of Aaron? For the priesthood being changed, there is also a necessary legal change. For he of whom these things are spoken has part in a different tribe from which no one served at the altar.

---

15 Josephus, Life, 1.1-2, in *The Works of Josephus: Complete and Unabridged,* ed. William Whiston (Peabody: Hendrickson, 1987).

16 David Frankfurter recognizes the temple-centric narrative as dominant throughout Revelation: "Revelation offers remarkably detailed images of this heavenly temple cult, from the blowing of trumpets and pouring of bowls in chs 6-9, details that would have conjured sights of non-Jewish and civic ritual in Asia Minor cities, to the use of incense at the altar (8.1-3). The heavenly temple of John's apocalypse functions not just as the site of angelic service (cf 16.17) but also as the spectacle of divine power, alternatively veiled (15.8) and visible (11.19) according to the stages of the liturgical process through which the eschaton unfolds. Most importantly, both the angels (including the mysterious twenty-four elders, 4.10-11) and the righteous function primarily as priests and liturgical choristers (4-7; 15.2-8; 20.6), . . ." Frankfurter, *The Jewish New Testament*, 478.

> For it is evident that our Lord has risen up out of Judah, of which tribe Moses said nothing about priesthood. And yet it is abundantly apparent that there arises according to the likeness of Melchizedek a different priest, who has been made not according to the law of fleshly commandment, but according to the power of an incessant life (Heb 7.11-16).

While the early epistle of Peter uses the patterns of the temple cult and a compact smorgasbord of scriptural references and allusions to paint a picture of the church as God's new temple and priesthood, the epistle to the Hebrews addresses the implications of graduating from one Jewish cult to another. Although he does not explicitly rely—as Peter's epistles do—on apostolic authority, the author of Hebrews likewise engages a wide body of Jewish literature. In this instance, he appeals to the authority of a psalm that conveniently blurs the structures of the Mosaic and Davidic orders, a psalm that seems to conflate the offices of king and priest (Ps 110, cf Mark 12.35-37), and argues that the immortality of Jesus is evidential enough to justify a hierarchical rearrangement of the priesthood in consideration of the tribe of Judah, with which Jesus is associated. For the author of Hebrews, the Christ event justifies the reengineering of the Jewish faith, with Jesus taking charge of the priesthood. This is precisely the scene written by the Revelator:

> And one of the elders said to me, "Do not weep—behold, the Lion who is of the tribe of Judah, the root of David, has triumphed to destroy the seven seals and to open the scroll." And I looked and beheld—in the middle of the throne and of the four living creatures, and in the middle the elders—a lamb standing, as slaughtered, having seven horns and seven eyes (these are the seven spirits of God sent into all the earth).
>
> He came and received the scroll out of the right hand of him who sits upon the throne, and when he received the scroll the four living creatures and the twenty-four elders fell before the lamb, each having a harp and golden bowls full of incense, which are the prayers of the saints. And they sang a new song,

> saying, "You are worthy to take the scroll and to open its seals, for you were slain, and have purchased us for God with your blood out of every tribe and tongue and people and nation, and made us kings and priests to God, and we shall reign over the earth" (Rev 5.6-11).

Some time after Hebrews was written, the Revelator constructed a scene in which only the Lion of Judah—an Old Testament tribal emblem (Gen 49.8-12)—is competent to open the scroll of God's mysteries, while the Aaronic heads of the Levitical cult celebrate his coming with great relief. These Aaronic leaders do not seethe with resentment or plot to protect their priestly prerogatives, but rather praise God for the arrival of someone who can do what needs to be done. The author of Hebrews and the Revelator drive home the same point—out with the old, in with the new—but while the author of Hebrews emphasizes the inferiority of the former to the latter (Heb 7.11-19, 8.3-13, 9.6-19, cf Rev 5.5-7), the Revelator is more generous, demonstrating in the elders a spirit of cooperation with the lamb, rather than a spirit of antagonism.

Who are the twenty-four elders? They are the Aaronic leaders of the Levitical priesthood (1 Chr 24). And before whom do the elders gratefully bow? The lamb from the tribe of Judah (Rev 5.8, 14). Where do we find similar events presented and explained? The epistle to the Hebrews.

3.6 A HEBREW PRECEDENT

There are further similarities between what the Revelator has written and what the author of Hebrews has argued. For example, the Revelator describes the lamb as singularly qualified among all beings to open the scroll, having spiritual eyes that have been sent through all the earth (Rev 5.6-7), while the author of Hebrews describes a personified Word of God who can "discern the thoughts and intentions of a heart, and there is no created thing hidden from his sight, but all are naked and open to his eyes, before whom is our word" (Heb 4.13). Like the author of Revelation, the author of Hebrews expresses close familiarity with the Jewish temple and its culture, "of which we cannot now speak in detail" (Heb 9.1-4, cf 9.11-14, 25-28, 10.1-2, 10-12, 19-22), and describes the physical temple as "a sanctuary that is a copy and shadow of what is in heaven" (Heb 8.5). He also argues that Jesus "has now obtained a more excellent ministry, inasmuch as he is also the mediator of a better covenant which has been established on better promises" (Heb 8.6):

> And almost everything is purified with blood according to the law, and without bloodshed there is no pardon. Therefore, while it was necessary for the copies of things in heaven to be purified thusly, the celestial things themselves required better sacrifices than these. For Christ did not enter into a sanctuary made by hands, a copy of the true sanctuary, but into heaven itself, to appear now before the face of God for us. Neither should he often offer himself annually—as the high priest enters into the holy place with the blood of another—since it was necessary for him to suffer often from the foundation of the world. But now, once, in fulfillment of the ages, he has been manifested to remove sin by his sacrifice (Heb 9.22-26).

In Revelation, John describes a scene in which the eternally-slain lamb of God enters into the heavenly temple, approaches the heavenly throne, and receives a special revelation that he alone is qualified to open. The author of Hebrews describes Jesus similarly, as having suffered "often from the foundation of the world," entering into the prototypical, heavenly temple, being "manifested to remove sin by his sacrifice," "in the fulfillment of the ages." While it is probable that they both worked independently, the many similarities between these two authors are palpable; Revelation seems to provide an in-depth look at the archetypes and spiritual realities assumed or implied in Hebrews.

Further, the author of Hebrews interrupts his own arguments about Melchizedek to register some complaints (Heb 5.11-6.19). His project, he says, is complicated by the deficiencies of his audience. While he wants to move on to advanced teaching, he does not expect his listeners to be able to comprehend his doctrine; they require remedial attention: "And although by this time you should be teachers, you have need of someone to teach you again the beginning principles of God's oracles, having come to need milk and not solid food" (Heb 5.12, cf 5.11-6.3).

Already in the first century of the Common Era, at least one Jewish evangelist—the author of Hebrews—described a typological realm responsible for his Christian reality, expressed a desire to develop his teachings further, and lamented the inability of his audience to keep up, being mired in the rudimentary principles of oracular interpretation.

What type of literature might have materialized, if an evangelical author had labored to reveal a similar typological reality to a prepared audience?

3.7 A NEW TESTAMENT

The scroll sealed with seven seals, produced by the one on the throne and opened by the lamb, symbolizes the covenant that is sealed in the blood of Christ (cf Mark 14.24, 1 Cor 11.25), that newly-forged testament which guides the apostolic mission (2 Cor 3.4-18). You might already possess this knowledge if you are familiar with the opening line of Revelation, which introduces the book as "the revelation of Jesus Christ, which God gave him, to show his servants" (Rev 1.1). This language is ambiguous, open to at least two different readings—this could be a revelation that *belonged* to Jesus Christ, a special insight he uniquely beheld and broadcasted; it could also be a revelation *about* Jesus Christ.[17] Probably the safe money is on the double affirmative; both are true. The revelation of Christ is that gospel which Jesus himself disclosed, and it is also a revelation concerning the discloser.

Because the canon would not fully emerge for centuries, it would be anachronistic to imagine this scroll with seven seals as the New Testament, the traditional literary collection that Christians know as

17 David L. Barr's significant insights into this aspect of the book seem to lead him to conclusions that are often parallel to my own: "The Apocalypse is, in its most basic sense, a retelling of the story of Jesus in a new way and with new images. ... If we fail to recognize that this is a gospel story, it is because it does not come in a gospel form. It is a different kind of literature." Barr, *Tales of the End*, 202/6687, cf 182-202/6687. For a moment I thought I had found someone in the academy who had beaten me to the punch.

the second part of the Bible. More precisely, this scroll is that new testament confirmed in human experience and history, the new covenant of which Paul can speak before the Christian canon was fully conceived or assembled (2 Cor 3.5-6). In this sense, the seven-sealed scroll is the Apocalypse, representing a new testament, embodying the good news, in the form of a Mystery (cf Eph 3).[18] As it is opened, we are taken on a tour of heavenly things concerning the Christ, which are fully revealed by and through him.

A structurally similar scroll is created in the Revelator's introductory sequence, wherein the Alpha and Omega tells John to prepare himself for visions: "What you see, write in a scroll and send to the seven churches in Asia" (Rev 1.11).[19] Subsequently John meets the Son of Man, who stands in the middle of seven lamps and proceeds to deliver seven enigmatic messages, each tailored for an individual congregation (Rev 2-3).[20]

---

18 This is not an earthshattering declaration; F. G. Smith was already resisting this implication in 1906: "The book in the hand of God is symbolical of something. Most of the commentators think it represents the book of Revelation, in which case, of course, it would not include the present description of the book itself, but only of its contents as applied to subsequent chapters. But this view, of itself, is unsatisfactory for many reasons. The rules governing the use and the interpretation of symbolic language would forbid the thought of one book's symbolizing another book; for the main idea conveyed by the term *symbol* is, that the symbolic object stands as the representative, not of itself, but of something analogous. Reasoning by analogy, what would the contents of a sealed book in the hand of God symbolize?" Smith, *The Revelation Explained*, 66.

Note: I might answer that it symbolizes the Mystery of God, not merely the literary construction known to the audience, but the disclosure delivered to the evangelists through the event and person of the crucified Christ. The opening of the symbolic scroll is analogous to the revealing of the new testament, not to the physical construct of the literature of the New Testament—unless we embrace a minor anachronism for the sake of brevity.

19 "The so-called seven letters are not actual letters, but they are formalized in such a way that they function as prophetic proclamation to the churches. The introductory formula "thus saith" has in Greek, just as in English, an archaic ring to it. It was used as an introductory formula by the Hebrew prophets (250 times in the LXX). ... The seven messages are thus best understood as royal edicts or divine oracles in letter form." Fiorenza, *Revelation*, 689/2255.

20 "The designation "one like a son of man" in an early Christian context suggests to the reader that the risen Christ is meant. But the description of the figure includes also some characteristics ascribed elsewhere to angels and some elsewhere attributed to God. The reader's assumption that the figure in the epiphany is the risen Christ is confirmed when he says "I became dead and behold! I am living forever and ever (1:18)." Adela Yarbro Col-

In each of these seven epistles, the Son of Man employs images of things yet unrevealed, which are also derivative of things contained in the Old Testament.[21] He for instance promises the Philadelphian congregation that he will turn those who persevere into pillars "in the temple of my God," and mark them with the name of "New Jerusalem" (Rev 3.12, cf 4.1, 21.2), while the temple and the city have not yet been presented. The other six churches are similarly tantalized with proleptic promises of rewards and also punishments, and in every case the Son of Man includes a summons: "He who has an ear, let him hear what the spirit says to the churches" (Rev 2.7, 2.11, 17, 29, 3.6, 13, 22). The declaration is both invitation and challenge, signaling an opportunity—for those so inclined and so equipped—to pursue a further understanding (cf Mark 4.9, 23, 7.16), so that the church may discover the harmony between its experiences and God's revelatory declarations.

These seven introductory salutations are followed by John's vision of the heavenly temple, wherein the whole universe is riveted by the mysteries of a seven-sealed scroll that only the lamb can open (Rev 4-5). Once upon a time in Israel, the prophet Isaiah saw a similar sight:

> For the Lord has poured out on you the spirit of deep sleep, and has closed your eyes, prophets, and he has covered your heads, seers. The whole vision has become to you like words of a scroll that is sealed, which men deliver to one who knows

---

lins, *Cosmology and Eschatology in Jewish and Christian Apocalypticism* (Leiden: E. J. Brill, 1996), 172-173.

21 "Revelation is not a mere book of riddles originating from a shallow post-Christian mind; it is a book of symbols deeply rooted in Old Testament history. We mistake their meanings when we fail to hear the background music of the Old Testament. The *tree of life* referred to in Jesus's letter to the church in Ephesus first appears in Genesis; the *ten days of testing* in Smyrna find their referent in Daniel; the heavenly *manna* promised to the church of Pergamum first fell from heaven in Exodus; the *Jezebel* who promoted sexual immorality in Thyatira is the mirror image of the idolatrous Jezebel in Kings; the *seven spirits* of the letter to the church in Sardis hark back to the Spirit as described by Zechariah; the *key of David* referenced in the letter to Philadelphia echoes the words of Isaiah; and Christ's rebuke to the church in Laodicea alludes to the words of Proverbs, "My son, do not despise the Lord's discipline and do not resent his rebuke" (3:11)." Hanegraaff, *The Apocalypse Code*, 117.

> scrolls, saying "Read this, please," and he says, "I cannot, for it is sealed." Then the book is delivered to one who does not know scrolls saying, "Read this, please," and he says, "I don't do scrolls."
>
> And the Lord said, "Because these people draw near with their mouths and honor me with their lips, but have removed their hearts far from me, and their respect for me is but the traditions of their rulers, therefore—behold—I will again do marvelously among this people, a marvelous work and wonder: the wisdom of their wise shall perish, and the understanding of their prudent shall disappear" (Isa 29.10-14, cf 6.9-10).

If you are familiar with the gospels you may especially recognize the last half of the above passage, as it plays a central role in the ministry of Jesus, who applies Isaiah's image of hypocritical sycophants to those who would force their customs upon his own disciples (cf Mark 7.5-11). The gospels thus demonstrate sympathy between Isaiah's vision of a people unable to understand God's revelation and the evangelical portrayal of a widely misunderstood Christ. Jesus' citation of this passage implies that he sees something that his own audience is missing due, in large part, to its traditional commitments.

In Revelation, the lamb takes the scroll and opens it for John, leading us right into the violence and destruction of the first six seals (Rev 6-9). But before the seventh seal is opened the author first takes us down to earth, to hear seven secret thunders (Rev 10.1-3). John remembers or records the seven revelations, but is instructed by heaven to "seal up that which the seven thunders said, and do not write them" (Rev 10.4). With a concern that his audience should clearly identify the climax of God's "Mystery," an angel makes an oath and then—oddly—he makes John eat those words. It seems John the Revelator is sent out into the world with an evangelical agenda and secret knowledge of the divine Mystery—specifically, the timing of its full unveiling (Rev 10.5-10).

At the very end of Revelation, John tells us that "the angel who showed me these things" instructed him to publish abroad what he has seen and heard: "And he said to me, 'Do not seal the words of the prophecy of this scroll, because the time is near.'" (Rev 22.8). The voice of Jesus then closes Revelation with a warning that no one should tamper with the words of the scroll, lest God blot out his name and place (Rev 22.1-5). This is language taken from the sealing of the Mosaic covenant (Deut 4.1-2, 28.58-61, Ex 32.33-34), and helps readers confirm what they ought to suspect, given that by the end of Revelation they are standing in the middle of the city of God and are able to drink from the waters of life: a new deal is now in effect (Rev 22.1-5).

3.8 THE HOUSE OF GOD

The Revelator's temple sequence dramatically corresponds to the dedication of Solomon's temple (2 Chr 5.1-7.4, 1 Kgs 8.1-66):

> Then Solomon assembled the elders of Israel and all the heads of the tribes, the leaders of the ancestral houses of the people of Israel, in Jerusalem, to bring up the ark of the covenant of the Lord out of the city of David, which is Zion. And all the Israelites assembled before the king at the festival that is in the seventh month. And all the elders of Israel came, and the Levites brought the ark. So they brought up the ark, the tabernacle of meeting, and all the holy furnishings that were in the tabernacle. The priests and Levites brought them up. Also King Solomon, and all the congregation of Israel who were assembled with him before the ark, were sacrificing sheep and oxen that could not be counted or numbered for multitude. Then the priests brought in the ark of the covenant of the Lord to its place, into the inner sanctuary of the temple, to the Most Holy Place, under the wings of the cherubim (2 Chr 5.1-7 NRSV, cf 1 Kgs 8.1-6).

The scene established in this short section of scripture is similar to the scene into which John is swept; the Revelator sees the spiritual prototypes of many things seen in the oracles of God. The scriptures describe the placement of the ark under the cherubim; we see a throne held aloft by cherubim (2 Chr 5.2, Rev 4.2-3, cf Eze 1.1-14). The scriptures detail the involvement of the Levitical priesthood; the Revelator witnesses the deeds of their twenty-four Aaronic captains (2 Chr 5.3-4, Rev 4.4). The scriptures portray Solomon assembled with the congregation of Israel before the ark, sacrificing an innumerable host of victims; we find the lamb standing before the throne with 144,000 saints gathered out of Israel, with a host of martyrs that cannot be numbered (2 Chr 5.6, Rev 7.4-10). After a song of praise accompanied by trumpets, smoke fills Solomon's temple and drives out those therein; this too occurs in Revelation (2 Chr 5.13-14, 1 Kgs 8.10, Rev 15.4, cf 2 Chr 7.1-3). These several close parallels seem to suggest that John's temple sequences are patterned on the dedication of Solomon's temple, and that we are perhaps witnessing a similar ceremonial dedication, one taking place in a higher house of God, one of distinctly Jewish design, though clearly of universal capacity.[22] [23]

There are elements of Hellenistic mystery culture in this scene, as well, primarily in the central presence of a closed scroll that finally discloses the "Mystery of God," around which most of the narrative action in Revelation seems to revolve.[24] The arrangement of the elders

---

22 The scene of Solomon's dedication frames the opening and closing of 2 Chronicles and made a significant impression on at least one other author, cf 2 Chr 35.1-6, 1 Esd 1.1-6.

23 "Indeed, the Apocalypse, as a whole, may be likened to the Temple services in its mingling of prophetic symbols with worship and praise. But it is specially remarkable, that the Temple-references with which the Book of Revelation abounds are generally to *minutiae,* which a writer who had not been as familiar with such details, as only personal contact and engagement with them could have rendered them, and scarcely have even notice, certainly not employed as part of his imagery. They come naturally, spontaneously, and so unexpectedly, that the reader is occasionally in danger of overlooking them altogether... " Alfred Edersheim, *The Temple, Its Ministry and Services as They Were at the Time of Jesus Christ* (Bellingham, WA: Logos Bible Software, 1874-2003), 140.

Note: Edersheim concluded that thus the Apocalypse was written while the temple was still standing. This seems unlikely, but it seems plausible that the Revelator, or those working in his name, might have been intimately familiar with the Jewish temple traditions in a way that contemporary audiences were and are not, ibid, 141-142. For a contemporary argument that Revelation was written before the fall of Jerusalem, see Hanegraaff, *The Apocalypse Code*, 123-124.

24 "There were also many associates of initiates (*mystai*) in "the mysteries" in Asia Minor, including those devoted to Isis and Serapis, the Great Mother (Cybele), Demeter and Kore, and Dionysos. Alongside the staple ritual of sacrifice, "mysteries" (*mysteria, orgia, telete*) were among the most respected ways of honoring the gods in various contexts (cf Burkert 1987). The term "mysteries" could encompass a variety of practices, including sacrifice, communal meals, reenactment of the myths of the gods, sacred processions, and hymn sing-

and the lamb is similar to the hierarchical structure of other religious cults in the ancient world, with initiates gathered in a circle around their privileged hierophant.[25] The implication may be that the ceremony underway in Revelation is both dedicatory and revelatory, and that this complete revelation of the divine Mystery inaugurates a new era, establishes a new kingdom, governed by a new covenant, authored and unveiled in the highest house of God.

3.9 THE LAMB

The lamb is Jesus (cf John 1.29-32, 14.22-24, 1 Cor 11.23-26, Ex 12.1-32, Gen 22.1-14).[26]

3.10 THE FOUR HORSEMEN

The four horsemen of the Apocalypse are seen as villains, vile and venomous sowers of chaos and evil. Yet these are not antagonists, but protagonists—agents of the Lord. They are four of God's highest-ranking angelic warriors, specialists to whom he outsources unpleasant wet work, spirits contracted as enforcers under the Mosaic covenant. The tasks with which they are saddled—conquering, making war, causing famine, and bringing death—are all anticipated in the Torah, as part of the punishments God will pour out on his people if they should prove themselves to be less than perfect. In this regard, there are two especially pertinent passages near the end of Deuteronomy; one is prose, while the other is poetry often billed as "The Song of Moses" (Deut 28.15-68, 31.30-43).

The prose passage is a laundry list of horrors bordering on gratuitous. In it, madness, rape, cannibalism, and other unpleasantries are the instruments by which God will correct the faithlessness of his

ing; most important for initiation into such associations was the unveiling of sacred symbols (associated with a particular deity) by the "revealer of the sacred objects" (*hierophantes),* often in lamplight." Philip A. Harland, *Associations, Synagogues, and Congregations: Claiming a Place in Ancient Mediterranean Society* (Minneapolis: Fortress Press, 2003), 45.

25 Cf Philo, *On the Posterity of Cain and His Exile*, 173

26 "The central figure of the composition is the lionlike Lamb, an image which occurs twenty-eight times in Revelation and always appears to signify the resurrected Christ. Although the reasons why the author employs this image for Christ remain unclear, his diction and imagery are quite different from those of the Fourth Gospel." Fiorenza, *Revelation,* 918/2255.

people (Deut 28.15-55). This curse-list makes mention of invasions, war, famines, various deaths and other tortures (Deut 28.56-61). Near its climax the passage speaks more generally:

> If you do not diligently observe all the words of this law that are written in this book, fearing this glorious and awesome name—the Lord your God—then the Lord will overwhelm both you and your offspring with severe and lasting afflictions and grievous and lasting maladies. He will bring back upon you all the diseases of Egypt, of which you were in dread, and they shall cling to you. Every other malady and affliction, even though not recorded in the book of this law, the Lord will inflict on you until you are destroyed (Deut 28.56-61, NKJV).

In ancient Israel, the people of God did not always expect their Lord to deal with his beloved tenderly and mercifully, as a loving father corrects his wayward son; theirs was a covenant sealed in suffering and blood.[27]

But it is the Song of Moses which most-effectively demonstrates the spirit of cooperation between Deuteronomy and these four riders in Revelation: the breaking of the first seal heralds the arrival of a rider on a white horse, carrying a bow and destined to conquer (Rev 6.2, cf Hab 3). The breaking of the second seal introduces a rider on a red horse, carrying a sword and tasked with bloodshed (Rev 6.4, cf Eze 21.8-17). The breaking of the third seal reveals a rider on a black horse, balancing a scale and charged with famine (Rev 6.6). The fourth seal releases Death on a pale horse, with Hell following close behind (Rev 6.8a). A look at the Song confirms that the four horsemen—armed to the teeth with swords, bows, famines, plagues, wild beasts, and more—have received their arsenal under Mosaic provision:

> They made me jealous with what is no god, provoked me with their idols.
> So I will make them jealous with what is no people, provoke them with a foolish nation.

27 "The pattern of sevenfold judgment against unfaithfulness on the part of Israel is spelled out in dreadful detail in Leviticus. Four times God tells his covenant people, "I will punish you for your sins seven times over." Hanegraaff, *The Apocalypse Code*, 117; Lev 26.18-28.

> For a fire is kindled in my anger, and burns to the depths of Sheol.
> It devours the earth and its increase, and sets on fire the foundations of the mountains.
> I will heap disasters upon them, spend my arrows against them:
> Wasting hunger, burning consumption, bitter pestilence,
> The teeth of beasts I will send against them, with venom of things crawling in the dust.
> In the street the sword shall bereave, and in the chambers terror,
> For young man and woman alike, nursing child and old gray head (Deut 32.21-25, NKJV).

The Song of Moses depicts a betrayed and enraged God who unleashes the fires of hell upon those Israelites by whom he has been so rudely disappointed, along with every other imaginable distress—the sword, the bow, famine, pestilence, wild beasts, and more. No one in the nation is safe from his wrath. Male and female, young and old, innocent and guilty, all are subject to the curses of the covenant. The Revelator's horsemen are imbued with these powers in concert with this pact, empowered to punish sinners.

And John was not the first Jewish author to depict heavenly beings as individually responsible for certain destructive tasks (1 Chr 21.11-22.5, Ps 78.49-50, cf 1 Cor 10.9-10, Hab 3). The experiences of plague, sickness, famine, and sword are extensively elaborated upon in histories and prophets.[28] Jeremiah records God's promise to Israel that he will "appoint over them four kinds of destroyers," and in Ezekiel the Lord God promises to "send upon Jerusalem my four deadly judgments: sword, famine, wild animals, and pestilence" (Jer 15.3, Eze 14.21).

Like the four living creatures upholding the throne of God, the Revelator's four destroyers are composite images, with their details alluding not to just a single prophetic source, but to literature scattered across a wide Old Testament body. For example, their careful

---

28 2 Chr 20.9, Isa 51.17-20, Jer 5.12-17, 14.12-18, 15.1-3, 18.18-23, 21.7-9, 24.10, 27.8-13, 29.17-18, Eze 5.12-17, 6.11-12, 7.15, 12.13-16. This is not an exhaustive list.

color-coding—white, red, black, and pale—is a detail paralleled in the book of Zechariah, which describes chariots transporting the "four spirits of heaven" (Zec 6.1-5).

The scales or balance in the hands of the third horseman is an emblem of judgment perhaps most famously associated with Daniel (Dan 5.25-28). The same horseman is given a detailed inflationary table that corresponds—inversely—to a passage in which the prophet Elisha predicts that the gates of heaven's storehouse are about to open unexpectedly (Rev 6.6, 2 Kgs 7.1). The Revelator's subtle but clear reversal of oracular language may indicate that we are likewise about to witness the opening of heaven's storehouse, but that the surprises inside are of an opposite, destructive nature—this, too, corresponds with the Song of Moses (Deut 32.34-35).[29] Not all of the Revelator's details neatly agree with the Song, however; the third horseman is told not to hurt "the olive oil and the wine," while the end of Deuteronomy places even those products under the curse (Rev 6.6c, Deut 28.38-42, cf Rev 7.3, 9.4, 14.14, Isa 24.12-13).

John's fourth horseman is not the first instance in which a biblical author has personified death and/or hell (Job 18.13, 28.22, cf Rev 9.11). Yet the release of Death by the lamb may be problematic for many readers of Revelation because the New Testament often presents death as antagonistic towards Christ and Christians (Rom 6-18, 1 Cor 15.20-28, 15.54-56, 2 Cor 3.7-9), and because at the climax of Revelation, Death and Hell are both tossed into a lake of molten fire in a paradoxical act of judgment called "second death" (Rev 20.14). It is a melancholy end for one who once wielded so much power, and yet this fate parallels a familiar New Testament assertion; by the end of Revelation, antagonistic Death is downsized, while his responsibilities are reassigned to a more-merciful agent (Gal 4.1-5, 2 Cor 3.7-9, Rom 6.23, Heb 9.16-20): "Fear not—I am the first and the last and the living one; I became dead, and behold: I am living into the ages of the ages, and I have the keys of Death and Hades" (Rev 1.17b-18).

29 Note that Moses is now taking aim at the Gentiles, cf Gen 7.11, Isa 24.18.

3.11 A JEWISH-GENTILE HOST

In another Ezekielian parallel, God's destroyers are held back while 144,000 people from the tribes of Israel are sealed "upon their foreheads" (Rev 7.3-8, Eze 8). While the repetitious listing of each tribe in Revelation may seem tedious—and, in some translations, is therefore eliminated—the time and space John spends on the roll-call creates a strong parallel between his numbering of the saints from Israel and the first chapter of the book of Numbers, in which Moses tallies the those fit for war "after they had come out of the land of Egypt" (Num 1.1-3, cf 4-53).

John's list is a little different. While his roll-call likewise represents the combat-ready (Deut 23.9-10, Rev 14.4),[30] his 144,000 Israelites are those special Jewish saints who have remained faithful to the covenant even in the face of trials, tribulation and, specifically, martyrdom (Rev 12.11). John is not the first evangelical writer to affirm their election. You may already recognize an alternative description of these pre-Christians:

> Therefore, from one man, and him as good as dead, were born as many as the stars of the sky in multitude and without number, as the sand which is by the seashore. In faith, these all died, not having received the promises, but having seen them from afar, and having been persuaded, embraced them, confessing that they are strangers and sojourners on the earth. Indeed if they were in remembrance of the places from which they departed, they might have had opportunity to have returned, but now they rise toward a better—that is, heavenly—place. Therefore God is not ashamed to be called their God, for he has prepared a city for them... (Heb 11.12-16).
>
> And what more shall I say? For time would fail me, to tell of Gideon and Barak and Samson and Jephtha and Samuel and the prophets who by faith overcame kingdoms, worked righteousness, obtained promises, stopped the mouths of lions,

30 Cf Barr, *Tales of the End,* 3575-3589/6687; Wright, *Revelation for Everyone,* 124; Pagels, *Revelations,* 50.

> quenched the power of fire, escaped the edge of the sword, from weakness were made strong, became mighty in war, made armies of foreigners turn back, women received their dead by resurrection while others were tortured, not accepting release so that they might obtain a greater resurrection. Others received trials of scourging and mocking, even of chains and imprisonment. They were stoned, sawn in two, tempted, slain with the sword, wandered in sheepskins and goatskins, being destitute, oppressed, and treated with evil; these—of whom the world was not worthy—wandered in deserts and mountains and caves and dirty holes. And all these to whom faith bore witness did not receive the promise, God having proved something better for us, that they should not be made perfect apart from us (Heb 11.32-39).

These heroes of faith are extensively profiled in Hebrews 11, which describes all of human history, starting with creation, following major Old Testament and intertestamental events, and concluding with the establishment of the Christian institution. Although there are noticeable differences between this passage and the Revelator's depiction, both authors divide the Christian body into two distinct halves: the faithful saints of past tradition, and the present-day recipients of a faith which those saints anticipated but never realized.[31] The two

---

31 "Revelation 7:9 sees the promise fulfilled in the great multitude which exceeds the possibility of a census because it is *international*. This is a distinctively Christian understanding of the promise in which probably it is being interpreted by reference to its other form in Genesis: the promise of a multitude of nations (Gen 17:4-6; 35:11; 48:19; cf Rom 4:16-18; Justin, *Dial.* 119-120) ... suggesting perhaps that the tribes of Israel are not excluded, but included in the greater, international multitude of Abraham's and Jacob's 'descendants'. Or perhaps it would be better to say that the redeemed of all nations have been included with them among the 'descendants' of Jacob. Both forms of the patriarchal promise (innumerable descendants, a multitude of nations) were given not only to Abraham but also to Jacob (Gen 32:12; 35:11). So the international multitude of 7:9 are all 'sons of Israel' (7:4), though not all are of the twelve tribes. ... This is consistent with the picture of the new Jerusalem in chapter 21, where gates inscribed with 'the names of the twelve tribes of the sons of Israel' (21:12) stand open to the nations (21:24-26)." Richard Bauckham, *The Climax of Prophecy: Studies on the Book of Revelation* (London: T&T Clark: A Continuum Imprint, 1993), 224-225. **Note,** further, that this international city is hedged about by a wall of 144 human-like cubits, Rev 21.17.

evangelists—the Revelator and the author of Hebrews—draw from the same rhetorical pool on behalf of different audiences. The epistle to the Hebrews is aimed at those who identify themselves as Hebrews, while Revelation's appeal is a little more explicitly universal. Yet despite these shifts in posture, both authors represent the saints of today and yesterday as a body united in experiences of suffering—they have all "washed in the blood of the lamb" (Rev 7, 14.1-4, Heb 12.1-4). Both authors show their respective audiences the international, intercultural people of God, joined together out of the long course of time through Jesus their Christ.

Unlike the author of Hebrews, however, the Revelator assigns the Jewish multitude of saints a very specific sum.

4.1 FUN WITH NUMBERS

Then Joseph said to Pharaoh, "Pharaoh's dreams are one and the same; God has revealed to Pharaoh what he is about to do. The seven good cows are seven years, and the seven good ears are seven years; the dreams are one. The seven lean and ugly cows that came up after them are seven years, as are the seven empty ears blighted by the east wind. They are seven years of famine. It is as I told Pharaoh; God has shown to Pharaoh what he is about to do."

"There will come seven years of great plenty throughout all the land of Egypt. After them there will arise seven years of famine, and all the plenty will be forgotten in the land of Egypt; the famine will consume the land. The plenty will no longer be known in the land because of the famine that will follow, for it will be very grievous. And the doubling of Pharaoh's dream means that the thing is fixed by God, and God will shortly bring it about" (Genesis 41.25–32, NRSV).

The genre of apocalypse allows for abrupt shifts in metaphor, enabling the Revelator to illustrate the same things from a variety of perspectives, to more-fully illuminate what may already be partially apprehended. For example, in an opening sequence the reality of the church is illustrated as the heavenly house of God, while in a closing sequence the reality of the church is illustrated as a city on earth (Rev 4-5, 21-22, cf 3.11-13). As in the gospels, numerical devices help hold many of the evangelist's illustrations in parallel, but in Revelation these markers are more prominent, and take up more narrative space, because they cover a much wider range of allegory. While numerical symbols and patterns are low-key in the rest of the New Testament, in the Apocalypse they are unavoidable and explicit, and the reader who abuses them will be locked out.

Although in Revelation symbolic quantities are inescapable, the field of their interpretation has proven especially hazardous. Through its long history the church has been plagued by mathematical missteps. From pew to pulpit to ivory tower, it seems no one at all is comfortable with the numbers. But because the Apocalypse is of a genre that begs interpretation, there is an open expectation that readers will examine certain figures and utilize them as clues in conjunction with their contextual associations. We may ascertain, for example, that the twenty-four elders are Aaronic leaders not only by the specificity of their number (1 Chr 24.1-19), but also because John has dressed them as priests and gathered them around an ark in the house of God as part of a sequence modeled on the dedication of Solomon's temple (2 Chr 5.2-13). Hypothetically, contextual relevance prevents readers from attaching the wrong value to John's numerical symbols.

But as with non-numerical details, any authority—real or imagined—can reinterpret the numbers of a text, can invest the numbers of any passage with a new range of meaning. It happens all the time. The author of Daniel seems to do this to a famous prophecy of Jeremiah, the later prophet reinterpreting his predecessor by perceiving a new symbolic meaning within the older prophecy—seventy years become seventy weeks of years, or four hundred and ninety years (Jer 25.11-12, 29.10, Dan 9, 2 Chr 36.21, Zec 7.5). Interpreters of John's Apocalypse do something similar when they speculate that the seven epistles to the seven churches prophetically reveal the seven ages of the universal church (Rev 2-3). While there is no clear directive to interpret the text thusly, there is no clear injunction against it.

Being frequently ambiguous, numerical devices are inherently volatile, vulnerable to mishandling and therefore prone to misfire. But the detection of numerical patterns and cues was an integral part of many discipleship programs in the ancient and antique world.[1] In

1 "Ignorance of numbers, too, prevents us from understanding things that are set down in Scripture in a figurative and mystical way. A candid mind, if I may so speak, cannot be anxious, for example, to ascertain what is meant by the fact that Moses and Elijah, and

many circles, including religious and philosophical circles, students studied many subjects, including math and geometry—the sciences of figures and patterns—before graduating to higher levels of inquiry.[2] Christian readers today may rightly be grateful that the apostolic authors never ascended to the mystic numerical heights attained by Jewish philosophers like Philo, who never met a number in scripture he couldn't allegorize.[3]

Most biblical texts employ numerical symbolism sparingly, and often when they do, they merely rely on significant quantities to bridge related passages, to highlight an interrelationship between events, scenes, or characters.[4] Likewise, numbers and numerical patterns in one part of Revelation often correspond to numbers and patterns in other parts of Revelation. This is demonstrated in the two chains of seven plagues organized under the parallel images of seven trumpets and seven bowls (Rev 8, 16). This type of intratextual parallel encourages readers to pay close attention to patterns of similarity and dissimilarity in pursuit of cohesion.[5]

---

our Lord himself, all fasted for forty days. . . . And in the same way, many other numbers and combinations of numbers are used in the sacred writings, to convey instruction under a figurative guise, and ignorance of numbers often shuts out the reader from this instruction." Augustine, *On Christian Doctrine*, 2.16.25, in *A Select Library of the Nicene and Post-Nicene Fathers of the Christian Church, First Series: St. Augustine's City of God and Christian Doctrine*, ed. Philip Schaff (Buffalo: Christian Literature Company, 1887).

2 cf Philo, *Preliminary Instruction*

3 cf Philo, *Allegorical Interpretation* I-III

4 "This kind of associative link was particularly important in the exegesis of Scripture. Jewish exegetes had a name for it, *g*^{e}*zerah sh*^{e}*wa,* which signified the explication of one text by cross-reference to another which had some verbal link with it; and Christian exegetes followed their example." G. B. Caird, *The Language and Imagery of the Bible* (Philadelphia: The Westminster Press, 1980), 108.

Note: Caird emphasizes verbal similarity, such as verses focusing on "stone" in 1 Peter 2, ibid. I would like to add—in anticipation of my own proposal—that it is hard to get more verbally specific than "six hundred and sixty and six," even crossing through the barriers of language (from Greek to Hebrew and vice versa) with numerical precision.

5 "The early fourth century commentator Victorinus of Pettua proposed a theory of recapitulation—arguing that later scenes in Revelation merely repeat the action that has been portrayed in earlier accounts—a theory adopted by many subsequent commentators. This duplication of events can be seen most clearly in the series of seven bowls, which is nearly identical to the series of seven trumpets." Barr, *Tales of the End*, 4874/6687.

The Revelator's numbers can also correspond to biblical passages outside of his apocalypse, as in the numbers twenty-four and 666 (1 Chr 24, 2 Chr 9.13). This type of exegetical reference can be more difficult to navigate, because it requires access to, or knowledge of, a specific passage, book, collection, or culture. As with so many of his non-numerical images, details, and references, John's numerical allusions to various oracles seem to anticipate—even necessitate—the development and acceptance of a scriptural canon.

4.2 AN OLD TESTAMENT FORMULA: A = B

The Revelator's special use of numbers is nascent in what is often called the Joseph novella, the longest and final story of Genesis (Gen 37-50). This novella is a conclusion well-suited to a book of spectacular beginnings, and contains many episodes that revolve around the principles of interpretive deduction. One of the points hammered home in the life of Joseph is that a few are gifted with a special kind of insight, while many fail to adequately evaluate the evidence right in front of them (Gen 37.27-36, 39.12-20, 41.38-46, 42.7-8, cf Gen 38).

The Joseph novella also demonstrates important principles of numerical interpretation. In three pivotal sequences, separate dreams occur in pairs, and each pair contains parallel numbers; these sequences operate on an assumed logic that Joseph eventually discloses (Gen 37.5-11, 40.7-23, 41.1-37).

In Joseph's first dream, the sheaves of his eleven brothers bow down to his own; in his second dream, eleven stars bow down before him, along with the sun and the moon (Gen 37.6-7, 9).

In the second sequence, which is more complex, Joseph interprets the dreams of a cupbearer and of a baker. Their two dreams are similar—the cupbearer dreams of three branches which produce wine, while the baker dreams of three breadbaskets which are consumed (Gen 40.9-11, 16-17). Joseph determines that the cupbearer will return to normal life after three days, whereas the baker will be executed (Gen 40.12-13, 18-19).

The third dream sequence is the most complex. Pharaoh has two troubling dreams in one night, and these also are numerically similar. In his first dream, Pharaoh watches seven fat cows get eaten by seven skinny cows; in his second dream he watches as seven healthy ears of corn are followed by seven skinny ears. Joseph interprets: there will be seven years of surplus followed by seven years of shortage (Gen 41.1-7).

In these episodes, thematic elements of the dream sequences tend towards contrast: abasement versus exaltation, replenishing versus depleting, plentiful versus sparse. At the same time, certain numbers—twelve, three, and seven—arrange these juxtapositions in some significant order: twelve sheaves and twelve stars represent twelve brothers; three branches and three baskets represent three days; seven cows and seven ears of corn represent seven years (Gen 41.24-32).

In Genesis, readers are encouraged to identify patterns of similarity and dissimilarity in divine revelation, which can be received in duplicate forms, having value that may be discerned according to numerical patterns, structures, and cues.[6]

For example, Joseph does not conclude that the fourteen cows and fourteen ears of corn represent a combined total of twenty-eight years. Instead, he determines that the two dreams are episodically concurrent, and represent the same fourteen-year period of time. The same is true of the separate visions of the cupbearer and the baker. Even though the two men experience different outcomes, their dreams iterate the same three-day period of time.

In Genesis, sets of visions are harmonized and interpreted based on their numerical parallels and thematic contrasts. "God will show you the same thing in different ways," explains Joseph, "to make sure you get the point" (Gen 41.25, 32).[7]

---

6 I imagine that this might have some relevance to the field of source-critical theory, which takes great care to identify the original sources that the biblical authors arranged, synthesized, and otherwise harmonized. For an introduction to this field of biblical research, see John J. Collins, *Introduction to the Hebrew Bible* (Minneapolis: Fortress Press, 2004), 49-65. See also Richard Elliot Friedman, *The Bible With Sources Revealed: A New View Into the Five Books of Moses* (San Francisco: HarperSanFrancisco, 2003).

7 The biblical author(s) of this Joseph story may have had a special interest in demonstrating and defending this particular point, if we accept the hypothesis that the biblical version of the Joseph novella is the product of (at least) two older literary traditions, as seems to be the case, cf Collins, *Introduction to the Hebrew Bible*, 101-103. That is, the Joseph novella—situated at the end of Genesis—is a composite work concerned with epistemological hermeneutics that hinges upon and defends a multiplicity of sources.

4.3 MARKAN FIGURES: A + B = C

In the Gospel of Mark, Jesus—while on his way to heal a dying twelve-year-old girl—is interrupted by a woman who has been suffering from a menstrual issue for twelve years. The older woman gets her cure, but she causes a delay, and by the time Jesus arrives at his destination, the girl seems to be dead (Mark 5.22-43). Many readers might be tempted to treat the numerical parallel between the two females as a minor coincidence, and such is their prerogative. Nevertheless, this parallel number of years helps illustrate the link between the two episodes, which belong to a whirlwind sprint of signs and wonders, many of which overturn established traditions and taboos, including biblical purity regulations.

Contrary to what his actions might imply, the scriptures contain clear injunctions against coming into contact with menstrual women and with dead bodies (Lev 15.19, 22.4-7). Yet Jesus, it seems, is invulnerable to impurities that would inhibit healers of lesser degree. It is almost as if the Mosaic laws do not apply to Jesus in quite the same way as they do to other authorities, and though we might not understand why, we perhaps should not be surprised. The sequence does, after all, start with Jesus commanding the wind and the sea, and then demonstrates him to be invincible against the incalculable contamination of a foreign graveyard inhabited by thousands of pigs and a legion of demons (Mark 4.35-5.20, cf Ps 65.7, Lev 11.7-8).

Following these great deeds, while on his way to heal a sick child, Jesus pauses for a few moments to discover who has unexpectedly drawn his healing power out of him. Though he blesses the supplicant when he finds her, the news of the girl's death arrives "while he is still speaking" (Mark 5.35). Until he reverses the situation by changing the meaning of death, it is the first sense of limitation to Jesus' power one encounters in the gospel. Though he is master of demons and spirits, he cannot be everywhere at once. The woman sick for twelve years is made well, but at greater cost to a girl as old as her illness. While subtle, Mark's numerical detail draws further scrutiny upon episodes that, in his account, are joined together in a wider narrative arc emphasizing the unprecedented, unexplained strength of Jesus' charismatic power.

Another scene from Mark may offer further insight into the way the evangelists could signal an audience through the structures of their stories: the short but famous pericope in which Jesus heals a blind man in two steps, rather than all at once (Mark 8.22-26). It is an oddity precisely because it again seems to represent a limitation to an otherwise irresistible power. It is an unusual portrayal of Christ, in the sense that it defies superlative expectation. Some readers may be inclined to accept the scene as a clinically historical account grounded in an early Christian tradition that wasn't worried about portraying Jesus as an invincible superman.

To make better sense of the scene, it may be productive to consider the immediately preceding episode, in which a frustrated Jesus reminds his disciples that they've witnessed the same miracles twice, and that they therefore have no excuse for failing to understand his doctrine (Mark 8.11-21).[8] His subsequent encounter with a blind man who needs doubled attention reflects the experience of an audience that has been treated to duplicate signs (cf Mark 6.32-43, 8.1-6).[9] "I've demonstrated the same thing twice," Mark says. "Do you now see?"

4.4 JOHANNINE FIGURES: 5A + 2B = 7C

The symbolic use of numbers in Mark's Gospel is subtle, and rarely intrudes into the story's open action. This is also true of John's Gospel, which similarly employs numbers, though with a heavier hand for a broader audience—what Mark does discretely, John does with flair. As befits a Johannine work, seven plays an especially pivotal role; the five miracles that are unique to John are keyed to the number seven (John 2.1-11, 4.46-54, 5.1-16, 9.1-14, 11.1-43). Two of these miracles—the first and last miracles of Jesus' earthly min-

8 "This miracle and its structural parallel (7.31-37) are the only miracles recorded in Mark alone. It is the only recorded two-stage miracle which Jesus performed. Sight was a widely used metaphor for understanding. This miracle depicts the correct but incomplete understanding of the disciples." John D. Grassmick, "Mark," in *The Bible Knowledge Commentary: An Exposition of the Scriptures,* ed. J. F. Walvoord and R. B. Zuck (Wheaton: Victor Books, 1985), 138.

9 Burton Mack nicely lays out the parallel miracle chains preceding the transfiguration; Burton L. Mack, *A Myth of Innocence* (Philedelphia: Fortress Press, 1988), 216-217.

istry—take place on the seventh day of their respective sequences, though to detect this one must bravely wade into simple addition (John 1.29, 35, 43, 2.1, 11.1-43). The remaining three miracles are less subtle. Jesus heals a certain son "at the seventh hour" (John 4.52),[10] and the other two miracles explicitly occur on the Sabbath, the seventh and final day of the week, which becomes the occasion of controversy (John 5.16, 9.14).

While in Mark the number twelve briefly functions to emphasize the figurative overlap between back-to-back pericopes—perhaps we might even speculate that the number twelve helps Mark coordinate two older pericopes—the unique miracles of John are synchronized with the number seven, a longstanding symbol of completion or perfection, paradigmatic of God's finished work (Gen 1ff). With this number, the fourth gospel bridges five distinct signs that are remarkably similar in structure and function, but which are dispersed across multiple sequences. Yet not all of the miracles in the fourth gospel are unique to John. The five Johannine oracles are arranged around two older signs: Jesus feeding five thousand and walking on water (John 6.1-21, cf Matt 14.13-52, Mark 6.30-51).

Because the Johannine audience is different from the synoptic audience, the fourth gospel lays it on thick. Jesus is quickly surrounded by five—rather than twelve—disciples (John 1),[11] meets a woman-in-waiting with five ex-husbands (John 4), cites five witnesses to his authority inside a shrine with five porches (John 5), and performs five uniquely Johannine signs (John 2-12). In order to help us make sense of this heavy-handed pattern, John—like Mark and the twice-touched blind man—embeds a structural key or map of his gospel within one of his oracles, his account of Jesus at Bethesda.

Although we should not forget that the pool of Bethesda actually did have five porticoes, the arrangement of the five porches around

10 The Greek manuscripts read, "ὥραν ἑβδόμην," or "at the seventh hour." Some translations harmonize John's clock with the modern schema, so that the miracle is said to take place "at one o'clock." This unfortunately obscures the Johannine numerical cue. John's Jesus does not use a clock with twenty-four hourly divisions (John 11.9).

11 The twelve disciples are mentioned in passing on a few Johannine occasions, cf John 6.67, 70-71, 20.24.

mystically moving waters in the Gospel reflects John's arrangement of five new oracles around the older accounts of Jesus breaking bread and walking on a troubled sea. To help us interpret all these signs together, John's Jesus begins his ministerial wrap-up with *explicit instructions on how to interpret his works*: the earthly ministry of the Son is the activity of the Father at a higher level (John 14.7-11).

Like Mark, the fourth gospel uses numerical cues to link episodes, and to map the structure of the larger gospel within a specific scene, bringing hermeneutical implications into the narrative foreground for readers who may otherwise fail to detect a certain point. Unlike Mark, John provides explicit hermeneutical instructions for its newly-minted sign segments, and by their arrangement seems to encourage the gospel audience to follow those instructions when interpreting older material. Whether or not we can satisfactorily determine how John would have us understand those miracles, it remains difficult to miss the careful organization of his gospel around the numbers five and seven.

Other numbers in John are also important, functioning not as intratextual links between significant scenes or as hermeneutical keys, but as exegetical bridges between John's Gospel and relevant Old Testament passages. At the pool of Bethesda, for example, Jesus heals a man who is thirty-eight years old. If we were to search the scriptures for a coordinate reference, we would find only one: during its exodus, Israel spends thirty-eight years languishing in the wilderness near an oasis known for its miraculous waters (Deut 2.14, cf Num 14, 20). To a reader who follows Jesus' hermeneutical instructions and examines the works of the Son to find the Father, this sign in which Jesus incurs the wrath of an irate mob by healing a lame man on the Sabbath may begin to look like a scene in which God restores an ungrateful Israel (John 14.8-11, John 5.5, Deut 2.14-15, cf Isa 35.3-7).

A similar numerical cue in the epilogue to John is a little more tenuous, but deserves honorable mention: Peter & Co. catch an astounding 153 fish with one net, in a scene that reverses traditions recorded in Matthew and Luke (John 21.1-12, Luke 5.1-11, Matt 14.28-31). It is an oddly specific number, and has provoked its share of speculative proposals. To these I add that Solomon netted just over

153,000 foreigners to build the house of God (2 Chr 2.2, 17, 1 Kgs 5.15-16).[12] Fishers of men, indeed.

But these exegetical connections are not a vital part of John. They are almost entirely peripheral. Though the presence of oddly specific numbers in an otherwise meticulously scripted gospel may induce inquiry, we make whatever connections we make off the main stage. The project of deciphering numerical intertextuality in the gospels is one (mercifully) reserved for the interested few, and is supplemental to the primary thrust of the story. Just as one may read the famous "in-the-beginning" of John and fail to make any connection to the "beginning" of Genesis, one may fail to appreciate the lame man in John as a representation of an exiled Israel, suffering in the wilderness, and the latter case one may even be forgiven. John's legendary prologue is packed with images and phrases that seem consciously evocative of Genesis 1, whereas 38 and 153 are just digits. Even if there are very few places in the biblical canon that use those specific numbers, numerical cues or referents are harder to demonstrate. Numbers can be just numbers; a detail is not always a cue.

4.5 THE END OF TIMES: x + 2x + ½x = 3½x

While the Revelator has already employed numerical signifiers—like four and twenty-four—in his depiction of certain icons, his numbers become increasingly specific and complex after his introduction of the 144,000 saints who are marked out of Israel. While it would be a very serious mistake to approach this proliferation of digits with arithmetical literalism—John was not a Pythagorean—there is some actual math involved. In Revelation, one prime set of numbers is used to coordinate several scenes; 3½, 42, and 1260 link together the tale of two witnesses, a woman, a sinful city, and a vengeful beast, demonstrating major points of contact between their respective narrative arcs, even when their causal connections are otherwise obscured. Fortunately, these numbers do not command even the majority of John's Revelation. Most of his complex quantities, including his calendar, are introduced shortly after the 144,000 first appear, and vanish again

12 2 Chr 2.2, 17 counts 153,600; 1 Kgs 5.15-16 counts 153,300.

shortly before the 144,000 are reintroduced—it is as if almost all of the Revelator's special numbers are carefully synchronized to illuminate the circumstances from which the saints of Israel have been extricated, the means by which they have been rescued, and the purpose of their ingathering (cf Rev 7.4-14.3).

1260 days = 42 months = 3½ years. These chronological qualifiers are related to the well-phrased "time, and times, and half a time" of prophetic delay in the book of Daniel (Dan 12.7).[13] Revelation borrows this specific turn of phrase to describe the length of time a particular woman spends hiding in the desert (Revelation 12.14), but reference to Daniel's "times" are evoked earlier, when the ceremonies in heaven are suddenly suspended, and an angel goes to great lengths to impress upon his audience precisely what the sounding of the final trumpet should mean. For best effect, the Revelator's passage should be seen in conjunction with its antecedent:

> Then I heard the man clothed in linen, who was above the waters of the river, when he held up his right hand and his left hand to heaven, and swore by him who lives forever, "It shall be for time, times, and half a time, and when the power of the holy people has been completely shattered, all these things shall be finished" (Dan 12.7, cf Deut 32.36).

> And the messenger whom I beheld standing upon the sea and upon the land lifted his right hand to heaven and swore to the one living to the ages of ages, who created the heaven and the things in it, and the earth and the things in it, and the sea and the things in it, "There will be no more time, and in the days of the sound of the seventh messenger, when he is going to sound the trumpet, the Mystery of God will also be completed" (Rev 10.5-7).

13 "The primary intention of Daniel 9 is to assure the persecuted Jews that the time of trial is coming to an end by locating it in an overview of history. This is achieved through the angel's revelation, which specifies the total duration of the postexilic period (from "the going forth of the word to restore and rebuild Jerusalem"). The profanation of the temple is to last for half a week (i.e., three and a half years, or a time, two times, and half a time). The attention to specific lengths of time is significant for its psychological effect and was noted in antiquity as a distinctive characteristic of Daniel's prophecy (Josephus, *Ant.* 10. 11.7, §267)." Collins, *Daniel*, 1602/2057.

Without reading the New Testament scene against its Old Testament referent, some—such as Thomas Aquinas—understand the angel's declaration as a prediction or promise of the end of the space-time universe.[14] Some translations better-convey the sense of the passage by using the word "delay" for the Greek word *chronos* (literally: time), but while this captures the sense of fulfillment that accompanies the sounding of the seventh horn, it buries the reference to Daniel's complex "times" at a critical moment, just before readers are exposed to a series of sequences and images that represent, in no small part, the duration and fulfillment of Daniel's "time, and times, and half a time" oracle.

The last half of Daniel looks forward to a day when Israel's captivity shall finally be concluded, which cannot happen until Israel undergoes total destruction. Readers who fail to appreciate Daniel's faith in a God who will rescue Israel only after destroying Israel may fail to appreciate the Revelator's dramatic story of a woman hidden in the wilderness for her own protection—it is a story of love, betrayal, violence, and reconciliation.

This drama, as with the rest of Revelation, is woven out of a wide array of prophetic visions, psalmic celebrations and laments, legal frameworks, and national histories. Unlike John's tour of the heavenly temple, this spectacle is choreographed across multiple platforms, and his leaps from sequence to sequence can be disorienting. Fortunately, he has included a calendrical scheme, inspired by Daniel's apocalyptic charter, that holds it all together: the two witnesses, the beast, the woman, and the temple of God are all tied to a calendar of 1260 days, 42 months, and 3½ years represented as days. This calendar of times holds multiple narrative streams in parallel (Rev 11.2-3, 9, 11, 12.6, 13.5). Like the dreams of Pharaoh in the Joseph novella, these allegorical sequences are chronologically concurrent and hermeneutically interdependent, representing intertwined narrative threads.

And that's not all: in addition to harmonizing multiple sequences based on the general schema of Daniel's prophetic times, the quantity

14 Bryan Kromholtz, *On the Last Day: The Time of the Resurrection of the Dead According to Thomas Aquinas* (Fribourg: Academic Press Fribourg, 2008), 175-177.

42 also here represents six periods of seven.[15] The Revelator is not the first evangelist to use this number symbolically. Matthew begins his gospel by measuring the distance between Abraham and Jesus by forty-two generations, in three clusters of fourteen generations (Matt 1.17).[16] These groupings position the subsequent Matthaean gospel as the beginning of a final chain of events, and portrays this climax as deeply rooted in the major actions and figures of Jewish history. Abraham and the patriarchs, the dynasty and kingdom of David, the Babylonian captivity—all are leading to the birth of Christ.[17]

---

15 Swedenborg notes this implication, and interprets it to represent the end of one age and the beginning of another: "... for the number "forty-two" arises from the multiplication of six into seven, six times seven making forty-two, therefore "forty-two" has a similar signification as "six weeks," and "six weeks" something similar to the "six days" of one week, ..." Swedenborg, *The Revelation Explained*, 663a.

16 Brown, *The Birth of the Messiah*, 68-69

17 Raymond Brown grappled with this Matthaean construction with mixed success (abracadabra: gematria!), and he pre-concluded that, "giving reign to a predilection for numerical patterns, Matthew thought that he had discovered the key to God's plan of salvation, a 3X14 pattern." Brown, *The Birth of the Messiah*, 70. But his observations remain informative: "In light of these facts, how do we interpret Matthew's insistence (1:17) on the 3X14 pattern? ... True, some have calculated that Matthew's 3X14 is equal to 6X7, so that six periods of seven generations preceded Jesus and he opens the seventh or final period, a division of time attested in the *Book of Enoch*, as we shall see. But if that were Matthew's idea, one would have expected him to speak of 6X7 rather than 3X14. (A genealogy built on sevens is a perfect possibility, as we shall see in Luke.) Moreover, there is no explicit emphasis in the Matthean infancy narrative on Jesus' closing one period and opening another ... A catalyst to such Matthean calculation may have come from gematria, since in the ancient Hebrew orthography the numerical value of David's name was fourteen," Brown, *Birth of the Messiah*, 75-80.

Note: An adequate response to Brown's immaculate scholarship is impossible here, but: A) He objects to the 6 x 7 construction on the grounds that Matthew's infancy section itself doesn't reflect an "explicit emphasis" on Jesus' "closing one period and opening another," as if the numerical peculiarities of Matthew's genealogy should appeal to something intrinsic to its first two chapters, and B) He assumes that the author of Matthew should spell out six sevens (rather than clustering them together in three groups of two sevens) if he wishes to be read thusly. This seems unusually shortsighted for Brown, especially since he almost immediately went on to discuss additional numerical traditions associated with the Babylonian exile, ibid, 81. What he missed: Daniel divides Israel's salvation history into three clusters (7.25, 12.7) and also into a symbolic chain of weeks (9.1-2, 20-27). Matthew's genealogy does both things at once (Matthew 1.17). Could we read Matthew's opening genealogy against Daniel's calendar of "time" (14 generations), "times" (14 x 2 generations), with half a "time" (7) left?

The Revelator's use of this same numerical structure is not absolutely congruent with Matthew. Whereas the Matthaean number tracks the distance between Abraham and Jesus, in Revelation it tracks the time a woman spends hidden in the wilderness, and feeds on two witnesses while the beast rampages on. This period of forty-two excruciating months is brought to an end by a chain of seven plagues (Rev 8, 16). In the Apocalypse, the climactic completion of the Mystery of God seems to be the forty-ninth event in a chain of seven sevens (Rev 10.5-7, 11.2-3, 11-14, 13.5, 16.2, 14-17).

The structure of seven sevens is prominently celebrated in Leviticus, in the form of the Jubilee law. Every forty-nine years was a special Day of Atonement wherein a special sacrifice was offered, signaled by the blast of the trumpet in the seventh month (Lev 25.8-9, cf Rev 8.1-2, 6), and in the following year, the fiftieth year, the year of Jubilee, the land should lie fallow and everyone should return to his ancestral home in peace (Lev 25.10-17, cf Rev 21-22). In John, Jesus is apparently crucified on the eve of the forty-ninth Passover of the temple's rebuilding.[18] In the book of Acts, the Holy Spirit enters the church at the feast of Pentecost, taking place on the fiftieth day (Acts 2.1-2).[19]

4.6 SEVEN THIRDS

The proportion of thirds plays a significant role in John's Apocalypse, linking different sections of Revelation together by intratextual and exegetical reference. The first series of seven plagues in Revelation is

---

18 During the first Passover mentioned in John's gospel, the crowd asserts that the Jerusalem temple has been under reconstruction for 46 years (John 2.20). Almost exactly two Passovers later, Jesus is crucified in Jerusalem (John 6.4, 19.28). Someone might object that this means Jesus was crucified in year forty-eight (46 + 2 = 48). This deficit may be balanced by counting forward from the Passover *preceding* the beginning of reconstruction (1 + 46 + 2 = 49)—just like the year *zero* marks the beginning of the *first* century. Others, however, have proposed that the unnamed feast of John 5 represents an additional Passover. Both this reading and my proposed reading independently bring the implied number of Passovers to forty-nine. Obviously, accepting both of these theories would result in the congruence of the Christ's crucifixion and the fiftieth Passover in John's Gospel.

19 "A literal version of the Greek text has "when the day of Pentecost was being fulfilled." That is, when the fiftieth day arrives, the period of waiting is completed. For the apostles a new era dawns." Simon J. Kistemaker and William Hendriksen, *Exposition of the Acts of the Apostles*, (Grand Rapids: Baker Book House, 1953–2001), 75.

characterized by the destruction of "thirds"—the first plague destroys a third of the earth's vegetation, the second destroys a third of the ocean, the third destroys a third of the freshwater, the fourth destroys a third of the heavenly bodies, the sixth destroys a third part of mankind, and the seventh plague—when it finally happens—destroys a great city in three parts (Rev 8.7-12, 19, cf 10.7, 16.16-19, 17.1ff).

Unlike the other six, the fifth plague does not affect a third of some population. Rather, it is itself a third, one of three distinct "woes" that receive special attention as part of a narrative grouping that is, like the five Johannine signs, episodically dispersed (Rev 8.13, 9.12, 11.4, 12.12, cf 18.10, 16, 19). These three woes—the appearance of Abaddon, the resurrection of John's two witnesses, and the battle of Armageddon—are further entwined with a war in heaven, a series of plagues on earth, and the fall of a great city, through the proportion of thirds (Rev 9.7-18, 12.4, 16.17-19).

Intertwined with this structural chain of thirds is an exegetical reference to an Ezekielian passage in which God delivers Jerusalem to destruction in three parts: a third part of Jerusalem to the flame, a third to the sword, and a third to the wind—fire and sword refer to an impending siege; dispersal by wind is a prophetic metaphor for forced relocation (Eze 5). Certainly this allusion colors John's description of a city falling in three parts (Rev 16.19). It also colors the first series of plagues (Rev 8.6-19), so that the first set of plagues and the three woes are events that occur within a specific context, affecting a specific population; this is emblematic of the divine judgment(s) against Israel and Jerusalem as frequently described in the Old Testament. This may enable readers to distinguish between the plagues of destruction that are limited to the one-third range and the later plagues of destruction that affect the entire world (cf Rev 9.20-21), although neatly separating the two chains seems an impossible task (Rev 8, 16).

4.7 SEVEN AND TEN

There are two crafty points of apocalyptic obscurity in John's Revelation which discretely maintain a powerful and meaningful relationship.

The first concerns the effects of a notable earthquake that occurs in the wake of the first resurrection explicitly described by the Revelator (Rev 11.11).[20] Because of this terrible earthquake—which punctuates the resurrection of the two witnesses—"the tenth of the city fell," and seven thousand people seem to die.

These details are often dealt with through an appeal to two separate Old Testament references: God once preserved seven thousand saints in a nation of sinners (1 Kgs 19.18), and once discussed the fate of a tenth of a remnant (Isa 6.13).[21] This composite solution to the odd detail of the seven thousands and the tenth may be attractive as one that at least appeals to the Jewish sources which the author of the Apocalypse clearly favors. But it is problematic even beyond the frustrating and idiosyncratic Greek that characterizes his writing. Critically, the Revelator does not actually say that seven thousand people die in the earthquake. More precisely, he says that "names of men, seven thousands" are killed (Rev 11.13). It is perhaps easier to appreciate this cue in linguistic context, inasmuch as both Hebrew and Greek semantically associated hordes of a thousand with their captain or leader.[22]

This brings us to a second obscurity, identified and explained by an angelic guide as "the mystery of the woman and the beast carrying her having seven heads and ten horns" (Rev 17.1-18k cf 12.1-3, 13.1).

While the seven-headed nature of this terrible monster is a detail unique to the Revelator's description, the detail of his ten horns is straight out of Daniel's vision of a last, terrifying beast with "ten horns" (Dan 7.7).[23] In Daniel 7 the prophet's vision of beasts and a human-looking figure is kindly interpreted by an angelic atten-

20 This is the resurrection of the two witnesses (Rev 11.1-13). However, the Revelator explicitly identifies another event elsewhere as the "first resurrection" (Rev 20.5). I propose that these are parallel or congruent scenes.

21 The meaning of this passage is not absolutely clear, and may admit opposing translations. Some render the fate of the tenth in a positive sense, so that it will be saved or become salvific (cf KJV, NKJV), while many render the whole land, even the tenth part, as utterly damned (cf RSV, NRSV, ESV, ASV).

22 "χιλίαρχος (chiliarchos), *military tribune*. A compound of ἄρχω [to rule] and χίλιοι [thousand] ... Heb. equiv. fr. LXX: ףֶּלֶא (18×), ףוּלַּא (2×), ףֶּלֶא (2×), האָמ (1×)." *The Lexham Analytical Lexicon to the Greek New Testament* (Logos Bible Software, 2011); cf Ex 18.21, 25; Jdg 6.15.

23 Bauckham points out that the Revelator's beast has seven heads, whereas Daniel's four beasts have seven heads between them, Bauckham, *The Climax of Prophecy*, 404.

dant. His explanation details a specific succession of ten kings, with one king—probably Antiochus Epiphanes—proving to be especially problematic for the people of God (Dan 7.24-27).[24]

The angelic disclosure of the mystery of the Harlot and the Beast in Revelation is quite similar to the disclosure of the mysterious Ten Horns in Daniel—complete with angelic interpretation. It is not, therefore, surprising to find contemporary readers of Revelation attempting to solve the riddling passage with an appeal to a succession of Roman emperors, an association strengthened by Rome's well-known description as a city sitting on seven hills.[25]

> And the angel said to me, "Why are you so amazed? I will tell you the mystery of the woman and of the beast having seven heads and ten horns carrying her. The beast that you saw was and is not, and is about to ascend from the bottomless pit and go into destruction, and those living upon the earth—whose names have not been written in the book of life from the foundation of the world—will marvel when they see the beast, because it was and is not and is to come.
>
> Here is the mind having wisdom: the seven heads are seven mountains where the woman sits upon them—and they are seven kings. Five have fallen, one is, the other is not yet come, and when he comes he must remain a short while. And the beast which was, and is not, is also an eighth, and is of the seven, and goes into destruction.
>
> And the ten horns which you saw are ten kings which have received a kingdom, but they receive authority as kings one hour with the beast. These have one mind, and of themselves will distribute their own power and authority to the beast. These

---

24 cf Collins, *Daniel*, 1376-1384/2057

25 "Because the ancient world knew Rome as the City of Seven Hills, most readers in Asia Minor would have understood the clue. John's explanation of the imagery, however, displays how symbolism in Revelation is multilayered and fluid. In Revelation 13, the beast seems to be the entire Roman Empire. Now in Revelation 17, we see that the heads of the beast are seven hills of the city of Rome, and they also are seven kings!" Kraybill, *Apocalypse and Allegiance*, 2394/4079. **Note:** I suppose that Kraybill may mean something else by this observation than I do.

> will make war with the lamb, and the lamb will overcome them because he is lord of lords and king of kings, and those that are with him are called, and chosen, and faithful (Rev 17.7-14).

Understanding the Revelator to be a prognosticative prophet first and an evangelical artist second, many have interpreted the mystery of the five fallen kings—with another up to bat, and one more on deck—as an indicator of the political or social climate in which the book was written, and have thereby dated the book to reflect a turbulent era in Roman history. Nero and Domitian are favorite defaults.[26]

The seven-and-ten kings who violently turn on the Harlot are indeed rulers, but their historical identities are completely irrelevant to their function within John's prophetic story. Many ordinary readers may (and should) associate the imperial beast with Roman rule, but the Revelator's sources predate the contemporary situation of the church, and are meant to extend beyond. Roman political hegemony may be one of his concerns, but it is not his primary concern. The kings are not precisely referent to actual Roman rulers.[27] The mystery of seven-and-ten, delivered by the angel, is *not* designed to permanently embed the Apocalypse within a Romanesque framework. Rather, the seven-and-ten are sequential markers, intratextual signals which enable the reader to correctly group and order distinct visions, visions which otherwise may not immediately seem to be related.

In this case, the state of kingly affairs—with five fallen kings, one present king, and one coming king—alerts the reader to the sequential position of this vision in relationship to earlier, major portions of Revelation. This vision of a harlot and a beast is carefully positioned as the situation of Israel *before* the resurrection of the two witnesses and the riddle of

26 "Of course it cannot be denied [I deny it] that 17:9-11 provides in some sense a numbered sequence of emperors and locates the time of writing within the sequence. Consequently a great deal of inconclusive discussion has attempted to determine from this passage which emperor was reigning when Revelation was written." Bauckham, *The Climax of Prophecy*, 405.

27 "Since our problems are not due to any lack of historical information, there is no reason to think that John's first-century readers would have been in any better case than we are. It is probable, therefore, that we have been looking for the wrong sort of solution." G. B. Caird, *The Revelation of St. John the Divine* (New York and Evanston: Harper & Row, 1966), 218. **Note:** Caird had the right sense of it, but he settled for Nero, ibid, 219.

the seven names of "thousands" and the tenth which are overthrown (Rev 11.11-13, 17). When John sees the Prolific Prostitute, the seven-and-ten kings have not yet turned against her, and have not yet launched their war against the lamb and his saints, and have not yet fallen, being defeated, at the beginning of the thousand-year reign (cf Rev 19.19-20.3).

This is the meaning of the sevens and the tens: the woman sitting on the beast is Jerusalem. The seven-headed, ten-horned monster is a symbol of imperial power, evocative of Rome and embodying Satan. This monster will betray Jerusalem, who has betrayed her God (Rev 18, cf 11.7-11).

But the story does not end there—a hero will rise to rescue his damsel from the clutches of the beast (Rev 19.6-16, 14.1-4). He will face and defeat a two-horned subservient—the eighth who is of the seven (Rev 19.20, cf 13.1-18, 17.15-18). These two, the beast and the false prophet, will be overthrown, together, by the power of the spirit of resurrection, and Moses and Elijah will ascend to the heavenly plane (Rev 11.11-14, 20.4-6). This is the means by which the imperial beast is overpowered, being the seven "thousands" slain and the tenth overthrown (Rev 11.13, 17.9, 13-14). This is a military victory represented as a wedding supper for our hero and his bride (Rev 19.6-20.6), inaugurated by the first resurrection of the righteous saints to live and reign with Christ (Rev 20.1-6, 16.13-21). After this, only one thing remains: after a little while, Satan must be loosed from his prison, and again make war with the lamb (Rev 20.7-10).[28]

This narrative only emerges from Revelation if readers treat its peculiar numbers as exegetical and intratextual devices. These invest otherwise obscure symbols and sequences with a contextual or sequential value, linking together a series of visions with an otherwise ambiguous meaning in an apocalyptic yet logically coherent presentation of the gospel, one that is functionally dependent upon the Jewish oracles.[29] We are already acquainted with the story of Jesus the Jewish

28 As parallel to 14.14-20, 16.13-20. Cf Barr: "At least three times the same pattern holds: the forces of evil gather for battle against God's forces and are utterly defeated and destroyed (16:14; 19:19, 20:8). They seem more like three ways of telling the story rather than three stages of the same war," ibid, *Tales of the End*, 3693/6687. **Note:** Barr and I seem here to be moving in the same general direction, though our lists of parallel scenes vary somewhat.

29 Compare to Barr, lacking this theory, who reads three "independent" stories with vaguely similar themes and "echoes:" "I have presented one way of reading Revelation that sees

prophet who was executed for questionable messianic claims—John shows us that in a higher reality, this event was a (very important) part of an eternally-raging battle between a dragon and a lamb, a conflict crossing into multiple spheres, anticipated in multiple calendars, building to an inevitable conclusion. Though this familiar story is sealed within apocalyptic convention, the Revelator's interrelated sequences employ symbols molded and fashioned out of scripture and include a battery of numerical devices by which they may be aligned.

4.8 666 = $$$

The most notorious number of John's Apocalypse is the mark of the beast, which is given as 666 (Rev 13.18). Contemporary majority scholarship is eager to apportion the number to the Roman emperor Nero, arriving at this connection by assigning a numerical value to each letter of his name, based on their respective positions in an alphabet, and adding them together.[30] [31] The result is not a perfect

---

the book as three interrelated, inter-acting stories, tied together by a common story-telling framework. While these three stories are independent stories with virtually no connections in terms of the actions portrayed in each, the audience imagines connections between them because they are presented together. The author encourages this imagination by setting up a series of echoes between the stories. These echoes exist on the level of characters, actions, and mythic paradigms. These echoes allow the author to guide our reading of each story so that it is read in the light of the others." David L. Barr, *Reading the Book of Revelation: A Resource for Students* (Atlanta: Society of Biblical Literature, 2003), 23.

30 "The majority of modern scholars find a reference to Nero in Revelation 13:18, where the number of the beast is said to be 666. Since this number is also called 'the number of his name' (13:17; 15:2), John has usually and rightly been supposed to be employing the ancient practice of gematria, whereby any word could be given a numerical value. Since the letters of both the Greek and Hebrew alphabets were all used as numbers, it is possible to add up the numerical value of each letter of any Greek or Hebrew word and obtain the 'number' of the word. This, it is generally supposed, is what it would be to 'calculate (ψηφισάτω) the number of the beast' (13:18): John is inviting the reader 'who has intelligence' (ὁ ἔχων νοῦν) to reckon the numerical value of the beast's name and find it to be 666." Bauckham, *The Climax of the Prophecy*, 385.

Note: Bauckham notes further that this has been a majority position since its (re)formation in 1831, ibid, 387. His chapter "Nero and the Beast" is a good source for theories of numbers in the Apocalypse largely alternative to, and much more complex than, what is herein proposed, cf ibid, 385-452.

31 I love Beale's rejoinder: "Rev. 13:9 employs the metaphor of hearing to exhort believers to perceive spiritually the deceptive nature of the satanic, beastly institutions to which they are being tempted to accommodate. The exhortation in v 18 has the identical mean-

match—666 thus translated into Greek reads "Neron"—and some have even appealed to an early manuscript tradition that records the number as 616, which corresponds better with "Nero."[32 33] This sum and summation was rejected by the second-century St. Irenaeus, who identified 616 as a scribal error,[34] and reluctantly hazarded a guess that the mark—the intended number, 666—could perhaps refer to three or four different entities, including the Latins, the Titans, the recent emperor Domitian, or some unknown named Evanthas.[35] But

ing, except that the metaphor of an intellect able to calculate is used instead of the ear metaphor. If the exhortation to exercise intellect by calculating is taken literally, then the exhortation to "have ears to hear" absurdly must be taken in literal fashion to refer to hearing with physical ears!" G. K. Beale, *The Book of Revelation: A Commentary on the Greek Text* (Grand Rapids: Eerdmans, 1999), 24.

32 "When Greek letters are used as numerals the difference between 666 and 616 is merely a change from ξ to ι (666 = χξς and 616 = χις). Perhaps the change was intentional, seeing that the Greek form Nero Caesar written in Hebrew characters (קסר נרון) is equivalent to 666, whereas the Latin form Nero Caesar (קסר נרו) is equivalent to 616." Bruce M. Metzger, A Textual Commentary on the Greek New Testament, Second Edition a Companion Volume to the United Bible Societies' Greek New Testament (London, New York: United Bible Societies, 1994), 750; Ian Boxall, The Revelation of Saint John (London: Continuum, 2006), 199; Hanegraaff, The Apocalypse Code, 146-147.

33 Fiorenza points out the fatal flaw in this general approach: "Since the number 666 refers to different letters depending on whether the Greek, Hebrew, or English alphabets are utilized, it is difficult to establish an objective one-to-one meaning not only between numbers and letters but also between numbers and the historical referent. Despite centuries of puzzling over this problem, scholars have yet to agree on whether 666 refers to Nero, Caligula, Domitian, or any other historical referent. The number 666 is a polysemous symbol that defies referential analysis." Fiorenza, *Revelation*, 275/2255. She lost me at "defies referential analysis," but the rest is right on.

34 "I do not know how it is that some have erred following the ordinary mode of speech, and have vitiated the middle number in the name, deducting the amount fifty from it, so that instead of six decades they will have it that there is but one [666 – 50 = 616]... Others then received this reading without examination; some in their simplicity, and upon their own responsibility, making use of this number expressing one decade; while some, in their inexperience, have ventured to seek out a name which should contain the erroneous and spurious number." Irenaeus, *Against Heresies* 5.30.1, in Roberts Alexander, James Donaldson, and A. Cleveland Cox, *The Ante-Nicene Fathers*, 558.

35 "For if there are many names found possessing this number, it will be asked which among them shall the coming man bear. It is not through a want of names containing the number of that name that I say this, but on account of the fear of God, the zeal for the truth: for the name Evanthas contains the required number, but I make no allegation regarding it. Then also Lateinos has the number six hundred and sixty-six; and it is a very probable (solution), this being the name of the last kingdom. For the Latins are they who at present bear rule. I will not, however, make any boast over this (coincidence). *Teitan*, too, among all the names

he himself ventured back into the Revelator's source material—the Jewish oracles—to explain the number, and resorted to a composite approach as a means of interpreting the Apocalypse, when he turned to Genesis, where Noah is six hundred when the flood strikes (6--), and then to Daniel, where Nebuchadnezzar's golden idol is sixty cubits high (-6-) and six cubits wide (--6).[36]

In an age of electronic databases and search engines—an age with a canon, no less—it is easier to track down a more-likely referent. In the Old Testament, 666 appears in not one but two contexts. One is pertinent, the other superfluous. The irrelevant mention is found in Ezra, where 666 appears in reference to the number of returning exiles associated with the household of one Adonikam (Ezra 2.13). We know that this number is, in all likelihood, not the subject of John's reference not only or even primarily because the figure is disputed even within the canon (cf Neh 7.18, 1 Esd 5.14),[37] but because the Revelator surrounds the number 666 with highly specific, contextually relevant clues:

> And he causes all, the small and the great, and the rich and the poor, and the free and the slaves, that he should give them a mark upon their right hand or upon their foreheads, and that no one should have power to buy or to sell without having the mark or the name of the beast or the number of his name. Here is wisdom: let the one with understanding count the number of the beast, for it is the number of a man, and his number is six hundred threescore and six (Rev 13.16).

Because there is great potential for error in interpreting this number, John belabors the sum. He invites those with 1) wisdom to tackle this number of 2) a specific person, and lets us know that the mark is 3) monetary in nature. If we were to search the scriptures for a referent

---

which are found among us, is rather worthy of credit. ... Among many persons, too, this name is accounted divine, so that even the sun is termed "Titan" by those who do now possess (the rule)." Irenaeus, *Against Heresies.* 5.30.3.

36 Irenaeus, *Against Heresies*, 5.29.2

37 Ezr 2.13 records the number of Adonikam's descendants as 666. Neh 7.18, 1 Esd 5.14 record the number of Adonikam's descendants as 667.

that is compatible with all of these clues, we would find the number 666 in two (parallel) passages that describe a massive annual intake of golden talents, into the treasury of the wisest king of Israel:[38] [39]

> Now the weight of gold that came to Solomon in one year was six hundred and sixty-six talents of gold, beside that which the traders and merchants brought; and all the kings of Arabia and the governors of the land brought gold and silver to Solomon (2 Chr 9.13, 1 Kgs 10.14).

Even though the passage aligns with those clues with which the Revelator has bludgeoned us, we may be tempted to write off the congruity as a coincidence. Because talents are an abstract financial concept for most of today's readers, it may be difficult to appreciate the enormous quantity of hard currency this number represents, but it is the largest personal fortune recorded in the Old Testament.[40] The Jewish historian Josephus was impressed enough by the sum to retain it in his recountings of Solomon's glory.[41]

The import of 666 as it is utilized in Revelation may be more apparent if the reader also detects in the mystery of the number a reference to the Shema, a critical portion of scripture recognized by Christ as the greatest law of all (cf Mark 12.28-31):

> Hear, Israel: The Lord—our God, the Lord—is one. You shall love the Lord your God with all your heart, and with all your

---

38 "The mention in 1 Kgs. 10:14 of 666 talents of gold accumulated by Solomon may also be in John's field of reference. The 666 talents are mentioned immediately after Solomon has reached the peak of his kingship. After telling of such greatness, 1 Kings immediately tells how Solomon broke a series of God's laws for kings (Deut. 17:14–17) by multiplying gold, horses, chariots, and foreign wives and by becoming involved in idolatry (1 Kgs. 10:14–11:13). Consequently, the 666 from 1 Kings would have served as an excellent candidate for a number to symbolize the perversion of kingship through idolatry and economic evil," Beale, *The Book of Revelation*, 727.

39 The first exegete to note this connection appears to be the Venerable Bede in the eighth century, Wallis, *Bede: Commentary on Revelation*, 206.

40 In 4 Maccabees 4.17 Antiochus Epiphanes accepts a bribe of "three thousand six hundred talents annually" from a would-be Jewish high priest, but the passage is not precise about from where the money came, or about the value of the talents (e.g. gold vs. silver).

41 Josephus, *Antiquities* 8.179, cf 2 Chr 9.17-19, 1 Kgs 10.19-21

> soul, and with all your might. These words that I command you today shall be in your heart. You shall drill them into your children, and shall speak of them while at home and while you travel, when you lie down and when you rise. **Bind them as a sign on your hand and fix them before your eyes,** and write them on the doorposts of your house and on your gates (Deut 6.6-8, emphasis added).

This passage is an early anchor of Jewish piety, which makes it also a pillar of Christian faith. It reflects a core principle of monotheism and a core disposition of devotion. Moses insists on making this great commandment a staple of daily life, the subject of constant discussion, an object of constant instruction. It should not only be etched into architecture, but should also should be physically joined to the pious person as a binding reminder upon the hands or head. Although the imagery has allegorical implications,[42] this is not just a figure of speech. Phylacteries and frontlets remain a staple of Jewish orthodoxy.[43]

The Revelator's vision joins these two Jewish references together—Solomon's treasury and Israel's Shema—to relate a symbol of false worship, a mark placed upon the hands and foreheads of people who are overwhelmed by force and submissive to power, a mark for those who are fooled by political dominion masquerading as divine order. These "marvel and follow the beast" based on his apparent durability and longevity (Rev 13.4). They are subservient devotees of wealth, and of the power it brings. The Revelator's portrayal of their pretentious, false, and blasphemous piety is consistent with a wider evangelical vision of the doomed and desperate multitudes led astray by greed

---

42 cf *Letter of Aristeas*, 159

43 "Some Jews to this day literally place the words "The Lord is our God, the Lord alone..." in little boxes called phylacteries fastened on their hands and foreheads (fig 3.13; see Matt 23:5). These are symbols of devotion to God. Deuteronomy teaches the people of Israel always to make allegiance to God front and center—as we might say. Worship should govern every thought and action as completely as if God's name were bound to our hands and affixed to our foreheads. [paragraph] Just as reverence for God should be first in the mind of every Jew and Christian, so allegiance to the beast also is the controlling factor for people beholden to the empire." Kraybill, *Apocalypse and Allegiance*, 1196-1206/4079.

and lust for power (Matt 6.24, 26.15, Mark 11.15-18, 12.14-17, Luke 16.13, John 12.6, 1 Tim 6.10, Heb 13.5).

This group of the damned stands in stark contrast against the Revelator's vision of another multitude. Immediately after introducing the beast and his 666, the Revelator returns us to the lamb and his 144,000 (Rev 13.11-18, 14.1-4). In John's Revelation, these two numbers are symbolically incompatible, and represent two groups locked in conflict, engaged in an unavoidable battle between higher and lower spheres of influence: "You cannot serve both God and money" (Matt 6.24).[44]

44 Or, "You cannot serve both God and Mammon."

5.1 WAR IN HEAVEN

Finally my brothers, be empowered in the Lord and in the power of his strength. Put on the armor of God, so that you will be able to stand against the methods of the devil, because ours is not a struggle against blood and flesh enemies, but against first principles, against the authorities, against the cosmic powers of this darkness, against the spiritual forces of wickedness in the places of the heavens. Because of this, take up the armor of God, so that you might be able to resist in the day of evil, and having finished all things, to stand (Ephesians 6.10-13).

While the gospels usually keep the cosmic scope of the conflict between good and evil in the background, it is definitely a subject of interest, and occasionally bubbles to the surface of the story. The best example of this may be found in a uniquely Lukan scene, as an army of disciples returns to the Christ to celebrate their ability to subdue demons through his authority (Luke 10.17). In response, Jesus clues them into his own private vision: Satan had plummeted from heaven. Their invincibility against demons and serpentine stingers is connected to that revelation. Yet, although the battle seems to be going well, the Christ encourages his followers to rejoice in a higher victory: their names are marked down in heaven (Luke 10.18-20).

The scene is unlike anything else we have in the gospels, and it isn't over. Luke transitions into an internal Christological dialogue, giving to us a triune image of Christ talking through the Spirit to his Father, thanking him for these reinforcements—even if they aren't exactly the brightest of the bunch (Luke 10.21-22).

Jesus turns to his merry band of protoevangelists and tells them, privately, that what they have been experiencing is something that has been a long time in the making. And then Luke returns us to Christ's more mundane ministry, to an argument about the greatest law of all, resolved by a good Samaritan (Luke 10.23-24). The gospel continues.

In Luke, the account of Christ's apocalyptic vision is a brief glance into the higher realms that Jesus quietly navigated and manipulated through his ministry. This is consistent with earlier Mark's overall portrayal of the Christ, though in that gospel, Jesus' cosmic command of the universe is submerged with great weight beneath a swiftly flowing narrative current. Although he is obviously keeping something under wraps, what or why is never made explicitly clear. Yet in incident after incident Jesus endeavors to maintain a low profile, tells his students, his clients, and their unruly spirits to keep his powers and identity to themselves (Mark 1.34, 43-44, 3.11-12, 5.6-17, 42-43, 7.24, 34-36, 8.29-30, 9.9-10). Peter is only able to partially grasp Jesus' messianic secret. "Sure you're the Christ," he says. "But the Son of Man isn't supposed to die" (Mark 8.29-32).

Jesus disagrees (Mark 8.33).

The second half of Revelation illuminates what Peter did not yet see. That is the beauty of apocalypse. It facilitates a change of perspective.

5.2 THE FIRST WOE

There are three climactic moments, explicitly identified as "woes," around which Revelation is arranged. These three calamitous signs of the end are pivotal, and bring to climax a chain of seven sevens, as the final three-act staging of God's Mystery (Rev 11.14-15).

The first of these woes is the opening of the bottomless pit and the releasing of a notorious Destroyer, king over those strange creatures which torment men for five months (Rev 9.10-11). The elaborate description of this swarm in Revelation relies on the lengthy description of an "army" in Joel, and also corresponds to a plague of locusts that preceded the exodus (Rev 9.7-11, Joel 2, Ex 10.12-14). One detail that corresponds to neither of these two sources is their strange tails, which sting men like scorpions and snakes. This may be yet another allusion to the Song of Moses (Rev 9.5, 10, cf 19, Deut 32.24, 32-33).

The depthless abyss from which these tormentors arise is the vault of the underworld, an ethereal realm of Hades. It is one of the rare images in Revelation without a strong Old Testament referent, though even in the biblical tradition the depths are frequently a subterranean realm inversely corresponding to heaven, often infested with monsters and spirits hostile toward wo/man and God.[1] It is from this dark region of shadow that the Destroyer's subjects swarm, obscuring the sun like a bank of smoke. They are destructive spirits released into the mortal world, and they feed not upon the fruit of the earth, but upon those not sealed in heaven (Rev 9.4-5).[2]

The master of this horde is called Abaddon in Hebrew and Apollyon in Greek. As with the four horsemen, there is often a strong impulse to recognize this Destroyer as the bane of creation,[3] and given his titles and company this impulse is natural. But readers of apocalypse know that things are not often what they seem. As the heavenly scroll has already revealed—and as the Mosaic law certainly affirms, and as the prophets would probably agree—the destruction of sinners is not Satan's responsibility alone, but is also God's department. And yet perhaps because the Destroyer's power is so terrible, it is hard to know exactly which side he is fighting for.[4] Many readers have identified him as Satan, or one of his associates.

---

1 Job 28, Psalm 69.14-15, 74.14, 27.1, 148.1-8, Proverbs 8.22-31, Sirach 1.3, 16.18, 24.5, 4 Esdras 6.49-52, 16.51-60, Luke 8.31, Romans 10.6-7, Isaiah 7.11, cf Isaiah 14.3-21, Ezekiel 26.19-21; this type of underworld seems to be assumed or anticipated in the incident with the witch of Endor, 1 Samuel 28.3-20, cf Deuteronomy 18.9-14.

2 "The bizarre description of the locusts as horse-shaped, long-haired flying insects with scorpion tails, wearing golden crowns above human faces that are not marred by lions' teeth, should not be allegorized. Rather, it should simply be seen as an exaggerated, repulsive depiction of unnatural, demonic power." Fiorenza, *Revelation*, 1105/2255.

3 "The Hebrew word means 'the place of destruction', and the Greek word means 'destroyer', indicating well enough the anti-creation energy here displayed." Wright, *Revelation for Everyone*, 86.

4 "While the meaning of these details remains obscure, the clear image of a ruler of diabolical forces that invade the world represents a dramatic shift in the telling of the story, where up till now evil has been largely seen in human terms." Barr, *Tales of the End*, 2433/6687.

This Destroyer is the commander of the army of the Lord, come to personally handle the crisis at hand (cf Ex 23.20-33, Josh 5.13-14). He is Jesus, in the role of God's anointed warrior.[5]

In all four gospels, the earthly ministry of Jesus begins with his baptism in the river Jordan. The Baptizer introduces Jesus as someone who will command the Holy Spirit. When the Christ emerges from the waters, the heavens themselves are "torn apart,"[6] and the spirit emerges to distinctively rest on the messiah while God thunders his approval (Mark 1.8-10, Matt 3.11-17, Luke 3.21-22). Matthew and Luke emphasize the apocalypticism latent in this Markan scene, asserting—just prior to Christ's baptism—that God's Anointed would command a fierce spirit, a harvester who would sweep the earth, separating wheat from chaff, gathering one and destroying the other with "unquenchable fire" (Matt 3.11-12, Luke 3.15-17).

In Mark this powerful spirit descends upon Jesus and "immediately" compels the Christ to enter the wilderness, where he is tried by Satan and attended by angels (Mark 1.12-13). Matthew and Luke expand this scene by detailing three specific trials that Jesus overcomes with reference to the oracles of God (Matt 4.1-11, Luke 4.1-13). Throughout this interpretive conflict, Jesus has his mind fixed on a very specific outcome: he is called to break a different kind of bread, to show the people a different kind of sign, to rule over a different kind of kingdom. Jesus successfully resists the devil and—most vividly in Luke—emerges from his tests unhindered by satanic influence, infused with divine charisma, respected and feared (Luke 4.13-15).

---

5 Contra Hoffmann, who briefly examines a similar series of exegetical connections between the Revelator's "Destroyer," Paul's "Destroyer," and the OT "Destroyer," and then concludes that there is no probable overlap, apparently because he cannot think of a plausible reason to contextualize both Johannine and Pauline christologies against the material of the Old Testament: "Taken together, these features may lead us to the conclusion that Christ should be identified with this angel—but this is unlikely—and a better suggestion is that the angel represents Satan, or even alludes to Domitian or another Roman emperor (Nero) as one of Satan's minions." Matthias Reinhard Hoffmann, *The Destroyer and the Lamb: The Relationship between Angelomorphic and Lamb Christology in the Book of Revelation* (Tübingen: Mohr Siebeck, 2005), 126, cf 117-134. **Note**: An explanation for this conclusion contra the evidence would have been most useful.

6 cf Eze 1.1, "the heavens were opened."

Thereafter, certain of Jesus' rivals are so threatened by his ability to influence, manipulate, and compel spirits of all sorts that they accuse him of leaguing with "Beelzebul," the "ruler of the demons," in order to accomplish diabolical miracles (Mark 3.22-28, Matt 12.46-50, Luke 8.19-21). The first parables of Mark's Gospel are told in response to this accusation, and these drive home an important point—it doesn't work like that (Mark 3.23-27). Jesus also carefully admonishes his critics not to confuse the "holy spirit" with an "unclean spirit" (Mark 3.28-29, cf Matt 10.24-25).

The Revelator's Destroyer is not the first evangelical icon to similarly blur the narratively convenient categories of monotheistic dualism. John's Gospel contains a famously uncomfortable comparison between the crucified Jesus and the image of a snake on a stick (John 3.14-15), and this unusual and controversial Johannine image has an early Pauline antecedent, a cryptic warning to the church that groups the Lord with "serpents" and "the destroyer" (1 Cor 10.9-10).[7]

All of these evangelical images rely upon an incident occurring after Israel's first holy war in pursuit of holy land, as the tribes depart from a region of wholesale slaughter thereafter dubbed "Destruction" (Num 21.1-4). The journey doesn't sit well with the congregation of Israel and it becomes sullen, dissatisfied with the manna and miracles that have sustained it (Num 21.5-6). When God is so irked by their ingratitude that he sends a plague of poisonous serpents among them, it's Moses to the rescue, and the lawgiver smelts a "fiery serpent" of bronze and mounts it to a pole: "and whenever a serpent bit, that person would look at the serpent of bronze and live" (Num 21.7-9). In this episode of the exodus, the destruction plaguing Israel becomes emblematic of Israel's salvation; this symbol of Israel's destruction accomplishes its larger salvation.

In Revelation, John introduces a king over a legion of beings that sting sinners like serpents, and names him "Destroyer" in Greek and "Place of Destruction" in Hebrew.[8] Though a grim apocalyptic persona obscures his identity and mission, he is a dark knight with an

---

7 Some manuscript copies of 1 Cor 10.9 read "the Lord," while others read, "the Christ," as noted in the footnotes of both the NRSV and the ISV translations. Cf Hoffman, *The Destroyer and the Lamb*, 117-118.

8 Cf Wright, *Revelation for Everyone*, 86

unnerving command of the shadows. His is even the key to the depthless abyss (Rev 1.18, 3.7, 9.1, 20.1). The Revelator's first woe is the emergence of God's chief Destroyer on the world stage, and is treated in the gospels as the christening of a harvester come to ingather, sort, and discard. Although the gospels contain images of Jesus and company as fieldworkers (John 4.31-39, Matt 9.37-38, 13.24-43, Mark 4.26-29, Luke 10.2, cf Rom 1.13), the Revelator works in a medium that enables him to more-adequately represent the emergent Son of Man in his apocalyptic glory, instructed out of heaven to begin the reaping of earth (Rev 14.14).

Appearing in many guises throughout Revelation, the Destroyer is not only depicted as a heavenly field hand. He is briefly a radiant angel "having great authority" (Rev 18.1-4); he is the commander of God's army, "Faithful and True," wearing many crowns, baptized in blood—yet retaining a secret identity and an inscrutable agenda—who rules with an iron rod and grinds the winepress of God's furious wrath (Rev 19.6-15, cf 14.9-10, 19-20, cf Josh 5.13-15).

In Revelation the Destroyer uses his key to the abyss to seal away Satan, at the start of a magnificent though temporary age (Rev 20.1-6, cf 9.1). In Luke's Gospel, this inaugural moment passes quietly: "And having finished every temptation, the devil departed from him until the time." (Luke 4.13). Although there are indications throughout the gospels that the span of Jesus' earthly ministry was a glorious era for those with eyes to see it (Luke 10.17-24, Matt 10.5-23, 13.36-44, Mark 9.1-12), there are also indications that this golden age would only be appreciated in hindsight by the early apostles of Jesus (Luke 17.22, cf 10.17-24), who spent the better part of their own ministries explaining the aftermath of the crucifixion, which brought a brilliant career to an unexpected conclusion: the destruction of the curse of the law, by someone who "became a curse for us" (Gal 3.10-13).

5.3 THE SECOND WOE

The first woe is the fifth event in a chain of seven plagues (Rev 9.12), and this chain is interrupted just before the critical moment, so that an angel in heaven can illustrate what the final trumpet should signify

(Rev 10.1-7, Dan 12.7).[9] In this context the Revelator first alludes to an apocalyptic schema inspired by Daniel: time, and times, and half a time.

The second woe is one of the first events of John's Revelation to be explicitly incorporated into this calendar. While the "holy city" is trampled by the nations for 42 months, two witnesses prophesy for 1260 days (Rev 11.2-3). Subsequently they are said to lie unburied in Jerusalem for 3½ "days" during the reign of the beast, which elsewhere is said to last 42 months (Rev 11.7-9, 11, cf 12.6, 14, 13.5-7). Their resurrection is the second woe (Rev 11.11-14).

The witnesses are described as the "two olive trees and two lampstands," a menorah-based image used in Zechariah to describe Zerubbabel and Joshua, key leaders of Israel's restoration associated with the offices of prince and priest, respectively (Rev 11.4, Zec 4, 6, cf Ezra 2.2, 4.1-2, 5.1-2, Neh 7.7, 12.1, Hag 1.1, 12, 14, 2.2-4, 21-23, 1 Esd 4-5). They are leaders of God's people in the time of his establishment.[10] The Revelator's witnesses are also mighty charismatic prophets, with the authority to call down fire, command droughts, turn the waters into blood, and "to strike the earth with all plagues, as often as they might desire" (Rev 11.6). These are miraculous powers associated with Elijah and Moses, respectively (1 Kgs 17, 2 Kgs 1.10-12, Ex 7-12).

The misfortunes that befall them—the trampling of their "holy city," their non-burial in the place "where also their Lord was crucified," the spectacle of their subjugation and scorn in front of the nations—are lifted, image for image, out of Psalm 79 (Rev 11.1-2,

---

9 "When the seventh trumpet is sounded, then this mystery revealed only to John will be made public. Since this seventh trumpet is already sounded toward the center rather than at the end of Revelation, the author indicates thereby that the narrative sequence of the book's visions is not chronological. The vision of the seventh trumpet thus appears to speak about the same final eschatological salvation that is also the focus of the last chapters of Revelation." Fiorenza, *Revelation,* 1167-1174/2255.

10 "Here the imagery of the lampstand and the two olive trees are reconfigured into an intricate linguistic tapestry, the threads of which are drawn from a host of Old Testament passages. In sum, they form a composite image of the Law and the Prophets, culminating in the life, death, resurrection, and ascension of a Prophet and Priest who is the earnest of all who are his witnesses and who will reign with him in a New Jerusalem wherein dwells righteousness." Hanegraaff, *The Apocalypse Code,* 301.

8-10, Ps 79.1-2, 3-4).[11] This same psalm laments that "they have given the bodies of your servants to the birds of the air for food" (Ps 79.2), and this passage should remain informative when we encounter a winged woman in the wilderness being "nourished for time, and times, and half a time" (Rev 12.14). While these two witnesses are called to prophesy on God's behalf, their ministry is a sacrificial one from the outset. They represent the oracles of God, the law and the prophets, that manna from heaven which fed the body of Israel in the wilderness, sustained Jesus in his combat against Satan, and still nourishes the Church (Ex 16.31-35, Deut 8.3, Matt 4.4, Luke 4.4, cf 1 Cor 10.1-21, John 6.22-66). Perhaps for this reason the Revelator proleptically encourages his readers to anticipate the delivery of "hidden manna" in the time of their own crisis (Rev 2.17).

The resurrection of these two witnesses is rendered only a little differently in the synoptic gospels: Moses and Elijah appear in splendor with the radiant Christ (Mark 9.1-8, Matt 17.1-8, Luke 9.28-36). The full encounter is an experience reserved for an elite few. Peter, James, and John are the only disciples to so clearly "see the kingdom of God having come in power" (Mark 9.1-2).

In the second epistle of Peter this moment receives brief treatment. Though there is a thunderous voice from the heavens and glorious majesty upon on the mountaintop, Moses and Elijah aren't even mentioned (2 Pet 1.16-18). This witness is one intended to confirm the prophetic message of the evangelist (2 Pet 1.19a), and is delivered after he expresses awareness of his own mortality (1 Pet 2.13-14). The author also expresses concern for his followers, knowing that after his departure they will be exposed to the dangers of irresponsible religious specialists. To keep his flock from being scattered and consumed by what he sees as predatory influences, he has delivered to them a testimony to dwell upon "as a light shining in a dark place, until the day should dawn, and the morning star should rise in your hearts" (2 Pet 2.19). This vision of the resplendent Christ upon the mountain is framed as an oracle meant to sustain the church in the circumstance

11 cf Isa 14.15-16, Jer 16.1-4

of apostolic absence, and is intended to gradually guide its audience into a fuller understanding of the gospel.

At the same time, the same letter rejects the notion that the apostolic witness is one of "ingeniously concocted myths" (2 Pet 1.16), and construes ancient Jewish oracles of wars in heaven, floods on earth, and fiery judgments on cities of sin as resources which congregations may consult concerning the present and future (2 Pet 2.4-11, 15-16). While the finer distinctions are still lacking—his use of the Greek "Tartarus," for example, is not widely considered to reflect a Jewish conception of the underworld,[12] and traditional canons lack a clear record of primordial angelic banishment (2 Pet 2.4-5, cf Jude 5-7)—the later epistle of Peter begins to draw lines of distinction between the sources and means of faithful Christian testimony and those "false prophets" who "lure unstable souls" and "will exploit you with deceptive words" (2 Pet 2.1-3, 14). Here the boundaries of evangelical resource are beginning to emerge: the Christian witness is one that endeavors to employ the law and the prophets, the images and narratives associated with the oracles of God. Ingenious (pagan) myths and fables are a resource of false apostles. This disposition towards outside influence and private interpretation would soon be known within the church as Gnosticism.

In the synoptic rendition of the transfiguration, Moses and Elijah appear with Jesus, a spectacle overshadowed by a heavenly cloud and loud voice exalting "my beloved Son" (Mark 9.1-7).[13] The vision abruptly ends, and there stands "only Jesus" (Mark 9.8). Perplexed, the apostolic trio ignores what Jesus tries to tell them about the Son of Man—instead they press him for answers regarding a scribal interpretation of the scriptures, one that portrays Elijah as the forerunner of Israel's restoration (Mark 9.9-12). This expectation is rooted in an oracle out of Malachi, which celebrates the arrival of Elijah as a final portent of the "day of the Lord" (Mal 4.5). But Elijah is not the only prophet in the passage:

---

12 The author uses the verb ταρταρόω (tartaroo) to describe the action of God "casting [the angels] into Tartarus." Many translations gloss over this inconvenient terminology by rendering the phrase, "cast them into hell."

13 The words of this pronouncement are a little different in each gospel.

> "For behold the day is coming, burning like an oven, and all the proud and all who do evil will be stubble. And the day that is coming shall burn them up," says the Lord of hosts, "that will leave them neither root nor branch. But to you who fear my name, the righteous sun will rise up with healing in its rays; and you will go out and play as satisfied calves. You will trample the wicked as ash under the soles of your feet on the day of my doing," says the Lord of hosts. "Remember the law of Moses, my servant, which I commanded him in Horeb for all Israel, statutes and judgments. Behold I will send you Elijah the prophet before the coming of the great and terrible day of the Lord" (Mal 4.1-5).[14]

In Malachi, Mosaic law and the prophet Elijah prefigure or anticipate the rising of the healing sun, and signal the "coming of the great and terrible day of the Lord." It is an oracle of cataclysmic judgment, one that utilizes Moses and Elijah as figures of a celebrated legacy, signifying a glorious dawn, a rising sun to scorch the wicked and illuminate the righteous. These are the signs of the impending end, a trial that will separate the just from the unjust.

In Mark and Matthew, after Jesus' innermost circle beholds his glory on the mountain, after he is flanked by Moses and Elijah, after his face illuminates the shadow of the heavenly cloud, apostolic minds immediately fly back to this oracle, which depicts Elijah's return as a sign of those things for which Israel impatiently waits. Jesus implies that this popular scribal expectation has already been met in the ministry of John the Baptist, and that Israel has failed to appropriately respond (Mark 9.11-13). This failure is especially ominous because, in Malachi, while the goal of God's rising sun is the restoration and reconciliation of a divided house, the alternative outcome is grim: "Or else I will come and strike the land with destruction" (Mal 4.6b).

The death of these two witnesses in Revelation, these witnesses who so keenly resemble the law and the prophets overthrown for a

14 For the sake of simplicity, I have chosen to follow the traditional Christian numbering, which splits the final oracle of Malachi into two chapters, rather than the Masoretic text, in which the final oracle is contained within a single unbroken chapter.

time, seems to parallel the sacrifices of the 144,000 who "washed in the blood of the lamb." Their resurrection—the second woe—is part of an event described by the Revelator as "the first resurrection," during which the martyrs are "given judgment" for the time of one thousand years (Rev 20.1-2, 4). This reference, "one thousand years," could signal to the informed reader that the duration of this glorious era is not actually a literal period of one thousand years. The second Petrine epistle makes precisely this same numerical citation, in reference to a psalm, to argue a related point (2 Pet 3.8, Ps 90.3-4).

The book of Revelation describes two different resurrections in connection with the millennial reign. The first resurrection is the vindication and empowerment of the fallen saints who then serve as international judges, and takes place at the beginning of the thousand years (Rev 20.5-6); the second resurrection concludes the thousand years and is universal in scope, and is a time where all the dead are judged according to the heavenly records that may finally be opened (Rev 20.11-13).

This is not the first time we find an evangelist doubling down on the resurrection.[15] John's Gospel likewise points to two different resurrections, the first of which Jesus says "is now" (John 5.25), during his earthly ministry, as he raises the dead to life "like the Father raises the dead," so that whoever believes his word "has eternal life, and does not go into judgment" (John 5.24). At the same time, throughout John the resurrection hour is constantly approaching, and is "the judgment of this world," when "the ruler of this world will be cast out;" this moment is a greatly anticipated incident during which Jesus will be somehow "lifted up from the earth" (John 12.31-32).

(Behold:) These three resurrection sequences in Revelation—the resurrection of the two witnesses, and the two-step resurrection of the thousand-year reign—harmonize two different evangelical traditions that emerge, separately, in the synoptic and Johannine gospels. The Revelator's second woe parallels the synoptic oracle of transfiguration,

---

15 Contra Wright: "No other writing, Jewish or Christian, has any mention of this 'double resurrection', let alone of the surrounding events." Wright, *Revelation for Everyone*, 176.

numerically incorporating the revival of Elijah and Moses within his apocalyptic calendar of final events, and is concurrent with the first resurrection of the thousand years (cf Mal 4, Mark 9.1-13, 12.18-27). The second resurrection at the climax of the millennial-year reign represents Jesus, in crucifixion and resurrection, as the anticipated revival of Israel (cf Eze 37.1-14), as also emphasized in John.[16]

5.4 IN THE BEGINNING

The Revelator's second woe is the sudden resurrection of two witnesses who have been feeding a woman in her wilderness (Rev 11.11-14). Though it is "quickly" followed by the third, our vision of this final woe is hindered by the sudden expansion of our view: as part of the celestial ceremonies, the ark is opened, and our narrator sees heavenly and primordial sights that predate even his apocalyptic calendar of times (Rev 11.19-12.4).

Earlier, the Revelator disrupted the celestial ceremony of mystery to show us what must happen to two prophetic witnesses outside the protective confines of the temple (Rev 9-10). Again he disrupts the unfolding sequence in order to facilitate the improvement of our perspective, placing the crux of Revelation—the final woe—at the center of a cosmological mural. Now the oracles of Israel in the time of the Gentiles begin to merge with images of primordial creation (Rev 12-14), as on the cosmic plane outside the heavenly temple we behold a beautiful woman, pursued by a serpentine dragon, in fear for her life and the life of her son (Rev 12.1-4). The exposure of God's innermost chamber reveals archetypal images reflecting our oldest biblical traditions (Rev 11.19-12.18). Here we are close to the heart of God.

16 Even synoptic Matthew likewise illustrates the crucifixion in the same light—as if the resurrection of Christ is the anticipated redemption of Israel—if briefly (Matt 27.50-52). We return briefly to the subject of resurrection in the subsequent chapter.

5.5 THE WOMAN

Lo and behold, a wondrous woman appears in the heavens (Rev 12.1-2). She represents the Beloved of God.[17] Her name is Zion.[18] [19]

In the Old Testament, Zion is a name for Jerusalem. This appellation is found throughout histories and psalms that celebrate the special status of Israel's most significant metropolis, and can refer to the city, the temple complex, or its general geographical precincts.[20] Though not all who lived in Israel would have universally approved of this portrayal (cf Amos 6.1, Neh 13.28-29, John 4.19-21), biblically Zion is God's favorite girl. As the "city of David," Zion also unites (with questionable foresight) Israel's political structures and religious institutions—Zion was first so-called when David took Jerusalem from its original occupants, and David's son transformed Moses' migratory tabernacle into a grand temple in his father's capitol, cementing the city's status as the seat of Israel's king and cult (2 Sam 5.7, 1 Chr 11.5, 1 Kgs 8.1, 2 Chr 5.2, cf Ps 69.35, 78.67-69).

Elsewhere, Zion is portrayed as a woman. In many oracles, she is the "daughter Zion" and "daughter Jerusalem" (2 Kgs 19.21, cf Ps 9.14, Isa 1.8, 10.32, 16.1, 37.22, 52.2, 62.11, Jer 4.31, 6.2, 23, Lam 1.6,

---

17 "The essence of Revelation is the unveiling of a bride. It is a wedding covenant from beginning to end—from first to last—from Alpha to Omega. It begins with seven love letters to *persecuted bride*—true Israel. It continues with the noxious vision of a *prostituted bride*—apostate Israel. In graphic Old Testament pictures, we see the judgment of God written on a seven-sealed scroll, announced by seven angels with seven trumpets, and depicted through the seven plagues that befall a prostitute in bed with a beast. It concludes with the unveiling of a *purified bride*—true Israel. She is carried over the threshold of Jordan into a New Jerusalem that "comes down out of heaven from God" (Revelation 21:10)." Hanegraaff, *The Apocalypse Code*, 116.

18 "Scholars have proposed that this glorious figure represents either the figure of Israel-Zion in the Hebrew Bible, or the heavenly church, or the historical mother of Jesus, Mary. In any case, it seems obvious that the vision intends a multivalent mythological symbolization of transpersonal divine realities," Fiorenza, *Revelation*, 1261/2255. **Note:** Obvious indeed.

19 A similar figure makes a crucial appearance in 2 Esdras 10.26-54, which may also remind us that even in the 90s CE diasporatic Jews were still grappling with the meaning of Jerusalem's decimation. Pagels, *Revelations*, 73-85.

20 2 Sam 5.7, 1 Kgs 8.1, 2 Kgs 19.21, 31, 1 Chr 11.5, 2 Chr 5.2, Ps 2.6, 9.11, 14. 14.7, 20.2, 48.2, 11-212, 50.2, 51.18, 53.6, 65.1, 69.35, 74.2, 76.68, 84.5-7, 87.2-5, 97.8, 99.2, 102.13-21, 110.2, 125.1, 126.1, 128.5, 129.5, 132.13, 133.3, 134.3, 137.1-3, 146.10, 147.12, 149.2, Isa 2.3, 4.3-5, 24.23. Not an exhaustive list.

17, 2.1-15, 4.22, Mic 1.13, 4.8-13, Zep 3.14-16, Zec 2.7, 10, 9.9; cf Matt 21.5, John 12.15.). Other times, she is more matronly—Isaiah's songs associate her with the barren wife of Abraham and portray her as a suffering mother who has been deprived of her offspring, eventually restored with more children than she ever anticipated (Isa 51.2-3, 49.13-23, 54.1-15). The husband of this woman is her "Maker," and "the Lord of Hosts is his name," her redeemer, called "the Holy One of Israel" and "God of the whole earth" (Isa 54.4-5). While this Zion is also clearly Jerusalem, her fate is bound up together with the larger fate of her nation; her salvation is for Israel's glory (Isa 46.13).

In Jeremiah, daughter Zion is a pregnant woman in the pangs of labor, gasping for breath as she flees from her killers, her lovers (Jer 4.29-31, cf 6.22-26, 30.10-17).

The Revelator beholds a pregnant woman in the sky, clothed with the sun and the moon and twelve stars (Rev 12.1, cf Gen 37.9-10). This woman is in the pangs of labor, and is being chased by a fearsome enemy, a dragon with an appetite for human flesh and an eye on her fertile womb (Rev 12.2-3). When he is deprived of his desire, the dragon is furious and so—for her own safety—the woman is sent into the wilderness, to a secret place in the wilderness that God prepared for her "so that there she can be nourished for 1260 days," or "time, and times, and half a time" (Rev 12.4-6, 13-14). The dragon is not strong enough to prevail in heaven, but he is crafty enough to change his tactics; he pursues the woman into the wilderness with a flood strong enough to sweep her away (Rev 12.7-9, 15-17). But then an abyss opens up in the earth, swallowing the flood produced by the dragon, and she is saved (Rev 12.16).

When next we find the figure of the feminine in Revelation, she has become entangled with a seven-headed beast that rises out of the oceans of earth and represents the kingdoms of the world (Rev 17.1-2, 15). Here her portrait is less flattering. Dressed now in robes of crimson, she is called "the great whore," has become intoxicated with the blood of martyrs, and bears upon her head a mysterious mark: "Babylon the Great, Mother of Whores" (Rev 17.1-6).[21]

---

21 With some exaggeration: "In biblical history only one nation is inextricably linked to the moniker "harlot." *And that nation is Israel!* Anyone who has read the Bible even once has flashbacks to the graphic images of apostate Israel when they first encounter the great pros-

In many Old Testament sources, Jerusalem is depicted as a prolific prostitute, including Jeremiah, who dressed her in crimson garments and golden ornaments (Isa 1.21, Jer 2.20-23, 3.1-6, 4.30-31, Eze 16.15-59, Hos 2.1-4.19). Ezekiel, who uses the metaphor of prostitution profusely in reference to Jerusalem, expands this image so that Jerusalem and Samaria are sister harlots descended from the same mother, some prototypical matron of harlotries (Eze 23, cf 16.44-59). The Revelator's image is also evocative of whoredom oracles out of Nahum and Ezekiel, aimed at Nineveh and Tyre respectively (Nah 3, Eze 27-28). Tyre's destruction echoes loudly in the Revelator's descriptions of a great, ruined city that sold its soul like so much merchandise (Rev 18, Eze 27-28).

The last woman to appear in Revelation is adorned as the bride of Christ, who has "made herself ready" and is dressed in white and pure garments (Rev 19.5-6). This woman is "prepared as a bride adorned for her husband," and is called "New Jerusalem," and also "holy Jerusalem, descending out of heaven" (Rev 21.1-2, 8-9). It is a city founded on the Lamb, a city surrounded by a wall of 144 cubits, a "measurement of men" (Rev 21.10-17).

Whatever her historical name may be in our various estimations—Jerusalem, Rome, or Washington D.C.—the progression of her story is parallel to the three stages of relationship that unfold in Ezekiel 16, a prophetic chapter which seems to provide a narrative template for the Revelator.[22] In it, Jerusalem is first presented as an abandoned young woman taken in by a loving God, who finds her attractive; he lavishes her with beautiful clothing and other trinkets of affection, and they get engaged (Eze 16.1-14). In the second stage of this oracle, God's favorite girl stabs him in the back, graphically prostituting herself to many lovers; "in fury and jealousy" God orches-

---

titute of Revelation. From the Pentateuch to the Prophets, the image is repeated endlessly." Hanegraaff, *The Apocalypse Code*, 119.

22 "Ezekiel's depiction of apostate Israel as an insatiable prostitute is particularly significant in light of the self-evident parallels to Revelation. ... Nowhere are the parallels more poignant than in Ezekiel 16 and Revelation 17—sequentially linked and memorable." Hanegraaff, *The Apocalypse Code*, 121-122. Like Hanegraaff I am inclined to identify the substantial referent of the Revelator's Babylon-is-Fallen oracle as the fall of Jerusalem in 70 CE, but I am not quite ready to embrace his early date for the Apocalypse, before Jerusalem fell, ibid, 123-124.

trates savage retribution at their hands (Eze 16.15-43, cf Rev 17.14-18). The Ezekielian oracle finally ends with their reconciliation and the establishment of an everlasting covenant between them through an atonement provided by God (Eze 16.60-63).[23]

This oracle is replicated in the experience of the Revelator's "Woman." It seems safe to call her Zion, and to identify her as God's beloved.

Why is she marked with the mystery: Babylon? It is like that mystery: 666—it is a mark of ownership, a sign that she has chosen the wrong side (Rev 13.16-18, 17.5).[24]

5.6 THE DRAGON

The dragon is that devil, Satan (Rev 12.9).[25]

5.7 THE BEAST

Perhaps in an effort to rescue the divine family, Michael and his angels fight against the dragon and his angels in a titanic clash of higher powers, and ultimately, the forces of light are successful (Rev 12.5-9). But it is not an easy victory. The dragon first knocks a third of the stars to the earth—four out of the twelve in the woman's crown—and then he and his angels are cast out of heaven (Rev 12.4, 7-9). Satan's defeat on the celestial plane does not signal his surrender on battlefield earth. In a last-ditch effort to overwhelm God's beloved, the Accuser transmogrifies into chaotic floodwaters, in the form of a monstrous beast (Rev 12.15, 13.1).

Like his satanic archetypal antecedent, this leviathan has seven heads, but while he is like the dragon, he is also like a leopard, a bear, and a lion (Rev 13.1-2). While this seven-headed beast is certainly a

---

23 This seems to be an essentially feminized representation of the Father-Son/God-Israel relationship patterned in the Song of Moses, cf Deut 32.1-14, 15-35, 39-43, cf 2 Esd 9.26-10.59.

24 Cf Jer 3.1-3: "You have the forehead of a whore, you refuse to be ashamed."

25 "John lived at a time when a general image of Satan was still taking shape, being forged out of numerous evil figures: Beelzebul, Azazel, Belial, Mastema, Semjaza, Satanel, Asmodai, and others. John participates in that process here with his listing of other aliases of the Dragon: the great Dragon… that ancient serpent, who is called the Devil and Satan, the deceiver of the whole world (12:9). Here is the process by which the novel villain gains an ancient pedigree." Barr, *Tales of the End*, 3349-3360/6687.

symbol sympathetic to the imperial influence of Rome, the Roman Empire known to John's immediate audience is merely one head of this conglomerate beast, which as the earthly manifestation of the typological dragon has taken many historical forms.[26] The Revelator's compressed image of empires is out of Daniel's first major apocalyptic vision, in which the same animalistic icons rise out of chaotic waters and are subjected to the Son of Man by the Ancient of Days (Dan 1.1-14, cf Hos 13.4-14). In Daniel 7 the rise and fall of these four beasts represents the rise and fall of certain empires, probably Babylonian, Median, Persian, and Greek.[27] In Revelation, these symbolic kingdoms are combined in a single image, representing various imperial powers that have risen throughout various ages.[28]

---

26 Bauckham says that the beast "sums up and surpasses the evil empires of history in itself," but also associates it with Rome: "The seven heads, interpreted as seven kings, represent the complete series of evil, antichristian rulers of Rome." Bauckham, *The Climax of Prophecy*, 404-405.

27 Collins, *Daniel*, 1374/2057

28 Much of the best current scholarship is hyper-focused on Rome, perhaps because its tangible presence in the historical record makes it a more-attractive exegetical target than the fantasmagorial projections of many apocalyptic literalists. Consider the work of Richard Bauckham, who writes: "Revelation has suffered from interpretation which takes its images too literally. Even the most sophisticated interpreters all too easily slip into treating the images as codes which need only to be decoded to yield literal predictions. But this fails to take the images seriously as images." Bauckham, *The Theology of the Book of Revelation*, 93.

This is an excellent point, and yet a tendency to overcompensate with Rome seems to lead him into some problematic exegesis: "The two major symbols for Rome, which represent different aspects of the empire, are the sea-monster ('the beast': especially chapters 13 and 17) and the harlot of Babylon (especially chapters 17-18). The beast represents the military and political power of the Roman Emperors. Babylon is the city of Rome, in all her prosperity gained by economic exploitation of the Empire," ibid, 36.

So in a reading of Revelation 17-18 that takes "the images seriously as images," Rome fornicates with Rome by sitting on Rome's face before tearing Rome to pieces? That's quite a circular contortion. But Bauckham is not alone in this approach, as Hanegraaff notes when logging a similar complaint: "Like LaHaye, hundreds of prophecy experts misidentify the great prostitute as the contemporary Roman Catholic Church. On the flip side of the coin, hundreds of commentators identify ancient (or revived) imperial Rome as the great harlot. The InterVarsity Press New Testament Commentary Series posits this as self-evident truth. The point is made with such force that anyone missing "the clarity of the identification" is left to wonder how he or she could possibly have been mistaken on something so painfully obvious. Like New Testament scholar Richard Bauckham, hundreds confidently identify the great harlot who rides the beast as "Roman civilization," which "as the corrupting influence rides on the back of Roman military power." Hanegraaff, *The Apocalypse Code*, 119.

In Revelation the beast fares well, at first, and prevails over every tribe, tongue, and nation for 42 months (Rev 13.5). At some point one of the heads of the beast is "slaughtered to death, but the plague of its death was healed" by the dragon's power, prompting the inhabitants of earth to worship him (Rev 13.3-5). This plague of death, also described as "the wound of the sword" (Rev 13.14), engages a key passage from Isaiah, in which the prophet describes a time of resurrection after Israel's long and painful captivity (Isa 26.14-20).

> For the Lord comes out from his place to punish the inhabitants of the earth for their iniquity. The earth will disclose the blood shed in it, and will no longer cover its stain. On that day the Lord with his cruel and great and strong sword will punish Leviathan the fleeing serpent, Leviathan the twisting serpent, and he will kill the dragon that is in the sea (Isa 26.21-27.1).

The Revelator, who was not the first Jewish writer to use the monster of the sea as a sign of empire, alludes to this oracle while elaborating further. Although Isaiah expects a definitive overthrow when God raises his mighty weapon against the twisting serpent, the Revelator understands that the watersnake is not the only monster with which God must contend (cf Eze 32.2-4). There is also his overlord in the heavens, and until this satanic problem is addressed, the beast continues to thrive, despite God's evident judgment against it (Rev 9.4-11, 12.16, 19.20-20.6). This problem is exacerbated by the arrival of a third beast, a deceptive false witness, who persuades men to worship what has weathered God's wrath.

5.8 THE RAM

First the Revelator saw a serpent in the sky, and then a monster from the sea—next he beholds "another beast coming out of the earth" (Rev 13.11). This beast has the authority of the "first beast," and speaks like a dragon, but has the distinctive appearance of a two-horned lamb (Rev 13.11-12). This two-horned villain is derivative of Daniel's ram "with two horns," representing the conjoined kingdom of the Medes and Persians in his second major apocalyptic vision (Dan 8.3-4, 20).

While early readers of Revelation were likely to identify this christological antitype as a menacing figure from the recent Christian present or past—perhaps as Nero, perhaps as Domitian, perhaps as some other notorious persecutor of the church (cf 2 Thess 2)—the author of the first Johannine epistle asserts that there are "many antichrists" already present in the world at the time of his writing (1 John 2.18, 22, 4.3, cf 2 John 7). The Revelator's ram likewise corresponds to many potential enemies of the gospel, just as there are many antitypes of Christ. Consider Judas, Caiaphas, or even Barabbas, that insurrectionist against Rome who sought to subvert the empire by use of force.[29] This is a soteriological model explicitly rejected by the Revelator as he rolls out the ram: "If anyone has an ear, listen: if one gathers captives, he goes into captivity; if one kills by the sword, he will by the sword be killed" (Rev 13.10). While Revelation never employs the term "antichrist," its image of a two-horned ram is one that contrasts vividly with the seven-horned lamb, an effect that is amplified by the ram's project of imposing the mark of the beast on all those he deceives with his great signs (Rev 13.13-18). Immediately after beholding this ram and his multitude of the 666, we are given to behold the lamb and his 144,000 (Rev 14.1).

The two-horned sheep also convinces the multitude to enter into the idolatrous worship of the apparently invincible beast he both serves and animates (Rev 13.13). This description probably resonated with the contemporary experience of John's audience with hostile, competing cults but—as is also true of the seven-headed leviathan—the subject of the Revelator's referent exceeds the contemporary kingdom of Rome.

---

29 Mark 15.6-14, Matthew 27.15-26, Luke 23.13-24, John 18.39-40; "*Barabbas was a robber* [lestes]: Josephus used the term *lestes* of the Zealots, whose false messianic pretensions, according to Josephus, caused God to abandon God's people and thus led to the destruction of the City and the Nation (cf Simonis, *Die Hirtendrede* 130-139). Against this understanding of "robber" in [John] 18:14 see Brown, *Death* 1:808. A link with 10:1-18, however, is likely where the discourse culminates in the revelation of Jesus as the messianic Good Shepherd (cf 10.14-18). But "the Jews" have chosen a *lestes*, a thief and a robber who came before him to plunder the sheep (cf 10:1, 8). See Meeks, *The Prophet-King*, 67-68. On the possibility that the name "Bar-abbas" might be a false "Son of the father" (Aramaic/Hebrew) see Brown, *Death* 1:796-800." Francis J. Moloney, *Sacra Pagina: The Gospel of John* (Collegeville: The Liturgical Press, 1998), 499.

In Revelation the antichristological beast with two horns has abilities similar to the powers of the two witnesses, including the specific ability to call down fire from heaven, and by these false miracles, he "deceives the inhabitants of the earth" (Rev 13.13-14). This deceptive replication of wonders recalls those miracles mimicked by the magicians of Pharaoh's court. These initially competed with the plagues Moses and Aaron delivered against the Egyptians (Ex 7.20-22, cf 8.18-19, cf Kgs 18.37-40). The ram's idolatrous fixation on wealth and gifts is similar to the ploys of Antiochus Epiphanes, a notorious persecutor of Israel who effectively utilized bribes and gifts to win the support of the faithless (Dan 11.23, 36-39, 43, cf 1 Macc 1.20-24, 41-62). For John's audience, Rome was the most recent global power to overrun the great city with great wealth, but in John's estimation, it was not the first.

5.9 BATTLEFIELD EARTH

After the seventh trumpet was delayed so that an angel could stuff an apocalyptic calendar of times down his throat, the Revelator's audience was subsequently subjected to a series of scrambled sequences.[30] These lurch backwards and forwards, sequentially and metaphysically, between the archetypal heavenly plane and the sphere of the earth, where spiritual realities are manifested. Through these disorienting pivots, we are given to know that God's beloved Zion on earth is a manifestation of God's beloved Zion in the heavens; the leviathan and the ram are emblems of kingdoms and kings generated from the mouth of the satanic serpent; Michael and his angels are victorious in the heaven, though on earth the dragon's beasts slay God's witnesses; during Satan's earthly reign of terror, those who capitulate under the pressures of the ram and the powers of leviathan are marked out; those

30 The Revelator's commandment to eat the scroll is very similar to the command given to Ezra right before a major series of apocalyptic revelations, most of which were recorded in sealed books (2 Esdras 14.38-41, cf 15.1-78). The ritual ingesting of certain substances as part of a spirit-world journey among religious specialists is well-attested; Pamela A. Moro, James E. Myers and Arthur C. Lehman, eds., *Magic, Witchcraft, and Religion: An Anthropological Study of the Supernatural* (New York: McGraw-Hill, 2008), 189-191, cf 147-154. It seems important to note that, in John's portrayal, the Revelator seems to be ingesting the Word or Mystery of God—not mushrooms, as a certain professor once suggested unto me.

remaining faithful until death are also marked, though under a different rubric (cf Matt 13.24-30, 36-43).

John sees this group of 144,000 saints, together with their commander, standing on the mountain of Zion, marked in their foreheads with the name of the lamb and "the name of his father" (Rev 14.1-2). Now they sing a "new song," a liturgical phrase represented in a handful of psalms (Ps 33.3, 40.3, 96.1, 149.9, cf Judi 16.13). In the Revelator's usage it is perhaps in reference to the "new song" in Isaiah (Isa 42.10), as the prophet dramatizes the national history of Israel in the figure of God's beloved anointed who must rise and fall before rebirth among the nations (Isa 40.27, 41.8-14, 42.23-43.15, 44.1-8, 46.3-8, 48.1-49.7, 53.1-55.13). In this reference, the new song is a war chant sung with the force of a woman in labor as the Lord goes forward "like a soldier, like a warrior" to prove himself against his enemies (Isa 42.13). With the lamb pitched against the ram, the battle promises to be bloody. Expecting heavy casualties on the Lord's side, a voice from the throne blesses the doomed (Rev 14.13).[31]

But before the battle is joined, three angels fly through heaven with declarations regarding what has happened, and what must happen. These declarations are especially useful in reorienting ourselves after John's dizzying leaps between heaven and earth, primordial past and narrative present. First we see the angel with the "eternal gospel," who sent out John to see every nation and tribe and language and people (Rev 10.6-11). This angel, who first announced the eventual sounding of the seventh trumpet, now announces that "the hour of his judgment has come" (Rev 14.6-7).

Another angel follows, announcing that fallen Babylon has "made all the nations drink of the wine of the wrath of her fornication" (Rev 14.8), and a third angel cries out that the worshippers marked with Mystery: 666 will "also drink of the wine of God's wrath" (Rev 14.9). These are the first mentions of wine since the breaking of the third seal, when the rider was instructed to strike the wheat and barley, but to avoid the "oil and the wine" (Rev 6.5). While this odd detail deviates slightly from the provisions of the Mosaic curse, it mimics

---

31 Parallel with 19.9

the seventh plague of the exodus, which struck "humans and animals and all the plants of the field in the land of Egypt," except for those crops which were not in season (Ex 9.22, 31-32). Now, in Revelation, a second wave of reaping is come (Rev 14.15).

Four angels—including the one like the Son of Man—orchestrate the harvesting of the earth (Rev 14.14-19). These are four generals, unleashed from their subterranean prison, where they have been waiting since they were first knocked from the sky, torn from Zion's crown (Rev 9.14, 12.1, 4, 16.12). This second harvest has been a long time coming—about a thousand years, or forty-nine cycles, depending on your calendar—"and they were gathered together in the place called in Hebrew, "Armageddon"" (Rev 16.15).

5.10 THE MOUNT OF MEGIDDO

The battle of Armageddon is a climactic scene of judgment that is visited again and again in Revelation,[32] but—as also the third woe—is never explicitly identified by the author. The place is named in Hebrew, "Armageddon," which translated means, "The Mountain of Megiddo." Megiddo, properly speaking, is an ancient city adjacent to an agriculturally rich area about eighty miles north of Jerusalem, heavily fortified as an integral part of a major trading route (Josh 17.11-13, Jdg 1.27-28). In the biblical record, this area is the site of several major battles (2 Kgs 9.14-28, 23.39-30, 2 Chr 35.20-25). The Song of Deborah celebrates the defeat of the Canaanite general Sisera, "by the waters of Megiddo," where "the stars fought from heaven, from their courses" (Jdg 5.19-20). It is also a place where the judgment of God falls hard on the just and the unjust alike, in eerily similar fashion (2 Kgs 9.27, 23.29-30, 2 Chr 22.7-9, 35.20-36.1).

More significantly, it is the place where Josiah, the last righteous king of Israel, meets his unfortunate end (2 Kgs 23.26-30). Josiah's contribution to Israel's religious life is difficult to overstate: born according to prophecy, he clashes with local rulers and cults, restores the temple and ark, reinstitutes a glorious Passover, and oversees the renewal of the covenant of the law (1 Kgs 13.1-10, 2 Kgs 21.24-26,

32 cf Barr, *Tales of the End*, 3693/6687

22.1-23.30, 2 Chr 34.1-36.1). But the (re)discovery of this book of the law—known to us now as Deuteronomy, containing the damning Song of Moses—was no cause for celebration:

> When the king heard the words of the book of the law, he tore his clothes. Then the king commanded the priest Hilkiah, Ahikam son of Shaphan, Achor son of Micaiah, Shaphan the secretary, and the king's servant Asaiah, saying, "Go inquire of the Lord for me, for the people, and for all Judah, concerning the words of the people, and for all Judah, concerning the words of this book that has been found; for great is the wrath of the Lord that is kindled against us, because our ancestors did not obey the words of this book, to do according to all that is written regarding us.
>
> So the [group of five] went to the prophetess Hulda the wife of Shallum son of Tikvah, son of Harhas, keeper of the wardrobe, and she resided in Jerusalem in the Second Quarter, where they consulted her. She declared to them, "Thus says the Lord the God of Israel, tell the man who sent you to me, thus says the Lord: I will indeed bring disaster on this place and on its inhabitants—all the words of the book that the king of Judah has read. Because they have abandoned me and have made offerings to other gods, so that they have provoked me to anger with all the work of their hands, therefore my wrath will be kindled against this place, and it will not be quenched."
>
> "But as to the king of Judah, who sent you to inquire of the Lord, thus will you say to him: Thus says the Lord, the God of Israel, regarding the word you have heard, because your heart was penitent, and you humbled yourself before the Lord, when you heard how I spoke against this place, and against its inhabitants, that they should become a desolation and a curse, and because you have torn your clothes and wept before me, I have also heard you, says the Lord. Therefore, I will gather you to your ancestors, and you shall be gathered to your grave in peace. Your eyes will not see all the disaster that I will bring on

> this place." And they took the word to the king (2 Kgs 22.11-20, NRSV, cf 2 Chr 34.11-28).

Although the omen is ill, Josiah does not surrender to the tide of inevitability. Immediately he summons the people of the kingdom, "small and great," and reads to them "all the words of the book of the covenant that had been found in the house of the Lord" (2 Kgs 23.2, 2 Chr 34.30). Reaffirming the Mosaic covenant in the spirit of the Shema (2 Kgs 23.3, 2 Chr 34.31), Josiah embarks on a merciless campaign against the polytheistic cults that have come to permeate Judah, including the annihilation of a prominent cult established by Solomon in reverence of the goddess Astarte and others, at a nearby place called in an obscure phrase, "The Mountain of Destruction" (1 Kgs 11.7-8, 2 Kgs 23.13).[33] Following this purge—in a ceremony explicitly modeled on the dedication of Solomon's temple (2 Chr 35.1-6)—Josiah reinstitutes the paschal feast: "No Passover such as it had been observed in Israel since the days of the prophet Samuel, and none of the kings of Israel had kept such a Passover as was kept by Josiah" (2 Chr 35.18).

And then, inexorably, the words of Hulda the prophetess are fulfilled. King Josiah rises to resist as Pharaoh passes through on his way to some larger battlefield. Though the foreign prince insists that he too is an agent of God, the king of Judah disguises his royal identity in order to fight with the troops, ignoring "the words of Neco from the mouth of God, and joined battle in the plain of Megiddo, and the archers shot King Josiah" (2 Chr 35.23). The people do not take the event of his death well.

> All Judah and Jerusalem mourned for Josiah. Jeremiah also uttered a lament for Josiah, and all the singing men and singing women have spoken of Josiah in their laments to this day. They made these a custom in Israel and these are recorded in the Lamentings. Now the rest of the acts of Josiah and his faithful deeds in accordance with what is written in the law of the Lord,

33 The Hebrew לְהַר־הַמַּשְׁחִית or, "le har hamashit," is translated "The Mountain of Destruction." The LXX has an uncertain meaning, and is often translated "Mount of Corruption."

and his acts, first and last, are written in the book of the Kings of Israel and Judah (2 Chr 35.24b-27).

5.11 THE PLACE OF THE SKULL

It has been variously proposed that some fragment of Jeremiah's tribute to Josiah remains embedded somewhere in the biblical record, but the best-known mention of a mournful lament focused on Megiddo is found in the book of another prophet, Zechariah.[34] His oracle is complicated by his inclusion of Hadad-rimmon, a phrase of indeterminate reference—is it the name of a city?[35] a warrior?[36] a foreign deity?[37]

---

34 Spence-Jones' comments on this passage, written over a century go, sternly anticipate the maneuverings of our contemporary academy, even to this very day: "This is generally supposed to refer to the death of King Josiah of a wound received at Megiddo, in the battle with Pharaoh-Necho (B.C. 609), and to the national lamentation made for him and long observed on the anniversary of the calamity (see 2 Kings 23.29; 2 Chron. 35.20-25). ... There is a difficulty about the identification of Hadadrimmon. ... The opinion that the name Hadadrimmon is that of a Syrian or Phœnician god, whose rites were celebrated as those of Adonis ("the weeping for Tammuz" of Ezek. 8:14), is preposterous; and the idea that the prophet would thus refer to the worship of an abominable idol is one that could have occurred only to disbelievers in revelation." H. D. M. Spence-Jones, *Zechariah: The Pulpit Commentary* (London and New York: Funk & Wagnalls Company, 1909), 137.

35 "The reference is generally supposed to be to the lamentation over Josiah, who was mortally wounded "in the valley of Megiddo" (2 Chron. 35:22). Hadadrimmon appears to have been a city in this valley, and Jerome speaks of such a city as still existing in his day, although he says that its name had been altered to Maximinopolis." John Peter Lange, Philip Schaff, and Talbot W. Chambers, *A Commentary on the Holy Scriptures: Zechariah* (Bellingham: Logos Bible Software, 1880-2008), 95.

36 "*Targum Jonathan* interprets the mourning of Hadad-rimmon as being, in fact, a weeping on behalf of Ahab, "who was killed by Hadad-rimmon," a clear expansion of 12:11 MT [Masoretic Text]. The Targum explains the MT's ambiguous geographical reference to the plain of Megiddo by suggesting that the mourning of Ahab will be just like that of the "weeping for Josiah who was killed by Pharaoh Neco on the plain of Megiddo." James E. Brenneman, "Debating Ahab: Characterization in Biblical Theology," in *Reading the Hebrew Bible for a New Millennium: Form, Concept, and Theological Perspective* (Harrisburg: Trinity Press International, 2000), 97.

37 "It is commonly supposed to be the name of a place near Megiddo and thus to be identified with modern Rummaneh, S of that city. However, the form of the name meaning '(the god) *HADAD is (the god) Rimmon', and the context, may show that it is a composite name. Both elements mean 'the thunderer' and are local names or epithets for Baal, and such a name can be compared with the deity Rashap-shalmon. The allusion would then be to the great mourning normally associated with this deity personifying the elements in ceremonies at Megiddo," D. J. Wiseman, "Hadad-Rimmon," eds. D. R. W. Wood, I. H. Marshall, A. R. Mil-

a pomegranate?[38] a second name like Zaphenath-paneah or Belteshazzar?[39]—but his interest in the place of Megiddo is clear enough:

> And I will pour out a spirit of compassion and supplication on the house of David and the inhabitants of Jerusalem, so that when they look on me whom they have pierced, they shall mourn for him, as one mourns for an only child, and weep bitterly over him, as one weeps over a firstborn. On that day the mourning in Jerusalem will be as great as the mourning for Hadad-rimmon in the plain of Megiddo (Zec 12.10-11).

The elusive signification of Zechariah's Hadad-rimmon is inconvenient, as it prohibits a definite connection to Josiah, which nevertheless remains highly plausible.[40] The precise meaning of Zechariah's allusion is often the subject of much discussion, but there are many other elements in the wider oracle that warrant further, closer attention. For your consideration, here are some other things that the prophet Zechariah says will also be happening as the people behold the one that they have pierced:

> Behold, I am to make Jerusalem, and also Judah, a cup of reeling for all the surrounding peoples. On that day I will make Jerusalem a heavy stone for all the peoples; all who lift it will seriously hurt themselves, and all the nations of the earth will gather against it (Zec 12.2-3, cf Rev 14.17-16.1, 20.7-9a).

---

lard, and J. I. Packer, *New Bible Dictionary* (Leicester, England; Downers Grove: InterVarsity Press, 1996), 437; Elwell, *Baker Encyclopedia of the Bible*, 911; Joel Burnett, "Hadad-Rimmon," eds. David Noel Freedman, Allen C. Myers, and Astrid B. Beck, *Eerdmans Dictionary of the Bible* (Grand Rapids: W.B. Eerdmans, 2000), 537.

38 "The LXX., mistaking the text, gives ὡς κοπετὸς ῥοῶνος ἐν πεδίῳ ἐκκοπτουένου, "as mourning for a pomegranate cut off in the plain." Spence-Jones, *Zechariah*, 137.

39 Gen 41.45, Dan 1.7, 5.12

40 "If a place is intended, then it may refer to an act of mourning commemorating the death of Josiah (609 B.C.) at the hands of the Egyptians in the plain of Megiddo (2 Kgs 23:29; 2 Chr 35:22). If it refers to a cultic act, it may indicate a practice not unlike the weeping for the Babylonian goddess Tammuz denounced in Ezekiel 8:14. ... The prophet's censure of idolatry later in the passage (13:2) does not necessitate a rejection of the latter option. The text is making comparisons to describe the depth of mourning and is not advocating the practice described." Clay Ham and Mark Hahlen, *Minor Prophets* (Joplin: College Press Publishing Co., 2001), 466.

> On that day I will make the clans of Judah as a bowl of fire upon the kindling, and as a fiery torch among sheaves, and they will devour to the right and to the left all the surrounding peoples, and Jerusalem will again be inhabited throughout, within Jerusalem (Zec 12.5-6, cf Rev 8.1-5, 20.9b).

> On that day the Lord will shield the inhabitants of Jerusalem, and the weakest among them will be on that day as David, and the house of David will be as God, as the angel of the Lord. And on that day I will seek to destroy all the nations that come against Jerusalem (Zec 12.8, cf Rev 14.1-4, 19.11-18).

> On that day a fountain shall be opened for the house of David and the inhabitants of Jerusalem concerning sin and impurity. And it will come to be on that day, says the Lord of hosts, I will remove the names of the idols from the land, and they will be no longer remembered, and also I will remove from the land the prophets and the unclean spirit (Zec 13.1-2, cf Rev 19.19-21).

While all these snippets read like close descriptions of scenes we find within the Apocalypse of John, Zechariah's vision of the day of the Lord—though often noted—is not best remembered for its connection to the Revelator's work. Instead, in Christian circles especially, this oracle is known as the subject of explicit reference in the Johannine scene of Jesus' crucifixion:

> Then came the soldiers and broke the legs of the first and of the other crucified with him, but when they came to Jesus and saw that he was dead already, they did not break his legs, but one of the soldiers pierced his side with a spear, and immediately burst forth blood and water. And he who has seen has born witness, and true is his witness, and he knows that he speaks truly, so that you may believe—for all these things took place, that the scripture might be fulfilled, "Not a bone of his shall be broken,"[41] and again another scripture that says, "They will look on the one they pierced" (John 19.32-37).

---

41 cf Ps 34.19-22

While also physiologically sustainable,[42] the image of blood and water pouring from the pierced side of the crucified savior is part of a long-running Johannine allegory, one stretching back to Jesus' first Johannine miracle, wherein he changes water into wine at the end rather than the beginning of a wedding (John 2.1-11). Both bride and groom are offstage in the Johannine account, but John introduces a friend of a bridegroom shortly (John 3.28-29), and then a woman-in-waiting with a disreputable practice and past (John 4.16-17). These Johannine courtship sequences are intertwined with sequences celebrating living bread and water, pointing to the blood and body of the sacrificial Son of Man (cf John 5-6). The water and the blood gushing from the side of the crucified Christ at Golgotha sustains a Johannine presentation of a communion in which the audience is invited to partake of the overabundant life of Christ by the sharing of his suffering. This is the wedding supper of the Lamb, in which we receive the water of life as the blood of our savior, which is the wine of our communion.

In Revelation this communion begins with the arrival of a glorious rider on a white horse, with a sharp sword, a rod of iron, several crowns, eyes of fiery flame, blood-soaked garments: "And his name is called, "The Word of God"" (Rev 19.11-16). While John's Gospel begins with an introduction of God's Word as beneficent co-creator of all that exists, John's Revelation formally introduces the Word of God at the revelatory climax of the story—not as creative force, but as destructive agent. As the Word leads the armies of heaven into combat against the beast and the false prophet, an angel summons the birds to dine upon the corpses of "small and great," as part of something called the "great supper of God" (Rev 19.17-19, Eze 39.17-20). The false prophet and the beast are defeated, and their satanic generator is sealed away (Rev 19.20-20.1).

---

42 That is, the description of blood and water pouring from the side of a crucified victim has been defended as a clinically accurate description of what happens to the fluids of a corpse stuck in an upright, hanging position when thus released. A. F. Sava, "The Wound in the Side of Christ," in *Catholic Biblical Quarterly*, (1960): 343-346; D. A. Carson, *The Gospel According to John* (Leicester, England; Grand Rapids: InterVarsity Press; W.B. Eerdmans, 1991), 623.

Following this initial success is a glorious era, identified as the "first resurrection" (Rev 20.4-6). Those saints who have been sealed by the "blood of the Lamb and the word of their testimony" (Rev 12.11) during the beast's reign of terror now "live and reign with Christ" (Rev 20.4, Eze 39.21-29, cf Eze 37.1-14). This is a group that has escaped the power of the "second death" by their willing entrance into the first (Rev 20.6, Eze 38-39, cf Luke 12.4-5, Matt 10.27-33).

After their glorious thousand-year reign, Satan breaks loose and gathers all the forces of Gog and Magog for a last confrontation of epic proportions (Rev 20.7-9, cf Luke 22.3, John 13.27). These forces surround "the camp of the saints and beloved city," and—finally—the fire that was cast from the altar of sacrifice at the breaking of the seventh seal finishes its long, plummeting arc and falls with destructive force on the mortal world below. Here is the end of that war in heaven.[43] Here is pressed the winepress of God's wrath, as the Word of God was always destined to do.[44] Now, in the proper season, the reaper hurls the fully ripe grapes of the earth into "the great winepress of God's wrath, and the winepress was trodden outside the city, and burst forth blood out of the winepress up to the horses' bits, to the distance of 1,600 stadia" (Rev 14.20), or—to chance a rough comparison—about as much wine as you could squeeze out of 144,000 perfect grapes (cf Gen 49.8-12, Num 13.17-24).

In John's Gospel blood and water burst out of Jesus' pierced side at Golgotha, a place that "was near to the city" (John 19.17-20), described in the epistle to the Hebrews as a sacrificial offering reserved for the faithful:

---

43 Concerning John's "war in heaven," (esp. Rev 12.7-11) Barr writes, "Again we find a radical symbolic inversion: images of power are replaced by images of suffering. Similar inversions occur at every point in the story—even in the climactic scene in which the heavenly warrior kills all his enemies, for his conquest is by means of a sword that comes from his mouth, not by the power of his arm (19.21)... Surely this story is built on the mythology of holy war (and that itself may be ethically problematic), but just as surely John consistently demythologizes the war—or perhaps more accurately, remythologizes the warrior with the image of the suffering savior so that the death of the warrior and not some later battle is the crucial event. At every juncture in this story where good triumphs over evil a close examination shows us that the victory is finally attributed to the death of Jesus." Barr, *Reading the Book of Revelation*, 101.

44 cf Rev 19.15: "He will tread the winepress of the fury of the wrath of God the Almighty."

> We have an altar from which those officiating in the tabernacle have no right to eat. For as the bodies of those animals whose blood is brought into the sanctuary for sin are burned outside the camp, also Jesus suffered outside the gate to sanctify the people through his own blood. Therefore, let us go with him outside the camp, bearing his reproach, for we do not have here an enduring city, but are seeking for the coming. Thus, through him we should offer sacrifice of praise to God always, which is the fruit of lips confessing his name (Heb 13.10-15).

In Hebrews, the Christian host is called to abandon the safe matrix of the camp—which has a priesthood inferior to its own—in order to enter into the sanctifying suffering of Jesus. The saints are asked to depart from the earthly city of God and to enter into the kingdom of heaven, following Christ in his own departure from his own city, to offer up a life of constant sacrifice in his name. In Hebrews, the suffering of Christ on the cross is congruent with suffering of the Christian in the church, which is congruent with the suffering of Israel's righteous. In Revelation, the winepress of God's wrath is filled with the harvest of the earth and pressed "outside the city" (Rev 14.19-20), by a Lamb and a Lion who is also the Son of Man, the Word of God, and a Destroyer (Rev 9.7-12, 14.1-14, 19.11-16). This third and final woe, this forty-ninth seven, is the crucifixion of Jesus from Nazareth, the Christ and Son of God. The Mystery is complete.

5.12 THE CRUCIFIED CHRIST

As the scene of evangelical fixation, the crucifixion of Christ is a moment frequently visited in the Apocalypse of John. It is referenced most clearly in the story of the two witnesses, who are murdered in the city "that is spiritually called Sodom and Egypt, where also our Lord was crucified" (Rev 11.8). But many of John's sequential climaxes are written to engage the scene of Christ's crucifixion implicitly, to more-fully reveal the heavenly reality incarnated in the sacrificial death of God's Son, for those who have already accepted this manifestation as a sign of salvation.

Here, then, are the words of the Book:

... Though I am the least of all saints, this grace was given to me: to bring to the nations the news of the boundless wealth of Christ, and to show to all what is the plan of the Mystery, hidden in the ages by God who created all things, so that, through the church, the rich wisdom of God might be made known to the rulers and authorities in the heavens (Eph 3.8-10)...

... And when I came to you, brothers, I did not come proclaiming with high words of wisdom the Mystery of God, for I decided not to know anything among you except Jesus Christ, and him crucified (1 Cor 2.1-2)... But we speak wisdom among the perfect, but wisdom not of this age, nor of the rulers of this age, who are becoming obsolete. And we speak the hidden wisdom of God in a Mystery, predetermined by God before the ages for our glory (1 Cor 2.6-7)...

... And the messenger whom I beheld standing upon the sea and upon the land lifted his right hand to heaven and swore to the one living to the ages of ages, who created the heaven and the things in it, and the earth and the things in it, and the sea and the things in it, "There will be no more time, and in the days of the sound of the seventh messenger, when he is going to sound the trumpet, the Mystery of God will also be completed" (Rev 10.5-7)...

... The second woe has passed; behold the third woe is coming soon. Then the seventh angel sounded, and there were loud voices in heaven, saying, "The kingdom of the world has become the kingdom of our Lord and his Christ, and he will reign in the ages of the ages" (Rev 11.14-15)...

... And it was the third hour when they crucified him, and the inscription of the charge against him was written, "The King of the Jews," and with him they crucified two rebels, one on his right and the other on his left, and those who passed by derided him (Mark 15.25-29a)... And having cried out with a loud voice, Jesus breathed out, and the curtain of the temple was torn in two, from top to bottom (Mark 15.37-38)...

... And the temple in heaven was opened, and the ark of his covenant was seen in his temple, and there were flashes of lightning, rumblings, peals of thunder, and earthquake, and heavy hail (Rev 11.19)...

... When therefore Jesus had received the wine, he said, "It is finished," and bowed his head, and surrendered his spirit (John 19.30)... And when they came to Jesus and saw that he was already dead, they did not break his legs, but one of the soldiers pierced his side with a spear, and at once blood and water burst forth (John 19.33-34)...

... And the angel swung his sickle over the earth and gathered the vintage of the earth, and he threw it into the great winepress of the wrath of God and the winepress was pressed outside the city, and blood burst forth from the winepress (Rev 14.19-20a)...

... And all the people answered and said, "Let his blood be on us and on our children!" (Matt 27.25)...

... And the seventh angel poured his bowl into the air, and a loud voice came out of the temple from the throne saying, "It is done!" And there came lightning and rumbling and thunder and there was a great earthquake, such as had not occurred since people were upon the earth, so great was the earthquake (Rev 16.17-18)...

... and the earth shook and the rocks were split and the tombs were opened, and many bodies of the sleeping saints arose and—having gone out of the tombs—entered into the holy city after his resurrection and appeared to many, and (Matt 27.51b-53)...

... Now is the judgment of this world; now the ruler of this world will be driven out, and when I am lifted up from the

> earth, I will draw all to myself (and this he said signifying by what death he would die) (John 12.31-32)...
>
> ... and the devil who had deceived them was thrown into the lake of fire and sulfur where the beast and the false prophet were, and they will be tormented day and night in the ages of the ages. And I saw a great white throne and the one sitting on it, from whose face fled the earth and the heaven (Rev 20.9-11)...
>
> ... who is the image of the invisible God, firstborn of all creation, because by him all things were created—the things in the heavens and the things upon the earth, the visible and the invisible, whether thrones, or dominions, or principalities, or powers—all things by him, and for him, have been created. And he is before all, and in him all things cohere. And he is the head of the body of the church, who is the beginning, the firstborn of the dead, so that he might come first in all things, because in him was all the fullness pleased to dwell, and by him to reconcile all things in himself, having made peace—whether on earth or in heaven—by the blood of his cross (Col 1.18-20).

These passages—from the Pauline corpus, from the synoptic tradition, from the Johannine gospel, from the book of Revelation—all detail the typography of the cross, though separately it may be difficult to appreciate their common ground. Though they are all unique, and together represent a colorful contextual variety, in concert they remind us that there is, indeed, a harmony produced by the evangelical choir. Paul and the Revelator, for example, have in common a preoccupation with the Mystery of God; they both suggest that it is primordial in its origins, and contemporary in its fulfillment. Matthew and the Revelator both imply that the blood of the Christ must be poured out upon those who have trampled the savior; Matthew, on the one hand, leaves the words of the bloodthirsty crowd hanging in the air—"Let his blood be on us and on our children!"—while on the other hand the Revelator portrays seven angels dumping the wine of the wrath of God on a great city, called Sodom, Egypt, and Babylon, "where also our Lord was crucified." In the synoptics, as Jesus exhales his last breath and dies upon the cross, the veil of separation in the Jerusalem temple is torn in half, while in Revelation the seventh trumpet sounds, bringing the Mystery of God to a climax, exposing the innermost chamber of God, revealing the beginnings of the Mystery: a woman, a son, a serpent (cf Gen 1-3). In Revelation, as the heavens declare that "the kingdoms of the world have become the kingdoms of our Lord and his Christ," on earth the sign is nailed above his head for all to see: "King of the Jews."

5.13 THE SUBSTANCE OF THE FAITH

As frequently befits the apocalyptic genre, every reader who would make sense of John's Revelation must bring something to the vision, and apply it to the text. Those who come to this mountainous project without substance to sustain them in their quest are likely to find an incoherent mess of wonton violence and depraved sex, an imminently entertaining, undeniably popular fantastical myth of destruction that successfully appeals to a wide, base audience.[45] Yet, while meeting the masses where they naturally congregate, the Revelation of John offers, to those in the crowd of critical interest, insight into the highest planes of reality.

Of those desiring to ascend the mount, many have undertaken the journey with inadequate provisions, bringing with them an insufficient substance. Some stumble across the way of truth, only to stagger at its offense, and depart empty handed,[46] while others plateau, exhausting

---

45 "It is good to remember, however, that despite its central tenets of love and peace, Christianity—like most traditions—has always had a violent side. The bloody history of the tradition has provided images as disturbing as those provided by Islam or Sikhism, and violent conflict is vividly portrayed in both the Old and New Testaments of the Bible. This history and these biblical images have provided the raw material for theologically justifying the violence of contemporary Christian groups. Attacks on abortion clinics, for instance, have been viewed not only as assaults on a practice that some Christians regard as immoral, but also skirmishes in a grand confrontation between forces of evil and good that has social and political implications." Mark Juergensmeyer. *Terror in the Mind of God: The Global Rise of Religious Violence* (Berkeley, Los Angeles, and London: University of California Press, 2001), 20.

46 Bernard McGinn, "Turning Points in Early Christian Apocalypse Exegesis," in *Apocalyptic Thought in Early Christianity*, ed. Robert J. Daly (Grand Rapids: Baker Academic, 2009), 81-82.

their interests before reaching the peaks of wisdom. Of these, a well-intentioned few have returned to the comfortable multitude at the base of the mountain with fractured answers and bad directions, and have led many into ditches, dead ends, and compound error.[47]

But for those willing to embrace the oracles of God and the gospel of his Christ, the way has been unlocked. The door has been opened, and no one may shut it. Yet to pass through, you must also accept the substance of our faith; you must eat the flesh of the dead, drink the blood of the slain, and even enter into the very waters of death in order to emerge upon the shores of the spiritual life. Every soul thus initiated into the Mystery of God receives a mark of our devotion, a sign of the faith granting its holder authority to bind and release higher powers in multiple spheres, thereby easing the upward path of ascent.

This key to the Mystery is nothing more and nothing less than that which Paul preached from the first: Jesus Christ, and him crucified—the evidence of that which we hope for, the substance of things unseen. Here is the missing piece, that pearl of wisdom, which the Christian initiate may bring to the Lord without fear of rebuke, for Christ has received the scroll from the hand of God, and has revealed all things therein. The lamb of God has already prevailed to open the book. All that remains for us is to follow the sign of his cross.

47 "Literal readings of the Apocalypse are perhaps more widespread today than ever. The attacks against John's Apocalypse by thinkers such as Whitehead, Shaw, and Lawrence, noted at the outset, have a foundation in history—the often sad and destructive story of those who have read the last book of the Bible as a literal blueprint for what is to come, and sometimes as a scriptural warrant for violence in God's name," McGinn, *Apocalyptic Thought in Early Christianity*, 105.

6.1 RESURRECTION

Therefore Martha said to Jesus, "Lord, if you had been here, my brother would not have died. But even now, I know that whatever you might ask of God, God will give you."

Jesus said to her, "Your brother will rise again."

Martha said to him, "I know that he will rise again in the resurrection, in the last day."

Jesus said to her, "I am the resurrection, and the life. The one believing in me, though he should die, he shall live, and everyone living and believing in me shall not die in the age. Do you believe this?"

She said to him, "Sure, Lord. I already believe that you are the Christ, the Son of God, the one coming into the world." And having said these things, she went away (John 11.21-28a).

The language of resurrection permeates the New Testament, as the event of resurrection permeates the life of the Christian believer. Resurrection is not an eventual concern of later evangelists. It is a primary subject even in the early writings of Paul.

Paul, for example, treats Jesus' death and resurrection as a model for the spiritual life of the believer, when he correlates water baptism with the event of Christ's crucifixion and resurrection in Romans (Rom 6.3-11). In Philippians he applies this same template to his own life, when he expresses his faith in Christ as a desire "to know him, and the power of his resurrection, and the sharing of his sufferings, being conformed to his death so that I might somehow come into the resurrection of the dead" (Phil 3.10-11).

But it is not the apostle Paul who generates the New Testament language and culture of resurrection. Resurrection images and expectations are ancient, being integrated with an Old Testament concern for the life of Israel and the survival of the righteous.

6.2 THE RESURRECTION OF THE SAINTS

At least two major Old Testament oracles use images of resurrection to describe the future life of Israel: the final apocalyptic vision of Daniel, and a vision received by Ezekiel in the Valley of Dry Bones (Dan 10-12, Eze 37.1-14, cf Isa 26). Both passages seem to have allegorical qualities—Ezekiel is carried out "by the spirit" to the middle of a valley, while "a thing was revealed to Daniel, who was named Belteshazzar, and the true word concerned great conflict, and he understood the word, having received understanding in a vision" (Eze 37.1, Dan 10.1).

Both prophets engage in the resurrection project personally—Ezekiel prophecies to the bones "as commanded:"

> and as I prophesied there was suddenly a noise and an earthquake, and the bones came together, bone to bone.... and I prophesied as he commanded me, and the wind came into them, and they lived and stood on their feet (Eze 37.7, 10).

By speaking the prophetic word to the dead, the prophet Ezekiel brings the people of Israel back to life:

> Then he said to me, "Son of Man, these bones are the whole house of Israel, for they say, 'Our bones are dried, and our hope lost, we are completely cut off.' Therefore, prophesy, and say to them, 'Thus says the Lord God: I will open your graves and bring you out of your graves, my people, and will bring you back to the land of Israel, and you will know that I am the Lord, when I open up your graves and bring you out from your graves, my people. And I will put my spirit in you, and you will live, and I will place you upon your own land" (Eze 37.11-14a).

According to the one speaking to the Ezekielian Son of Man, the vision of resurrection represents the restoration of Israel and the reconstitution of the people. Those in exile will exit their graves of despair and return to the land once lost, and it is through the words of the prophet that this resurrection is made possible.

Unlike Ezekiel the figure of Daniel plays a hands-off role in the event of Israel's resurrection. His job is not to facilitate this end, but rather to provide a record so that it may be opened in the day of the Lord:

> But at that time your people will be delivered, everyone who is found written in the book. Many sleeping in the dust of the earth will awake, some to everlasting life, and some to shame and eternal contempt. The wise will shine like the brightness of the sky, who will lead many as the stars forever. But you, Daniel, keep the words secret and the book sealed, until the end time (Dan 12.1b-4a).

One important difference between the Ezekielian and Danielic resurrection oracles is that the prophet Daniel makes finer distinctions than Ezekiel. Ezekiel's oracle is the resurrection of the house of Israel, while at least two groups are resurrected in Daniel. One group is "written in the book," while the other group is not. The former is rewarded with lasting life, while the latter is shamed. Unlike the final resurrection in Revelation (Rev 20.11-15), these oracles in Daniel and Ezekiel are not explicitly concerned with the resurrection of all human beings throughout history. Instead, they are focused on the future destiny of Israel, and on the trials and triumphs of God's (Jewish) saints on the stage of nations (cf Rev 20.4-6).

Resurrection and the end of times are doctrines that may be understood in many ways, some more literally than others. In John, for example, Martha the sister of Mary clings to the hope of her brother's eventual resurrection "on the last day" (John 11.24). Jesus responds to this declaration with a further saying, however, which indicates that the last day is at hand: "I am the resurrection and the life" (John 11.25a). He does not promise that faith in his resurrection will indefinitely ward off death. Rather, his is a resurrection that endures death (John 11.25b).[1]

This is not the only moment in the gospels that Jesus is prompted to counter popular resurrection notions, which in his day were many and varied. While some people passionately committed to the notion of their personal resurrection in the day of glory (2 Macc 7.1-42, 12.43, 45), others found the doctrine of the resurrection easy enough to ridicule. Such is the case of the Sadducees:

> And the Sadducees, who say there is no resurrection, coming to him also questioned him, saying, "Teacher, Moses wrote to us: "If a man's brother dies and leaves a wife and does not leave a child, his brother should marry the widow and raise up seed for his brother." So, there were seven brothers, and the first married and, dying, left no seed, and the second married her and died leaving no seed, and the third likewise, and none of the seven left seed. Last of all the woman herself died. In the resurrection, whose wife shall she be? For seven married her."
>
> Jesus said to them, "Have you not gone astray, not knowing the scriptures, nor the power of God? For when they rise from the dead they neither marry nor are given in marriage, but are as angels in the heavens. And as for the dead being raised, haven't you read in the book of Moses, in the part about the bush, how God spoke to him saying, "I am the God of Abraham and the God of Isaac and the God of Jacob?" He is God not of the dead, but of the living. You have gone far astray" (Mark 12.18-26, cf Deut 25.5-10, Ex 3.2-6).

---

1 "Jesus' response *corrects her misunderstanding.* He informs her that Lazarus will rise (v. 23), and the reader knows that Jesus will raise Lazarus from the sleep of death (vv. 11, 14). Martha, who was not present when Jesus spoke to the disciples (vv. 7-15), allows no space to Jesus, as she knows (*oida hoti*) about the resurrection of the dead. Breaking into Jesus' words, she tells him that she accepts a current Jewish understanding of a final resurrection of the dead. *She tells* Jesus what resurrection means: "resurrection at the last day" (v. 24). Jesus must wrest the initiative from the energetic Martha. His words transcend the limited eschatological expectation uttered by Martha and center on his person as the resurrection and the life (v. 25)." Moloney, *The Gospel of John*, 329.

Jesus mocks the Sadducees for dissecting the doctrine of resurrection with legalistic literalism, an approach that yields an unmanageable absurdity to which he refuses to be tied. Instead, he exposes a critical flaw in their proposal, an assumption that the laws of Moses will have the same application in the higher heavenly kingdom of God. And, even while he asserts that after their resurrection the saints cannot again die (Luke 20.35-36, cf Rev 20.6), Jesus' unexpected treatment of Abraham, Isaac, and Jacob does not affirm the notion of resurrection as a future event. Rather, it implies that the resurrection is somehow already underway: Abraham, Isaac, and Jacob are themselves already (or still) alive in the living God (cf Rev 20.4-5).

6.3 THE RESURRECTION OF THE CHRIST

Each gospel handles the resurrected Christ differently. Mark's original resurrection account is very brief, with three women encountering a mysterious young man at the empty tomb of Arimathea (Mark 16.4-7). This character sends Mary, Mary, and Salome out with a message to meet the risen Jesus elsewhere. Their encounter leaves the women in the throes of oracular awe: "And having gone out quickly they fled from the tomb, and they had tremors and ecstasy and said nothing to anyone, being afraid" (Mark 16.8).

It is a strange place to end a story, and is intended, I suppose, to provoke reaction and discussion at the close of the gospel presentation. Given its open-ended nature—being open to easy misinterpretation—it is no surprise that a later edition of the gospel was released with an appended ending, one apparently synthesized out of canonical literature—Matthew, Luke, (maybe) Acts, and John—to prevent potential misreadings of the gospel's conclusion.[2]

---

2 "External and internal evidence thus necessitates the conclusion that 16:9–20 is not the original ending of Mark but rather a later addition to the Gospel. The longer ending is a patchwork of resurrection appearances (or summaries) taken from the other three Gospels, ... Although the longer ending is clearly secondary, it is nevertheless very old. The earliest witnesses to the longer ending come from the *Epistula Apostolorum* 9–10 (c. 145), perhaps Justin Martyr (*Apol.* 1.45; c. 155), Tatian's *Diatessaron* (c. 170), and Irenaeus (*Adv. Haer.* 3.9–12; c. 180). This means that the longer ending "must be dated to the first decades of the second century." Of further interest in this regard is the fact that the resurrection harmony of the longer ending is composed of texts drawn largely from tradition that later became

Fear and trembling is not an unusual dynamic in the biblical encounter between mortal and spiritual beings. Consider the terrified reaction of Peter, James, and John at the spectacle of the transfiguration, demonstrated in the fumbling words of the chief apostle, who "did not know what to say, being terrified" (Mark 9.6). This common reaction to oracular encounter is attributed to Moses, demonstrated in Saul, Belshazzar, Tobit and Tobias, Manoah and his wife, Daniel, Ezekiel, Paul, and also the Revelator.[3]

It is also the reaction of the Roman guards, during the Matthaean account of the resurrection, a narrative climax that makes vivid what Mark left unsaid:

> Pilate said to them, "You have a guard; make it as secure as you know." And having gone they made the tomb secure, with the guard sealing the stone. And after the Sabbath, as it was becoming dawn on the first day of the week, Mary Magdalene and the other Mary came to see the tomb, and behold: there was a great earthquake, for a messenger of the Lord having descended, having rolled away the stone, was also sitting upon it, and his appearance was as lightning, and his clothing white as snow, and for fear of him those keeping guard trembled and became as the dead.
>
> And the angel answering said to the women, "Do not be afraid, for I know that you seek the crucified Jesus. He is not here, being risen as he said. Come see the place where the Lord was laid. And going quickly, say to his disciples 'He is risen from the dead,' and 'Behold: he goes before you into Galilee—there you shall see him.' Behold, I have told you." And having gone out quickly from the grave with fear and great joy, they rushed to proclaim it to his disciples.

canonical, and not from the plethora of apocryphal Gospels that were beginning to circulate in the second century. **This testifies to a collection of the four Gospels no later than early in the second century**." James R. Edwards, *The Gospel According to Mark* (Grand Rapids; Leicester, England: Eerdmans; Apollos, 2002), 499, emphasis added.

3 Heb 12.21, 1 Sam 28.15, 20-22, cf 1 Sam 10.10-11, 19.20-24, Dan 5.7-9, 10.15-17, Tob 12.15-22, Jdg 13.20-22, Eze 1.28-2.2, 3.23-27, 43.3-4, Acts 9.1-9, Rev 19.9-10

> And behold, Jesus came upon them saying, "Rejoice!" And they, having come to him, seized his feet and worshipped him. Then Jesus said to them, "Do not be afraid—go, proclaim to my brothers to go into Galilee, and there they will see me" (Matt 28.1-10).

Many things implied by Mark are explicit in Matthew. The unidentified young man is now clearly a heavenly agent (Mark 16.5, Matt 28.2). His simple white robe is now a brightly glistening outfit, better corresponding with the garments of Christ on the mount of transfiguration (Mark 16.5, Matt 28.3). The women do not merely discover him lounging inside the inexplicably open tomb, but actually sitting upon the rolled-back stone, which had been sealed by the Roman guard (Mark 16.5, Matt 28.2). Unlike Mark, however, in Matthew the women are not the primary victims of oracular terror, which falls heavily instead on those keeping watch (Mark 16.6, Matt 28.4). These watchmen, in turn, provide a credible witness of the resurrection to the chief priests and elders of Israel, who fail to respond to this witness in an upright manner (Matt 28.11-15, cf Heb 10.26-31). In contrast, the women—in obedience to the injunction against dread—rather than remaining mute successfully respond to their evangelical instructions, and "with fear and great joy they rushed to proclaim it to his disciples" (Mark 16.8, Matt 28.8).

But the most astonishing Matthaean development is the appearance of Jesus, who meets the women as soon as they depart to preach the good news (Matt 28.9-10). In (original) Mark, Jesus makes no post-resurrection appearance, while in Matthew he makes two—the first, to the women outside the tomb, and the second to his eleven surviving apostles on a mountain in Galilee "where Jesus had appointed them, and seeing him, they worshipped him" (Matt 28.16-17a).

If the Matthaean resurrection is like an extended edition of (original) Mark, the Gospel of Luke is like a director's cut with additional deleted scenes. Instead of a single mysterious witness or angelic agent, Luke introduces not one but two men in "brilliant clothes," and these terrify a group of women who are perplexed by the empty grave (Luke 24.1-4). Like the respective witnesses of Matthew and Mark, these two remind the women of Jesus' Galilean ministry (Luke 24.5). Unlike Matthew and Mark, however, Luke contains no command to return to Galilee. Instead, the women are reminded of a specific set of doctrines: "that the Son of Man must be betrayed into the hands of sinners, and be crucified, and on the third day rise" (Luke 24.6). These are those strange doctrines Jesus introduced at the mountain of transfiguration (Mark 8.31-3.1, 9.9-13, Matt 16.24-28, 17.9-13, Luke 9.21-24, 28-31).

The women do not encounter the resurrected Christ outside, as they do in Matthew. They carry the word back to the apostles and their associates, and almost all of them dismiss the strange news as crazy woman talk. Peter investigates, and finds only Jesus' burial linens (Luke 24.10-12).

At this ambiguous juncture, Luke cuts away to an alternate scene, with two disciples on a seven-mile journey out of Jerusalem and into Emmaus (Luke 24.13). Along the way, the two meet their resurrected teacher, but fail to recognize him, being caught up in their grief (Luke 24.14-27). Responding to the inquiry of the hidden Jesus, they sum up their whole experience of his ministry—their expectations, their disappointment and confusion, and even the strange news, from that very morning, of the empty tomb (Luke 24.18-24). Oddly, this stranger along the road is able to expound upon all things regarding their messiah: "and beginning with Moses and all the prophets, he interpreted to them the things concerning himself in all the scriptures" (Luke 24.27).

Arriving at the end of their journey as evening approaches, the two disciples persuade Jesus to linger for a bit. When Jesus breaks bread with them, "their eyes were opened, and they recognized him, and he became invisible to them" (Luke 24.31). That very hour they hit the road and make the seven-mile trip back to Jerusalem, where the company of the apostles is humming with the news that the risen Lord has also appeared to Simon (Luke 24.33-34, cf 1 Cor 15.5). This offstage appearance to Simon is upstaged by the onstage arrival of Jesus himself, startling his audience as if he were a ghost (Luke 24.36). This Jesus is full of encouraging words, and he carefully reminds his disciples that his life and death unfolded according to the plan of the scriptures, as they themselves have observed (Luke 24.44-48). Luke's grand gospel finale ends with a majestic procession out of Jerusalem to nearby Bethany, with the resurrected Christ leading a host of his followers, raising his hands in a final blessing, and being lifted into heaven, "they worshipped him, and returned to Jerusalem with great joy" (Luke 24.50-53). So begins a season of rejoicing which they carry even into the temple—setting the stage for a Lukan sequel.

6.4 THE WOMAN IN THE GARDEN

The Johannine resurrection contains elements of both Luke and Matthew, and thus, Mark. Mary Magdalene is a constant presence in all four accounts. In Mark and Matthew she is one of three to approach the empty tomb, a detail remembered almost as an afterthought in Luke (Mark 16.1, Matt 28.1, Luke 24.10). She is also, apparently, one of the women to whom Jesus appears as they leave the tomb to proclaim the good news (Matt 28.1, 8-9). In John, she is the only named woman to approach the tomb "while it was still dark," (John 20.2)[4] and—as similarly in Luke—she alerts the disciples to the detail of the stone's removal, and the absence of the Lord's body (John 20.3-7, Luke 24.10-11, cf John 20.20, 24-27, Luke 24.39).

As also in Luke, Peter responds to Mary's news by racing to the tomb, though in John a different disciple gets there first and enters second: "and he saw and believed" (John 20.5-8). This is not belief in Christ's resurrection, but in Mary's initial reaction to the empty tomb: "They have taken the Lord's body, and we do not know where they have placed him" (John 20.2b). This seems to also be the conclusion of both Peter and the other Johannine witness to the empty tomb and garment, "for they did not understand the scripture that it was necessary for him to rise out of the dead" (John 20.9).

As in Matthew Jesus himself makes a personal appearance to Mary, though in John she is not clearly grouped with the other women—instead, she seems to be alone outside the tomb, weeping, after the departure of baffled apostolic agents (John 20.10-11, Matt 28.8-9). When Jesus first appears, he is not recognized—a narrative element

---

4 The presence of others may be implied in John 20.2: "*we* do not know."

parallel to his appearance on the road to Emmaus (John 20.14, Luke 24.15-16). As also found in Luke, though chronologically displaced, she sees two dazzling figures, called "men" in Luke and "angels" in John (John 20.11-13, Luke 24.3-4),[5] before she encounters—as in Matthew—the resurrected Christ in person (John 20.14, Matt 28.8-9). When she does, he repeats verbatim words uttered inside the tomb, as also in Matthew.[6]

And when she figures out who he really is:

> Jesus says to her, "Do not hold on to me, because I have not yet ascended to the father. But go to my brothers and say to them, 'I am ascending to my father and your father and to my God and your God.'" Mary Magdalene went out and proclaimed to his disciples, "I have seen the Lord," and that he said these things to her (John 20.17-18).

This is somewhat different from Matthew's account of Jesus' appearance to Mary and her friends. In the Matthaean account, the women fall down, seize his feet, and worship him—in John, Jesus stops them before they start (Matt 28.9, John 20.17, cf Rev 19.9-10). Instead, Mary returns to Christ's disciples with one more riddle, one leaving little doubt as to what exactly the Son means when he talks about the Father.

Jesus doesn't give his disciples much time to ponder his saying. That evening he materializes inside a locked room where his friends are fearfully huddled (John 20.19). In order to fill them with gladness, Jesus is careful to show them his hands and his side—the places where he was pierced—and even repeats the gesture when he swings by again for a disbelieving Thomas, an element of doubt found also in Matthew (John 20.20, 27, cf Matt 28.15, Luke 24.38-40). In John, the resurrected Christ retains the image of the crucified Christ—though this is not his only visage, as the disciples from Emmaus knew—and

5 These two are "standing" in Luke's account, whereas in John they are sitting, a detail vaguely reminiscent of the lone sitter in Matthew and Mark, cf Mark 16.5.

6 "Do not be afraid," Matthew 28.5, 10; "Why are you weeping?" John 20.13, 14

he proudly bears the marks of his suffering.[7] As proof of his suffering, these signs link the resurrected Jesus to the historical cross.[8] They also bind him to the Jewish oracles of God (John 19.34-37, Zec 12.10). His shame has become his mark of distinction, and the enduring glory of his Israel.

6.5 THE RESURRECTIONS

There are multiple resurrections in Revelation. There is something called the "first resurrection" during the thousand-year reign, where the saints who died in faithful anticipation of their messiah's kingdom are finally given authority over the nations (Rev 20.4-6). In terms of narrative sequencing, this first resurrection seems to be congruent with the resurrection of the two witnesses on earth, and their upward ascension (Rev 11.11-13). The second resurrection is not explicitly labeled as such, but following the battle of Armageddon and the final defeat of Satan, John describes a great white throne hosting the divine presence, around which are gathered the standing dead (Rev 20.7-11). This second resurrection is more total. The subterranean realm of the sea, as well as death and Hades, surrender their dead to be judged, whereas before only the righteous had been resurrected to live and reign as judges (Rev 20.13, cf Rom 10.5-13, Eph 4.7-9).

As already noted, this two-step resurrection seems to be a structural feature in the Johannine Gospel, wherein resurrection is both a current and an impending event. On the one hand, throughout John,

---

7 "The disciples may need proof that the figure they see before them is the same Jesus of Nazareth whom they followed. Thus, closely associating a gesture with the greeting of peace (v. 20a: *kai touto eipon*), he shows them his hands and his side (v 20b). The risen Jesus is the person they had seen lifted up on a cross and whose side had been pierced with a lance (19:18, 34). Immediately the disciples respond with joy (v. 20c). His greeting, in vv. 19 and 21, brings peace midst of turmoil (cf 14:27). The certain proof that Jesus of Nazareth, the crucified one, is among them as risen Lord brings joy in the midst of confusion and suffering (cf 16:33)." Moloney, *The Gospel of John*, 531.

8 "That clear identification was to become critically important for the Church to maintain; the Crucified is *the risen Lord*, in the fullest sense of the term, and the risen Lord is *the Crucified*, the flesh and blood Redeemer, whose real death and real resurrection accomplished salvation for the whole person and the whole world. The disciples therefore were "filled with joy" as they grasped that he who stood before them was their own Master, alive from the dead." George Beasley-Murray, *John* (Nashville: Thomas Nelson, 2000), 379.

there is a final judgment just around the corner, when all the dead will hear the voice of the Son of Man and live. On the other hand, the Son of Man is, throughout John, already raising the dead (John 5.25-29). To an audience gifted with hindsight, these two eras of Johannine resurrection seem to correspond to 1) the active, personal ministry of Jesus in Israel, evangelically represented in astonishing signs such as restoring the lame, healing the blind, and raising the dead,[9] and 2) the crucifixion and resurrection of Jesus (John 3.14-16, 8.25-28, 12.30-34).[10]

But this duality is not entirely original to John's Gospel. The synoptic tradition also sends out some strange signals concerning the resurrection. We have already noted Jesus' unexpected rebuttal to the Sadducees' ludicrous hypothetical (Mark 12.18-23). His unorthodox treatment of resurrection posits an ontological change for the resurrected, so that they are less like humans on earth and more like the angels in heaven (Mark 12.24-25). It also posits a present-tense, ongoing resurrection for the patriarchal figures of Abraham, Isaac, and Jacob, who are apparently, in some immediate sense, already alive (Mark 12.26, cf Luke 20.35-36)—Jesus associates this immortal state of being with the nature (or, perhaps, presence) of God (Mark 12.27, cf John 1.52, 6.56-57). These unusual teachings, which are the only serious discussion of popular resurrection doctrines in the synoptics, receive no further explicit elaboration in the gospels.[11]

---

9 "The one who hears (*akouon*) the word of Jesus and believes (*pisteuon*) the Father who sent Jesus, the Son, *has already* passed (perfect tense: *metabebaken*) from death to life (*eis ten zoen*). Life can be achieved now through belief in the revelation of God in and through the Son of God (v. 25b). The passage from death to life is not a future promise; it happens now: *the hour is coming, and now is* (v. 25a)." Moloney, *The Gospel of John*, 179.

10 "The setting of the passion narrative in the life of Jesus requires no explanation, except that every Christian preacher and teacher who recounted it did so in the knowledge that this "end" of the ministry of Jesus in Judea and Galilee was its beginning for the world of nations. Ministry is service: the death of Jesus was the climax of his service of God and man, whereby the saving sovereignty of God was brought to humanity. No one knew this better than the Fourth Evangelist, who penned his narrative in the consciousness that every step of Jesus in those hours constituted part of *the* hour, whereby the Father was glorified in the Son and the Son was in process of exaltation to the throne of God." Beasley-Murray, *John*, 319.

11 Luke's Gospel briefly mentions "the resurrection of the righteous," Luke 14.14.

Synoptic Jesus does, however, discuss resurrection privately with his disciples. In conjunction with the transfiguration, Jesus begins to teach his disciples privately concerning the betrayal, trial, crucifixion, and resurrection of the Son of Man (Mark 8.31-34, 9.9-10, 10.32-34, Matt 16.13-18, 17.9, 22-23, 20.16-19, Luke 9.21-23, 43-45). Repeatedly, they fail to understand. Matthew and Luke both contain a public version of this doctrine, delivered to the masses in an enigmatic oracle which compares the Son of Man to the prophet Jonah (Matt 12.38-42, Luke 11.29-30): "For just as Jonah became a sign to the Ninevites, so also the Son of Man will be to this generation."

Although some dispute his authenticity, there is good reason to suppose that a first-century Jewish prophet like Jesus might identify personally with the figure of the Son of Man as he appears before the Ancient of Days.[12] In Daniel, this Son of Man appears to represent the saints of Israel as they enter the apocalyptic court of God and are vindicated on the stage of nations.[13] While this Son is a symbolic figure of hotly contested value,[14] it is useful to note that the adoption of prophetic personas—or symbolic identities—is a performative technique common to the Jewish prophets. In Hosea the prophet implicitly assumes the identity of God when he marries a prostitute who represents God's Beloved (Hos 1-3). Ezekiel's assumption is less grand, when he instead appears as the stricken Son of Man, representing at times the destitute future of Jerusalem's inhabitants (Eze 12.1-

---

12 "This narrative, the narrative that Jesus understood himself to embody, grows out of a reading of the story of the career of the "one like a Son of Man" in the Book of Daniel." Daniel Boyarin, *The Jewish Gospels: The Story of the Jewish Christ* (New York: The New Press, 2012), 38.

13 Cf Boyarin, *The Jewish Gospels*, 39-43; Collins, *Apocalyptic Imagination*, 183-187

14 "Much New Testament scholarship has been led astray by an assumption that the term "Son of Man" referred only to the coming of Jesus on the clouds at the *parousia,* Jesus' expected reappearance on earth. This has led to much confusion in the literature, because on this view it seems difficult to imagine how the living, breathing Jesus, not yet the exalted-into-heaven or returning-to-earth Christ, could refer to *himself* as the Son of Man, as he surely seems to do in several places in Mark and the other Gospels. This problem can be solved, however, if we think of the Son of Man not as representing a particular stage in the narrative of Christ but as referring to the protagonist of the entire story, Jesus the Christ, Messiah, Son of Man." Boyarin, *The Jewish Gospels*, 36-37.

16, 24.15-27).[15] The portrayal of the collective in the icon of the one is a bedrock feature of Jewish biblical narrative—consider Adam;[16] consider Abraham, Isaac, and Jacob.[17]

The human figure naturally lends itself to the symbolic representation of humanity, and to the artistic embodiment of the human experience. It should not, therefore, be surprising to find a variety of nuanced Old Testament passages employing the principles of personification to carry their messages forward:[18] Ezekiel's Son of Man personifies the doomed people of Jerusalem. Daniel's Son of Man personifies the victorious saints of the kingdom of God. The sin of Adam anticipates the sin of all. Isaiah's Suffering Servant personifies Israel, or "Jacob my servant" (Isa 41.8-16, 44.1-8, 21-28). Even the psalmist gets in on the action (Ps 80.1-2, 17).[19]

Jesus' apocalyptic sayings about the Son of Man are difficult for his first disciples—and for us—precisely because the Son of Man is a complex figure with many possible connotations. In evangelical representation, it is often difficult (impossible) to neatly distinguish between apocalyptic visions about a human-like son of man (as Daniel), prophetic gestures made through a mortal son of man (as Ezekiel), and the broader use of the human figure as an icon of Israel or even the human race (as throughout the law and the prophets). This is a problem compounded by many, frequent, and often contentious debates concerning ideal interpretations and preferred render-

15 Many translations render "Son of Man" in Ezekiel conceptually rather than literally, as an idiomatic phrase connoting human mortality, or "Mortal." This rendering obscures the otherwise clear use of the personal human agent as a symbol for the corporate body of the people in multiple instances.

16 Gen 1-3, cf Tob 8.6, Sir 40.1, 49.16, 2 Esd 3.21-26, 4.30-32, Rom 5.14, 1 Cor 15.22

17 Gen 17.1-16, 28.10-16, 32.28

18 Regarding the Son of Man, David Barr remarks: "Literally, a son of humanity; the Greek does not have the definite article. This phrase is rich in contextual meanings. In Ezekiel it refers to the prophet; in Daniel it refers to a heavenly archetype of Israel; in early Christianity it refers to Jesus. It is difficult to translate the sense into English, for it is built on a Semitic notion that "son of" indicates likeness to (as the "sons of thunder" in Mark 3:17). Thus, in the Daniel vision the contrast is between the beastly figures of the previous visions with the one like "a son of humanity" (i.e., a human being)." Barr, *Tales of the End*, 1335/6687.

19 A straightforward translation of Psalm 80.17 calls for a strengthening of God's "son of man you made strong for yourself," which seems to be the personified Israel mentioned at the psalm's opening, though some translations opt for a less-than-literal rendering.

ings of certain passages, which can become exceedingly polarized—in one contemporary translation alone, Daniel's "one like a son of man" becomes "one like a human being;"[20] Ezekiel's "Son of Man" is rendered "Mortal;"[21] the psalmist's personified "son of man you made strong" becomes, oddly, just "the one you made strong."[22] These translations may reflect the desire of an academy seeking to prevent exegetical misreadings—for example, those readings which oversimplify the scriptures by treating every Son-of-Man passage in the Old Testament as a prognostication of the New Testament Christ—but deleting the sons of men from the scriptures unfortunately obscures the value of the human figure in later evangelical rhetoric.[23]

One way to escape this current quagmire of dissenting opinions is to consider the way that canonical characters respond to Jesus' doctrine about the Son of Man.

In the canonical gospels, Jesus is introduced as a teller of symbolic stories, of parables, of dark sayings that are filled with characters and events that are frequently puzzling, and seem designed to prevent some of his listeners from understanding his message before the appropriate time. But Peter is able to at least partially discern Jesus' true identity: "You are the Christ" (Mark 8.29).[24] Many in Israel had a set of specific expectations for anyone they would call God's Anointed, and it seems likely that Peter had his own understanding of the role of the Messiah in the last days.[25] When, therefore, Jesus finally tells his followers

---

20 NRSV, Daniel 7.16. *The Holy Bible: New Revised Standard Version* (Nashville: Thomas Nelson Publishers, 1989).

21 NRSV, Ezekiel 2.1, with the footnote "and so throughout the book when Ezekiel is addressed."

22 NRSV, Psalm 80.17

23 "The Son of Man is an alternative to other symbols of authority, such as the Roman emperor and his agents, the heirs of Herod the Great, and the messianic pretenders who attempted to overthrow Roman rule by force. Jesus' teaching in this regard is similar to that of the book of Daniel, the Qumran community, the *Assumption of Moses*, certain teachers and prophets described by Josephus, and the book of Revelation." A. Collins, *Cosmology and Eschatology*, 158.

24 In Matthew, "You are the Christ, the Son of the living God," 16.16. In Luke, "You are the Christ of God," 9.20.

25 "Some groups among the Jews were not looking for any Messiah. The golden age had come with the Maccabean victories in 164 B.C. As long as the temple functioned, deliverance was not needed. Others (for example, the people who wrote the Dead Sea Scrolls) believed in two Messiahs. One would be a descendant of David who would rule as king, while the other

"openly" about the many things the Son of Man must endure—"the Son of Man must undergo many things, and be rejected by the elders and the chief priests and the scribes and be killed and after three days rise again" (Mark 8.31)—it is perhaps not surprising that Peter "began to rebuke him" (Mark 8.32). Jesus has apparently deviated from Peter's eschatological script. For the chief apostle, a story in which the Son of Man is helpless and defeated and carries a cross makes little or no sense in light of his own expectations.[26] Perhaps in his estimation, Jesus is telling the wrong story, or has confused his sources. But when these things occur in a tangible and demoralizing way, and the Son of Man is actually crucified upon an actual cross, Jesus' Son-of-Man sayings are proven true, as the language used in the prophets to describe the fate of Israel is manifested in the fate of Israel's Christ.

In all four Gospels, the crucifixion of the King of the Jews foreshadows the future Israel has chosen by idolatry, just as Josiah's death foreshadowed the inevitable destruction of Israel in the Old Testament. This sign, of a crucified king, was confirmed as a valid revelation in the eyes of the world when Jerusalem was viciously torn apart by the Roman "eagle," a standard symbol of the armies that razed the city in 70 CE (cf Mark 13, Matt 24.28, Luke 17.37).[27]

---

would be a descendant of Aaron who would purify temple worship as high priest. ... Still others were looking for a warrior-king who would deliver them from the Romans." Bruce, *Hard Sayings of the Bible,* 407.

26 But: "The notion of the humiliated and suffering Messiah was not at all alien within Judaism before Jesus' advent, and it remained current among Jews well into the future following that—indeed, well into the early modern period. ... That the Messiah would suffer and be humiliated was something Jews learned from close reading of the biblical texts, a close reading in precisely the style of classically rabbinic interpretation that has become known as midrash, the concordance of verses and passages from different places in Scripture to derive new narratives, images, and theological ideas." Boyarin, *The Jewish Gospels*, 132-133.

27 "And the prophecy, "He shall be the expectation of the nations," signified that there would be some of all nations who should look for Him to come again. And this indeed you can see for yourselves, and be convinced of by fact. For of all races of men there are some who look for Him who was crucified in Judæa, and after whose crucifixion the land was straightway surrendered to you as spoil of war. And the prophecy, "binding His foal to the vine, and washing His robe in the blood of the grape," was a significant symbol of the things that were to happen to Christ, and of what He was to do. For the foal of an ass stood bound to a vine at the entrance of a village, and He ordered His acquaintances to bring it to Him then; and when it was brought, He mounted and sat upon it, and entered Jerusalem, where was

Thankfully, the evangelical story does not end with the crucifixion and burial of the Son of Man—just as the trial, tribulation, and burial language found in the prophets and espoused by the Christ proved to be true in a poignant, personal sense, so also does the resurrection language of the Old Testament manifest itself unexpectedly in something New. The evangelists portray the resurrection of Christ as an intensely personal event. The historical person known as Jesus from Nazareth is resurrected, indeed as he said. Though he is changed—and, at times, unrecognizable—this resurrection is a vindication of his messianic claims.[28]

But—as the gospels are careful to further suggest—Jesus thought of himself as a different kind of messiah, and his words contained contradictory elements. Sometimes, Jesus speaks about the Son of Man as the judge dread, but other times as the judged (Mark 8.31-39, 9.11-13, 30-31). This oracular polarity, attributed to Jesus himself, may imply that the evangelical Son of Man is a messianic model *consciously developed* out of multiple sources, particularly out of passages and traditions which represented Israel or the saints as a single son of God, as a human being, as a son of man. If Jesus acted with this intention, he would not be acting very differently than other Jewish prophets, and

---

the vast temple of the Jews which was afterwards destroyed by you. And after this He was crucified, that the rest of the prophecy might be fulfilled. For this "washing His robe in the blood of the grape" was predictive of the passion He was to endure, cleansing by His blood those who believe on Him." Justin Martyr, "The First Apology of Justin," in *The Apostolic Fathers with Justin Martyr and Irenaeus*, ed. Alexander Roberts, James Donaldson, and A. Cleveland Coxe, vol. 1, The Ante-Nicene Fathers (Buffalo: Christian Literature Company, 1885), 173; *First Apology* 32.

28 "If, then, Jesus was telling a story which belonged genetically within this group of Jewish narratives, as I have argued that he was, there is a strong probability that he envisaged for himself a similar fate of suffering and vindication. The language placed on his lips at various points of the passion narrative probably reflects an awareness of vocation that, historically, had preoccupied him for much longer. **In bringing Israel's destiny to its great moment, the story Jesus was telling would include, as part of its climax, the 'woes', the great tribulation, that characterized Israel's vocation in bringing to birth the reign of her god.** The 'trials' and the crucifixion were not simply the last great controversy between him and his opponents. **Jesus must have perceived them as the climax of that larger battle of which all the controversies were in fact part.**" Wright, *Jesus and the Victory of God*, 454, emphasis added.

would not seem to be stepping very far beyond the bounds of Jewish narrative theological tradition.[29]

If the evangelical Son of Man is indeed an exegetical composite of multiple figures found in various Jewish works, the personal resurrection of the Son of Man may therefore be also a sign of the resurrection of Israel, God's beloved—the resurrected body of Christ is emblematic of the resurrected Body of Christ, the "Israel of God," which is also a heavenly temple (Gal 6.16, cf Mark 14.58, John 2.19). As similar to Ezekiel, the Son of Man's painful fate upon the cross represents the doom of Israel just on the horizon, while his glorious (re)appearing to the apostles represents and inaugurates the restoration of God's people, kingdom, house, and throne in the tangible and ongoing life of the church among the nations. Similarly, Paul frames water baptism as a ritual departure through symbolic death and a reemergence into a righteous Body—this is the very first resurrection of the believer (Rom 6.1-11). The Johannine Jesus congruently presents water baptism as a ritual means of spiritual rebirth, by which one may come to see and enter the kingdom (John 3.3-6). Here is the kingdom which the Revelator introduces subsequently to the universal resurrection and judgment (Rev 21-22): New Jerusalem.

6.5 NEW JERUSALEM

After the resurrection and judgment, John the Revelator beholds the arrival of a city out of the heavens called New Jerusalem, described as the bride of Christ. This city-as-bride image is prominent in Isaiah, wherein God promises Zion that the children of her restoration will flock to her from every corner of the globe, "and you shall put all of them on like an ornament, and like a bride you will wear them" (Isa 49.18). In the larger passage, Isaiah dramatizes Jerusalem's suffering as

29 However, the Son-of-Man/Jonah oracle contained in Matthew and Luke (being, therefore, perhaps—I suppose—original to hypothetical Q) represents the Son not only in a prophetic context, but also in an evangelical context. In Matthew and Luke, the Son of Man is as a figure who will emerge from his trials to rescue not the Jews, but the Gentiles. Just as Jonah emerged from the belly of the beast and preached among the Ninevites, so also would the Son of Man emerge from the tomb, resurrected, a Jewish signifier of salvation among the nations (Matt 12.38-42, Luke 11.29-30). The international significance of the Son of Man is not something that seems to be as heavily stressed in Mark's Gospel.

the suffering of a woman who has been made desolate (Isa 49.8-26, 52.1-12) and intertwines her story with the tale of Jacob, known as Israel (Isa 48.1-49.7, 51.1-23).

Isaiah's best-known Suffering Servant oracle had a substantial impact on the gospels' renderings of Christ, being referenced in the synoptic tradition and independently in the Johannine gospel.[30] The oracle graphically describes the sacrificial death of Israel, who bears the sins of many and intercedes for transgressors (Isa 53.12). His death is followed by a pivot in voice, with the narrator then addressing Zion, the "barren woman" who "never bore a child" (Isa 54.1, cf 26.14-19, Rev 12.5), informing her that the time to celebrate has come, because the Lord is flooding her with promised children.

Underpinning Isaiah's portrayal of Israel-and-Jerusalem in death-and-rebirth—with Jacob as the divinely conceived Servant, and Zion as God's spouse (Isa 44.1-2, 24, 54.5-8, cf 43.1)—seems to be a prophetic apologetic explaining Israel's spectacular, diasporatic shame and suffering on the stage of kingdoms as the means by which God has spread his revelatory light (word) to the world (Isa 49.6-8, 52.13-15). The outcome is a restored Zion that glitters with the glory of God, receiving patronage from every corner of the globe, even from the halls of power (Isa 44.28, 45.1ff). Israel's shame, suffering, and death is portrayed as the means of God's unprecedented glory and the means by which he will manifest his love for Zion through all the world.

The Revelator adapts several images used in Isaiah to describe Zion as a restored bride and city (Rev 21.2ff), merging them with other significant symbols of Israel's establishment, portraying New Jerusalem as a city founded upon the lamb and his twelve apostles (Rev 21.14). This New Testament establishment is adorned with precious stones in loose correlation with Isaiah's Zion (Rev 21.11, Isa 54.11), but the detailed list of "every jewel" which beautifies her corresponds more closely to ornaments associated with the office of the Jewish priesthood (Rev 21.19-21, Ex 28.17-21, 29.10-14).

John's description of "a new heaven and a new earth" also corresponds to another, later portion of Isaiah, a well-known description

30 cf Isa 52.13-14, 53.7-8, Matt 26.62-63, Mark 14.61, 15.5, Luke 23.9, cf John 19.9, 12.32-33.

of utopian Jerusalem (Rev 21.1, Isa 65.17). Elements of this passage appeared in the Revelator's earlier thumbnail sketch of paradise, and some of these elements are revisited in the longer closing of this final section (Rev 7.17, 21.4, Isa 25.19). In this New Jerusalem the thirsty are granted "a gift from the spring of the water of life" in affirmation of the heavenly declaration at Golgotha, which resounded also when the totality of God's wrath was poured out at Armageddon: "It is done" (Rev 21.6, 16.17, cf John 19.30).

To get an adequate perspective of the holy city coming down out of the heaven, John is caught up in the spirit to a great, high mountain (Rev 21.10). This spiritual vantage point is proximate to the view enjoyed by Ezekiel when he too saw God's temple restored (Eze 40.1-4). These two scenes of institutional manifestation are significant counterpoints to the experience of Christ in the wilderness, when "the devil took him to a very high mountain and showed him all the kingdoms of the world and their splendor," promising him power in exchange for obedience (Matt 4.8-11, cf Luke 4.5-8). This episode demonstrates the worldly temptation that Christ rejected, while the Revelator shows us the bride to whom he gave himself.

Similarly, the prophet Ezekiel also spiritually toured an Israel restored, to see the glory of the Lord return to a Jerusalem reestablished; so also does the Revelator's tour of New Jerusalem reflect upon many of the same wonders (Eze 40-48). Both prophets fixate on similar architectural features (Rev 21.16, Eze 48.17, 20). Ezekiel's measurements of the wall around the temple and city are precise and minute, while the Revelator measures it differently, saying that it is of 144 cubits, "a measure of men" (Rev 21.12-17, Eze 48.30-35). The Revelator's description of the water of life flowing from the throne of God and through the city, lined with the tree of life "on either side of the river," is abbreviated from a vision recorded in Ezekiel, lacking its lengthy description of the watery depths (Rev 22.1-3, Eze 47.1-9, cf Zec 14.8).

But these images go back further than the prophets. The tree of life especially has primordial origins in Genesis, with its ambrosial fruit offering eternal life to those privileged with access (Gen 3.22, cf John 6.35). Its presence and accessibility in New Jerusalem indicate a reversal of humanity's original sin for those within its walls (Gen 3.1-19, cf Rom 5.12-21). The Revelator seems to be setting the ancient curse placed by God on humanity for its original sin in parallel with the curse of the law endured by Israel (Rev 3.22, Gen 3.14-24, Deut 11.26, 32.1-43, cf Zec 14.11). Earlier, the Revelator's oracle of heavenly Zion brought together passages of primordial genesis and apocalyptic images of Israel's exodus and exile (Rev 12.14, Ex 19.4, Deut 28.49, 7.4). This oracle of the heavenly Jerusalem is similarly a composite blueprint out of the law and prophets, remodeled and expanded to shelter both Israel and the rest of the cosmos; the city of God enshrines the paradise of Eden. Yet, while New Jerusalem offers shelter and sustenance to God's saints, and will be a home to the nations and to the "kings of the earth" (Rev 21.24), grievous sinners are not so lucky—they are barred from entrance into the city (Rev 21.27, 22.15).

This carrot-and-stick vision of God's kingdom may seem like an unreasonable and merciless binary, but the angel who "showed me these things" does not exhort John to go out and stop the unrighteous with either force or persuasion. Instead he is to "let the unjust still do unjustly, and the unclean still be unclean, and the righteous still do right, and the holy still be holy" (Rev 22.10). In the final episode of Revelation, even as the city descends and settles onto its earthly geography, there remain those who decline to enter—and this is the same situation faced by the seven churches at the beginning of the book (Rev 2-3).

6.6 SEVEN CHURCHES

New Jerusalem—descended from heaven and surrounded by sinners—seems also to be the same city anticipated briefly at the beginning of Revelation. From the first, the Son of Man spoke to the Ephesians about "the tree of life that is in the paradise of God" (Rev 2.7). Likewise spake he to the Philadelphians of becoming "a pillar in the temple of my God," inscribed with "the name of the city of my God, the new Jerusalem coming down from my God out of heaven" (Rev 3.12). To the Laodiceans the Son of Man promised a throne closely resembling the one that appears at the center of New Jerusalem, the source of God's regenerative, creative powers (Rev 3.24, 21.1-5, 22.1-3). To Thyatira he mentioned the "morning star," which is finally integrated into John's evangelical invitation to "the whosoever will" to enter into the communion of saints inside the holy city of God (Rev 2.28, 22.16-17).

But not all the promises delivered to the churches in the beginning of the Apocalypse correspond directly to the Revelator's closing New Jerusalem sequence—the church in Smyrna, for example, is promised an escape from "second death," which anticipates the vision immediately preceding the arrival of New Jerusalem, regarding the first and second resurrections (Rev 2.11, 20.6, 14). And while the "new name" promised to the saints of Pergamum might refer to the name of New Jerusalem (Rev 2.17, 3.12), mention of "hidden manna" better corresponds to the emblems of the broken word embedded in the middle of the book—the two witnesses who feed Zion during her exodus among the nations, and seem to be revived concurrently with the first resurrection (Rev 11-12). The promise delivered to Sardis, on the other hand, corresponds clearly to the scene of universal judgment that is the second resurrection (Rev 3.5, 20.11-15).

These intratextual links establish points of correspondence between the situations of the churches in Asia Minor and John's visions of a heavenly temple, war, and city—but they do not create linear points of interdependence. The apocalyptic sequences of Revelation Major (Rev 4-22) do not rely upon the local situations of the saints in Revelation Minor (Rev 1-3) for narrative logic or symbolic inspiration. The Revelator did not write about a Great Harlot simply for the benefit of a single Jezebel (Rev 2.20, 17.1-19.2).[31] Instead, he has highlighted a parallel between Jezebel and the Babylonian Whore,

31 "Feminist scholars of Revelation have also taken up my argument but have made John's polemics against "Jezebel" the predominant hermeneutical key for the whole book. They have argued that Revelation is a misogynist tract, which advocates the dehumanization of wo/men and eradicates them from its community because the only actual historical wo/man mentioned is vilified. Tina Pippin's work, which is an original and creative attempt to reread the book of Revelation in and through the unmasking of its gender codes, has greatly contributed to such a reading of Revelation." Elisabeth Schüssler Fiorenza, "Babylon the Great," in *The Reality of Apocalypse: Rhetoric and Politics in the Book of Revelation*, ed. David L. Barr (Atlanta: The Society of Biblical Literature, 2006), 247.

an independent figure within the larger apocalyptic narrative of Revelation (Rev 4-22). In drawing the attention of the Thyatiran congregation to a certain (contextually relevant) portion of the story, the author encourages his audience to understand its Jezebel's actions and destiny in light of the bigger picture: in Revelation Major, a typological Zion flees the devil, betrays God, allies with his enemies, is destroyed, and is born again as a purified body that is both temple and city. The Son of Man invites the local churches to view a disobedient and defiant prophetess as a figure likewise doomed to condemnation, but even then there is still—perhaps, in some sense—potential for redemption (Revelation 2.20-25, 19.1-9, 21.2).[32]

This local appeal to the bigger spiritual picture is not unlike what we find in 2 Thessalonians, which contains an oracle very similar to the seven letters delivered to the seven churches (2 Thes 1-2, Rev 2-3). The central missive is apocalyptic in tone, and retains familiar themes: a "mystery of lawlessness" unfolds (2 Thes 2.7). A "lawless one" and "son of destruction" appears, to do the work of Satan with "power and signs and lying wonders" (2 Thes 2.3, 9-11) until "the Lord Jesus will destroy him with the breath of his mouth, destroying him by the manifestation of his coming" (2 Thes 2.4). This oracle is marked by an intentional ambiguity often required of mystical specialists; though the author cannot seem to pinpoint the source of controversy, he is compelled to correct a rumor that the day of the Lord had already come (2 Thes 2.2).

32 Contra Pippin: "The prophetess Jezebel and her unrepentant followers will be thrown upon a bed and will die (2:22-23). The Whore of Babylon is dethroned and made desolate and totally destroyed, as the ceremonial line proclaims: "Fallen, fallen is Babylon the great!" (18:2). Even the Woman Clothed with the Sun is "banished" for protection and safekeeping to the wilderness, "to her place where she is nourished for a time, and times, and half a time" (12:14). The bride figure (the New Jerusalem) alone is left standing, but only briefly, for she is replaced by the imagery of the city. The female—whether depicted as the cause of evil or as the cause of good in the world of the story—is nonetheless in the end erased from the text. Hence, all the females in the Apocalypse are victims..." Tina Pippin, "The Heroine and the Whore: The Apocalypse of John in Feminist Perspective," in *From Every People and Nation: The Book of Revelation in Intercultural Perspective*, ed. David Rhoads (Minneapolis: Fortress Press, 2005), 2075-2080/4278.

Note: Although I have some reservations about Pippin's method, agenda, and conclusions, it seems both fair and necessary to note that many of the basic assumptions and perspectives which underlie Revelation do indeed reflect the patriarchal culture and values of the ancient Mediterranean world.

This is not the only time we hear the Pauline voice dealing with the difficult implications of complex resurrection rhetoric. Young Timothy is exhorted to avoid men like Hymenaeus and Philetus, who speak "profane and idle babblings," "saying the resurrection is already past" (2 Tim 2.16-18a). Paul knows, of course, that there are many different shades of meaning when it comes to resurrection. In one of his earliest epistles he is forced to acknowledge the issue, and he still insists on addressing "resurrection" by carefully parsing the language, and then by slipping into the ambiguous rhetorical mode of oracular mystery (1 Cor 15.12-56). The voice of Paul, then, perhaps steers Timothy away from Hymenaeus and Philetus not merely because they have the audacity to inspect the meanings and timing of the evangelical resurrection, but because they also do so indelicately, even ineptly, and thereby "overthrow the faith of some" (2 Tim 3.18b).

We could perhaps exhaust ourselves by trying to imaginatively reconstruct the historical situation behind the oracle of 2 Thessalonians 2, or the way(s) in which Hymenaeus and Philetus fumbled the doctrines of the church. But, because there is an unsurpassable void in our information, we can only guess at the historical identity of "the restrainer" and "the man of sin," or the specifics of the earliest resurrection heresies.

The book of Revelation, on the other hand, retains both the Revelator's apocalyptic exhortation to local churches *as well as* an archetypal metanarrative which governs their eschatological experience: the churches of Revelation Minor (Rev 1-3) are explicitly informed by the complex and nuanced visions of Revelation Major (Rev 4-22). Accordingly, to appreciate the experiences of the seven churches, it is critical to first understand the major visionary sequences to which the seven epistles are attached.

The introductory epistles function, therefore, as a demonstration of evangelical discourse in multiple and apocalyptic dimensions. To an attentive audience, they reveal a variety of ways to leverage and direct biblical visions of dragons, heroes, and maidens for various groups in various situations within the Body of Christ. The words of the Son of Man to each of these churches were tailored for specific circumstances, and these situations are now only remotely accessible. It may still be possible, of course, to extract truth from Revelation 2-3 that applies to the contemporary church. These extractions, however, remain largely informed by our private perceptions and personal biases, and will typically shift and evolve with the passage of time—this process of exegetical evolution is not entirely inappropriate, as the seven oracles themselves are not, for us, primarily prognosticative, but demonstrative. They show us what might occur, and how to react.

Ephesus

Each of the seven epistles begins with a description of the speaker, the Son of Man that appears in the collective light of the seven churches, and has authority over them (Rev 1.12-13, 19, 2.20). These make it clear that the oracular agent speaking to the churches and the Son who first appeared in lamplight are the same person. This careful linking could imply that the seven epistles were secondarily conceived and inserted into an original introductory scene that was somewhat briefer.

The Ephesian church is praised for steadfastly examining and rejecting "those calling themselves apostles and are not," (Rev 2.2) and for hating "the works of the Nicolaitans which I also hate" (Rev 2.4). In the letter to Pergamum it becomes evident that the Nicolaitans are associated with the "doctrine of Balaam," a prophet who—for a fee—taught Israel's enemies underhanded tactics to derail God's plans for their establishment (Rev 2.14-15, Num 31.16).

In Jude and 2 Peter, Balaam is a figure of error-for-hire (2 Pet 2.15, Jude 11), and it is possible that the false apostles weighed and found wanting in Ephesus are not unlike the false apostles also critiqued in 2 Peter as false teachers espousing destructive heresies, privately imported (2 Pet 1.19-2.3). These competing groups may represent, in part or in whole, an early gnostic(ish) threat to the epistemological structures of the church. But the clearer danger is not an encroachment upon Ephesian freedoms by outsiders. Rather, it is inward desiccation. For all his labor and patience, the angel of Ephesus has departed from his "first love" (Rev 2.4).

This reminds me of a church that loves tradition and hates sinners.

Smyrna

The Son of Man introduces himself to the Smyrnean church as "the first and the last, who was dead and came to life" (Rev 2.8). Explicit reference to the personal resurrection of the Son of Man presupposes knowledge of the evangelical gospel, as it is never openly revisited in the book of Revelation, though it may be presupposed or implied in certain scenes.

This branch of the church is one that seems to be losing social influence or prestige, being locked in conflict with a "synagogue of Satan" (Rev 2.9-10). The dispute regards their religious identity, as both Christians and their opponents laid claim to a distinctly Jewish identity or heritage. The Christians seem to be losing the debate, at least in the public sphere, while their opponents are ascending. The Son of Man does not promise the saints victory in the first degree, and predicts the severe curtailment of their privileges, but at least "they will not be harmed by the second death" (Rev 2.11).

This reminds me that Christianity is not always popular, profitable, or politically expedient.

Pergamum

The Son of Man addresses the angel that is the church in Pergamum as "the one having the sharp two-edged sword," which—as with the markers of identity offered to Ephesus and Smyrna—connects back to the initial appearance of the Son of Man to John amidst the seven-fold candlestick (Rev 2.12, 1.16). This sword is probably identical to the one proceeding from the mouth of the King of Kings during the overthrow of the beast and false prophet (Rev 19.15, 21). In Hebrews a two-edged sword is compared to the living and powerful word of God (Heb 4.12). Isaiah describes the mouth of God's servant Israel as "a sharp sword" (Isa 49.2).

In Revelation the Son of Man juxtaposes the militant image of God's blade against the "throne of Satan" which is in Pergamum. Some identify this as a major temple of Zeus.[33] Some have noted the

33 Pagels notes the temple to Zeus but emphasizes the presence of a relatively new temple built to honor Augustus and the goddess Roma, ibid, *Revelations,* 11, 14.

presences of a massive Asklepion.[34] Others have noted the presence of imperial temples, cults, and governors.[35] All these seem equally possible.[36] According to the Revelator's epistle, there have been righteous, victorious saints in Pergamum (Rev 2.13), but unlike as in Smyrna, here the Nicolaitans have a foothold among a few "holding to the teaching of Balaam" (Rev 2.14-15). The Son promises to purge those who remain stubbornly committed to this avaricious doctrine with the oracular (s)word (Rev 2.16).

Their false for-profit preaching reminds me of the prosperity gospel and the number of the beast.

Thyatira

Thyatira is introduced to the "the one having eyes as a flame of fire and whose feet are like burnished bronze," as the Son of Man is initially described by John (Rev 2.18, 1.14-15). Yet he calls himself not the Son of Man, but rather the Son of God, demonstrating clearly that the same messenger may wear dual mantles of identity. This is the

---

34 Wright notes "the shrine of the healing-god Asclepius, whose symbol was a serpent," Wright, *Revelation for Everyone*, 20, while Barr describes a "major Asklepion—a temple-health complex dedicated to Asclepius, God of Healing," Barr, *Tales of the End*, 1511/6687.

35 Kraybill emphasizes the imperial cult, *Apocalypse and Allegiance*, 992/4079, cf Fiorenza, *Revelation*, 818/2255. Wright also emphasizes "the imperial cult of Rome and its emperors" in Pergamum, but his insight represents a significant distinction: "John does not identify Rome with the devil." Wright, *Revelation for Everyone*, 20.

36 "Perhaps in order to rival the Egyptian city [Alexandria], the third-century rulers of Pergamon adopted an architectural scheme which exploited the steep terrain of the city's acropolis to best effect. A Hippodamian plan was not imposed, no doubt because of the rugged contours, but, as in Alexandria, the public buildings were grouped in successive locations, in this case on different terraces mounting up the acropolis. Each terrace held an imposing group of monuments forming an architectural unity. The visitor moved from the grand lower agora to the gymnasium complex, followed by a sanctuary of Demeter, a second agora with, about it, the great altar to Zeus built by Eumenes II in the 170s to celebrate Attalos I's earlier triumph over the Galatai. On the highest part of the acropolis were a grand sanctuary of Athena, a theatre, the library, the palaces of the kings, and military installations. No single structure dominates the city; instead, the series of architectural spaces is designed to impress the visitor by its increasing scale and elaboration, assisted by the view over the plain that opens up as one ascends." Graham Shipley, *The Greek World After Alexander: 323-30 B.C.*, ed. Fergus Millar (London and New York: Routledge, 2000), 92.

only time the phrase "Son of God" is used in the entire Apocalypse (Rev 2.16).

Thyatira is that church which must deal with a Jezebel, who seduces the very elect. As Elaine Pagels notes, it is difficult to determine what the Revelator has in mind when he speaks about impurity in intensely sexual language—he could be talking about food, or about sex, or both.[37] Frequently, John's polemic against the impurity of Jezebel is decoded as a conflict between the Revelator and a permissive Pauline clique within the Thyatiran church, as an example of early inter-church politicking.[38] David Barr is kind enough to point out that the "city was also a center for an oracle of the Sibyl, a female prophetic figure who gave ecstatic prophecies."[39]

Thyatira reminds me of a comfortable church languishing in first-world comforts, craving pleasure and power and permission more than love and peace and obedience.

Sardis

According to the one "having the seven Spirits of God and the seven stars," the church of Sardis has a lively name in some quarters, but in reality is dead and dying, and largely imperfect (Rev 3.1-2). Sardis is a church which seems to have been abandoned or failed by many who have soiled themselves, leaving the majority of its saints vulnerable to sudden and unexpected judgment: "and you will not

---

37 "John clearly understands this language as a prophetic metaphor that warns against consorting with foreign cultures and flirting, so to speak, with foreign gods. [paragraph] But John also knew that these two issues—eating and sexual activity—aroused conflict whenever Jews discussed whether, or how much, to assimilate. Meat markets in Asia Minor and Greece, as throughout the empire, often sold meat left over from sacrifice in local temples... When John accuses "Balaam" and "Jezebel" of inducing people to "eat food sacrificed to idols and practice fornication," he might have in mind anything from tolerating people who engage in incest to Jews who become sexually involved with Gentiles, or worse, who marry them." Pagels, *Revelations*, 49.

38 i.e., "Both Paul's treatment of the issue of idol worship and his attitude toward the Roman government would have seemed inadequate to John of Patmos. Revelation is categorical in condemning the Roman Empire and any association with its pagan rites." Kraybill, *Apocalypse and Allegiance*, 3128/4079.

39 Barr, *Tales of the End*, 1514/6687, but he too suspects a point of Pauline/Johannine disagreement, which of course is not impossible, ibid 1829-1830/6687.

know what hour I will come upon you" (Rev 3.3). The Son of Man reminds these saints that God is watching, and that there will be a reckoning (Rev 3.4-5).

This makes me think of a scandal-plagued church.

Philadelphia

The one who speaks to the Philadelphians has a most interesting artifact—the key of David, which is like the "keys of hell and death" possessed by the Son of Man in his first appearing (Rev 3.7, 1.18), and also like the key possessed by a powerful angel who opens and closes the abyss at will (Rev 3.1, 20.1). In both Revelation and Isaiah, the "key of the house of David" is one that opens and shuts its doors contrary to the wishes of those in power (Rev 3.7-9, Isa 22.17-25).

As in Smyrna, the Philadelphian situation is complicated by a "synagogue of Satan" claiming Jewish identity over-against the Christians (Rev 3.9-10). As in either case, this could be Orthodox Jew vs. Jewish Christian. It could also be a case of Jewish Christian vs. Jewish Gnostic, or, I suppose, something entirely else. In any case, the most powerful key in the universe is held within the royal Jewish house, by the Christian messiah (cf Matt 16.18-20).

The grim situation in Philadelphia reminds me of the underground church.

Laodicea

The Son of Man identifies himself to the angel of the church of the Laodiceans as "the Amen, the Faithful and True witness, the Beginning of the Creation of God" (Rev 3.14). The "faithful and true" is not a title for the Son of Man in his early appearing. Rather, it is an appellation of the righteous judge and maker of war who appears late in the Revelation (Rev 19.11). It is also a phrase used twice as God remakes the world anew, according to the patterns of paradise, shortly thereafter (Rev 21.5, 22.6, cf 19.9-16), while the Son of Man as the "beginning of the creation" resonates with both Johannine "Word" theology and Paul (John 1.1-2, 1 John 1.1, 13-14, Col 1.15, 1 Cor 8.6).

This closing epistle seems to be intratextually linked to the introductory, central, and epilogical appearances of the Son of Man in Revelation; the final epistle to the final church connects with the Revelator's earliest vision and with his very last, and also with a central vision in the middle (Rev 3.14, 1.7-8, 14.13-14, 19.9, cf 21.5).

Laodicea is known as the lukewarm church, being "neither cold nor hot" (Rev 3.15-16). Disgusted by its waffling, middling nature, the Son of Man promises to "vomit you out from my mouth" (Rev 3.16). The angel of the Laodicean church has those riches and resources which he thinks he needs, but in reality he is "miserable and pathetic and blind and naked" (Rev 3.18). The Faithful and True begs this church to find real stability; to keep his clothes on; to take his medication. The Son of Man extends the promise of communion to even this detestable, dysfunctional, delusional spirit, if he will simply open the door and let him inside (Rev 3.19).

This church reminds me of me.[40]

6.7 SEVEN ANGELS

Though the seven letters are addressed explicitly to the seven angels which are the seven churches and the seven stars that are in the hand of the Son of Man, it is probably important to note that the Son does not tell individual Laodiceans to keep their white robes on and to apply medicinal salve to their eyes. Rather, this commandment is directed at the *angel of Laodicea*. Even in the Revelator's idiomatic Greek, this distinction is made obvious by the use of singular pronouns in several cases throughout the seven epistles.[41]

The Son tells the Philadelphian church angel that his enemies will "worship at your feet"—singular (Rev 3.9). He tells the angel in Sardis that he has still "a few names," as if the righteous members of the church are his constitutive possessions. Yet he himself is the one "alive and also dead," whose works are imperfect, and who should

40 cf Mark 5.1-20

41 "Note that in Greek the pronoun *you* (*your*) and the respective verbs in these letters are in the singular, which English is unable to transmit." Simon Kistemaker and William Hendriksen, *Exposition of the Book of Revelation* (Grand Rapids: Baker Book House, 1953–2001), 103.

return to his original mission (Rev 3.1-4). In Thyatira "love and service and faith and patience" are works done not by groups of saints, but by the spirit of the church. Likewise it is his lax toleration that has exposed Jezebel and her children to the Son of Man's higher judgment, which—says the Son—must be enforced as a sign to the other churches (Rev 2.19-23).

The seven angels are mediums of communication through which the Revelator, in conjunction with the Son of Man, may simultaneously address the entire church generally, and no one specifically. Rhetorically, this form of address appeals strongly to those readers or hearers of the word within each city who identify themselves as the animus of their local congregations, without explicitly demanding specific action from specific people. Leaders and laypeople alike are called to address (when they can) and endure (when they must) the difficulties facing the Body of Christ. Only when the Revelator characterizes particular Jezebels, Balaams, or Satans were specific opposition parties indirectly identified, and these could be confidently deconstructed only by active, informed church members associated with local congregations.

However, in several instances, it seems the seven-letter oracles involve widely-known figures and facts about the specific localities. The angel of Laodicea, for example, was described as lukewarm and instructed to take his eye-salve—two possible points of reference for those who knew about the lukewarm water piped in to Laodicea from far away, or those involved in its famous eye-salve industry.[42] Sardis, the angel warned to stay awake, was a city with a history of being caught off-guard in military matters.[43] Rhetorically, these inside references seem designed to represent the local churches as a corporate entity under a higher authority.[44]

42 Barr, *Tales of the End*, 1526-1531/6687

43 Barr, *Tales of the End*, 1859/6687

44 "Geographically, the list represents the cities one would come to if one left from Patmos and sailed to the coast of Asia Minor and then proceeded in a rough circle of about 60 miles in diameter, going first north then east. These are major centers, generally the dominant city of their regions." Barr, *Tales of the End*, 1326/6687.

Outsiders like ourselves—being about two thousand years removed from the time and the place—may still be able to uncover some of these generic allusions, though we may not be able to recover them all. Further, it is difficult to know with precision when the Son of Man is obliquely referencing well-known locational facts (for example, the Sybil who was active in Thyatira) or obscure doctrinal-praxical controversies (if the Revelator is bickering with a Pauline clique). By all means readers ought to continue exercising our best judgments regarding the substance and application of these oracles. And despite all the uncertainty they retain, these mini-mysteries in Revelation Minor are valuable as hermeneutical signals, alerting readers to the symbolic mode of communication in which the Apocalypse is transmitted.

Barring the discovery of lost records or the intervention of a prophet with private revelation, the personal details of each situation are largely lost to us, as they probably should be. What the church today may successfully extract from these seven oracles is not the precise name or crisis behind each mystery—though it is fun to imagine—but rather the social and spiritual probabilities that prompted John to draw each church in the colorful light of Revelation Major.

The oracles of Revelation Minor (Rev 1-3), delivered by the Son of Man—through the Revelator, for the benefit of the seven churches—seem to imply an organizational hierarchy conceived as spiritual reality, with a central authority exercising influence and agency over satellite bodies, setting an agenda for subordinate groups, tending to individual branches, and cultivating the larger whole. This may suggest that the late first-century church, already in the time of the Revelator's final writing, had developed a complex administrative infrastructure, spanning several cities and engaging multiple (sub)cultures, yet preserving a common ideological vision.

6.8 1000 YEARS

The structure of John's Revelation is complex and even a little convoluted, being prudently scrambled and conscientiously shuffled; it is an oracular maze that must be diligently and carefully explored by a devout readership. Certain skill- and knowledge-sets are useful in joining together the pieces: those who know the Jewish scriptures intimately will be able to identify a host of relevant references; those who know the story of an incarnated, transfigured, and passionate Christ may recognize a certain essential rhythm within the Revelator's narrative beat; those who can do basic math and recognize repetitive patterns may be able to harmonize visions based on their numerical congruencies—such as in seven-and-ten, or 144—so that dispersed narrative groupings are successfully conjoined, producing a coherent arrangement of plot.

But loose ends remain, even in an effectively ordered and exegeted reading. At the end of Revelation, even after the city of God has descended from the heavens, the nations of the earth continue to exist and sinners continue to thrive (Rev 22.2, 11-12, 14-15). The city of God rests upon the earth, being accessible to the nations, but independent from them.[45] This seems to be a consequence an eschatological dualism that is intrinsic to Revelation.

Being intentionally ambiguous, the book of Revelation supports two different but interrelated visions of the End. On the one hand, Revelation affirms the declaration that God's kingdom is coming, and that there will be a judgment that all must face (Rev 20.11-14). On the other hand, it simultaneously sustains the notion that the kingdom of God exists, is already among us, and is accessible to those having eyes and ears to see and hear (Rev 22.16-17).

Ending on an evangelical note, the Apocalypse invites the willing—in images and language associated with Christian communion—to enter into fellowship, and thereby become immortal (Rev 22.17). Accepting this invitation, the believer is not immediately delivered into a state of blissful pleasure. Instead, he or she enters into a church that is in transit, that faces pressures and threats from

45 Pagels notes that one of the earliest defenders of Revelation "boldly tried to drive a wedge between what we call *politics* and *religion*—and so to create the possibility of a *secular* relationship to government," Pagels, *Revelations*, 108. I might take this assertion a step further and argue that perhaps this early attempt at a separation of church and state is an effort inspired or supported by the theology of the book of Revelation, as it portrays the church among, but separate from, the nations.

within and without. Today, as then, the traditional rituals of baptism initiate spiritual newborns into a discipleship that is somewhat rigorous in its demands (Mark 8.31-34). These initiated have come into their first resurrection, but there is another inevitable judgment on the horizon which all beings must face. In the book of Revelation, the thousand year reign, spanning the distance between the first resurrection and the second, is but as a single day of the Lord. The inaugurated kingdom—which the apostolic trio similarly beheld upon the mount of transfiguration—endures even as Jesus' approaches the cross, to confirm before the whole world what had first been delivered to a select few.

Many, including St. Augustine, have regarded the thousand-year reign as symbolic of the era of the church.[46] Inasmuch as the church is following in Christ's footsteps, it will always be so. As long as we are sustained by the body and blood of Christ, we too are participating in the sacrificial wedding supper of the Lamb. In the synoptic gospels, the Day of the Lord is marked by the transfiguration (Mal 3-4, Mark 9.1-13). In Revelation, the beginning of the thousand years marks the inauguration of the kingdom, an era which closes after one last battle, and yet is contiguous with the following new age.[47] Believers united

46 "Although he had once held chiliastic beliefs, in *City of God* Augustine provides a sustained and developed understanding of the last times as the time of the church militant. This time had begun with the death and resurrection of Christ, and these events were the fulfillment of Old Testament prophecy; no events after these allowed for a further, more calculated determination of the end of the world. After Christ, in the world there is "nothing solid, nothing stable"; all of history is homogenous. Therefore, the thousand years of Revelation 20 symbolize all the years of the Christian era during which the church is always beset by the devil within through heresy and hypocrisy and without through persecution," ed. William C. Weinrich, *Ancient Christian Commentary: Revelation* (Downers Grove: InterVarsity Press, 2005), xxiii.

47 In this regard the exegesis of Oecumenius in the East is also illustrative, when he describes the "thousand years" as a "number used figuratively" to depict the totality of Christ's ministry from start to finish: "That which is effected spiritually by the Lord against the devil is shown to the Evangelist [the Revelator] as though on a painted tablet. For since John was a human being and could not see spiritual realities, that which occurred is depicted for him in material terms." Oecumenius' explanation could be a summary description of a prophetic hermeneutic that is uniquely Christian: apocalyptic images employed to illustrate the eschatological realities of Jesus' kerygmatic ministry. Cf Oecumenius, *Commentary* 20.1-3, trans. William C. Weinrich, *Ancient Christian Texts: Greek Commentaries on Revelation* (Downers Grove: IVP Academic, 2011), 87.

in and following after Christ are perpetually headed towards his cross; the age of ages, the final age, this present age, our present age—this is the thousand years; this also is the day of the Lord, and the coming of the Son of Man.

7.1 THE SON OF MAN

And he began to teach them that the Son of Man had to endure many things, and be rejected by the elders and the chief priests and the scribes, and be killed, and after three days rise again. And he said this all openly. And Peter took him aside and began to rebuke him. But turning and looking at his disciples, he rebuked Peter and said, "Get behind me, Satan—your mind is not fixed on the things of God, but on the things of men."

And—having summoned the multitude together with his disciples—he said to them, "If anyone desires to follow behind me, let him deny himself and pick up his cross and follow me. For whoever would save his soul will lose it, and whoever loses his soul for me and the good news will save it. For what do people profit, to gain the whole world and forfeit their souls? For what can people give in exchange for their souls? For whoever is ashamed of me and my words—in this unfaithful and sinful generation—the Son of Man will be ashamed of him, when he comes in the glory of his father with the holy angels" (Mark 8.31-38).

Then some of the scribes and Pharisees answered, saying, "Teacher, we desire to see a sign from you." But he answered and said to them, "An evil and adulterous generation seeks a sign, and no sign will be given it, except for the sign of the prophet Jonah—for as Jonah was three days and three nights in the belly of the beast, so will the Son of Man be three days and three nights in the heart of the earth" (Matthew 12.38-40, cf Luke 11.29-32).

> *"Now is the judgment of this world. Now the ruler of this world will be cast out. And if I am lifted up from the earth, I will draw all to myself." This he said signaling what death he would die. The multitude answered him, "We have heard out of the law that the Christ endures into the age—how can you say, 'The Son of Man must be lifted up?' Who is this Son of Man?" (John 12.31-34)*

The Son of Man question is a very early one, explicitly voiced in John and implicitly raised in the synoptic tradition. Yet many critics and scholars wisely question the noticeable absence of the peculiar term, so central in the gospels to the self-identity of Jesus, in the remainder of the New Testament corpus. Aside from two late appearances—in the introductory segments of Revelation and Hebrews[1]—the Son of Man makes scant appearance.[2] Significantly, Paul, writing before and not after the production of the gospels, never mentions him.

The sudden appearance of the Son of Man on the stage of the Christian gospels may therefore be disconcerting; is he an invention of the evangelists? Contrary to what is sometimes supposed,[3] the discernable narrative evolution of this icon is not necessary evidence that the Son of Man is fraudulently manufactured, or alien to authentic early Christianity—the Son of Man is a symbol of evangelical disclosure, appropriately timed.[4]

---

1 Revelation 1.9-3.22; Hebrews 2.5-10, cf Psalm 8.4-6

2 Contra Fiorenza, who disassociates the Son of Man in Revelation from the synoptic Son of Man based on slight semantic variance in the Greek, 736/2255.

3 e.g., "The Son of Man was an apocalyptic figure whose role was imagined as the royal judge at the end of time and whose decisions would be final on the question of rewards and punishments. To imagine that Jesus was the Son of Man who had authority to forgive sins [i.e. Mark 2.10] was a stupendous manipulation of imagery. But it can be understood without appeal to the normal scholarly opinion about "christology" explicating an implicit meaning to the event of Jesus' resurrection. It can be understood as Mark's desire to claim for Jesus absolute authority." Mack, *Myth of Innocence*, 238.

4 "The theology of the Gospels, far from being a radical innovation within Israelite religious tradition, is a highly conservative return to the very most ancient moments within that tradition, moments that had been largely suppressed in the meantime—but not entirely. The identification of the rider on the clouds with the one like a son of man in Daniel provides that name and image of the Son of Man in the Gospels as well. It follows that the ideas about God that we identify as Christian are not innovations but may be deeply connected

7.2 A THEORY OF CONSTRUCTION

It is sometimes suggested that what has become canonical Christian literature was not conceived as authoritative, binding scripture, and that any reverence now attached to the oracles of the New Testament is little more than an ill-advised religious fetish. Champions of this suspicious persuasion must also, of necessity, sweep aside the difficult implication that some Pauline works were already being classified as scripture by the time of 2 Peter (2 Pet 3.14-18), but to their credit it is probably not unfair to say that the early Christian evangelists considered the Jewish oracles—the law, prophets, psalms, and histories—to represent a distinct and unique body of scripture that was qualitatively different from the oracles which they themselves created.

C. H. Dodd (1884-1973), a scholar interested in the evangelical kerygma and an advocate for realized eschatology, sought to identify the reason for methodological similarities evidenced in the biblical writers: by what logic did they appeal to the scriptures when they themselves witnessed? Dodd identified the critical elements of Jesus' ministry—what he called the kerygmatic events of his life—as "a basic standard of reference for everything that is set forth as part of the Christian Gospel."[5] He also saw the Jewish scriptures as the other important half of the evangelical narrative equation.[6] He once speculated that perhaps—at some very early, unrecorded apostolic council—the church sat down and hammered out the tricky business of which Jewish oracles had prognosticated Christ and therefore fell within their own standards of fair use.[7] It was difficult for him to imagine that the late apocalyptic developments of the canon reflected an authentically apostolic disposition, and he regarded the Revelation of John with great suspicion.[8]

---

with some of the most ancient of Israelite ideas about God. These ideas at the very least go back to an entirely plausible (and attested) reading of Daniel 7 and thus to the second century B.C. at the latest. They may even be a whole lot older than that." Boyarin, *The Jewish Gospels*, 46.

5 Dodd, *According to the Scriptures*, 12

6 Dodd, *According to the Scriptures*, 13, 27

7 Dodd, *According to the Scriptures*, 14

8 "Thus it comes about that the typical apocalypse is full of a vindictive gloating over the downfall of national enemies, and an unhealthy indulgence of personal and corporate pride

His hostility towards the Apocalypse aside, Dodd may have been onto something with his realized eschatology. It is realized eschatology which may unlock the book of Revelation for many readers—both veteran and novice—as a lens through which its symbols and stories may be viewed in the proper kerygmatic light. In this capacity, the Revelation of John may function as an apocalyptic Rosetta Stone, against which the canonical gospels may be read and eschatologically contextualized.

Within the Apocalypse—or rather, within the reader, produced by the Apocalypse—is the startling realization that the kingdom of God is at hand in a real and tangible way, immediately present among those with seeing eyes and hearing ears. John's Revelation seeks to actualize the reality it portrays.[9] But, by design, this is not immediately evident in a simple or flat reading of the text. The characteristic ambiguity of the Apocalypse is part of a widespread oracular mode common to the cultural context of the early Christians. As an evangelist, the Revelator has wrapped an unconventional eschatology within the apocalyptic conventions of his wider culture, using the language and symbols of his heritage and faith. The result is a complex literary mystery filled with insider references and oracular puzzles, a mystery requiring near-mastery of the Jewish scriptures and an intimate knowledge of developing Christian tradition—in short, it is a puzzle that could only have been open to an elect few.

But once Revelation is sequentially aligned, and its referent images tracked down, the story that emerges is both intelligible and ingenious, relating a mythical, archetypal history through the scriptures and images of Israel, embodied by the evangelical Christ, climaxing in the triumph and good news of the gospel. To those who

---

with cupidity. The New Testament apocalypse is tainted with these vices no less than some of its Jewish congeners, and perhaps it would have been well for Christendom if those great scholars of the Eastern Church who disliked its presence in the Canon had had their way." Dodd, *Authority of the Bible*, 182.

9 "In other words, the visions do not just suggest a new future; they also create the future within the present." Brian K. Blount, "The Witness of Active Resistance: The Ethics of Revelation in African American Perspective," in *From Every People and Nation: The Book of Revelation in Intercultural Perspective*, ed. David M. Rhoads (Minneapolis: Fortress Press, 2005), 533/4278.

know where to look, prophetic portents of cosmic expectation—the arrival of a doomsday warrior, the dead rising from their graves, the last battle between good and evil—are revealed to have been fulfilled in the events of Christ's baptism, transfiguration, and passion, and resurrection.[10]

And yet, while these portents have been fulfilled, and the Mystery of God is complete, we ourselves—the church—remain united in this world with the Lord as he appeared in his life and death (John 6.46-59). For the followers of Christ, the kerygmatic events of Jesus' ministry have inaugurated a final age, an age of the kingdom of God, and they remain for us centrally informative images of faith; his faith is our faith, his life our life, his death our death, his resurrection our resurrection.[11] And though New Jerusalem is present among us, so also are the nations in need of healing. Those sinners that still choose sin continue to suffer the torments of destruction. John's Revelation does not champion a fully-realized eschatology. It does not claim that our utopian existence is now a static fact, or pretend that suffering has vanished from the earth. Yet neither does John's Revelation dissolve entirely into the popular cataclysmic and vindictive fantasies of his

---

10 "In all of this, the Christian use of apocalypticism is fully in accordance with its Jewish precedents. The primary difference between Christian and Jewish apocalypticism in the first century C.E. was that the Christians believed that the messiah had already come and that the firstfruits of the resurrection had taken place. Consequently, there is an element of realized eschatology in the Christian texts.[858] It is more pronounced in some texts (Colossians, Ephesians, the Johannine writings) than in others," Collins, *The Apocalyptic Imagination*, 268.

11 "Jewish apocalyptic, then, has been rethought, not abandoned, within early Christianity. But this rethinking of apocalyptic has nothing to do with a demythologization in which apocalyptic *language* conveys a gnostic or similar *meaning*, substituting the so-called 'vertical eschatology' of private piety or revelation (or, indeed, a 'world-denying' social critique) for the so-called 'horizontal eschatology' of Jewish thought. The early Christian rethinking has taken place because the crucified and risen Jesus has turned out to be the central character in the apocalyptic drama. The point of the present kingdom is that it is the first-fruits of the future kingdom; and the future kingdom involves the abolition, not of space, time, or the cosmos itself, but rather of that which threatens space, time, and creation, namely, sin and death. The vision of 1 Corinthians 15 thus coheres neatly with that of Romans 8:18–27, and, for that matter, Revelation 21. The creation itself will experience its exodus, its return from exile, consequent upon the resurrection of the Messiah and his people," Wright, *Jesus and the Victory of God*, 217-218.

contemporaries, but subverts them, reorienting the apocalyptic imagination of his audience toward the evangelical declaration of his Christ.

What emerges from the book of Revelation is an eschatological dualism that we find also developing in the gospels and even in Paul:[12] the kingdom is here, and the kingdom is coming. To a reader who is not interested in the intense discipleship of critical inquiry, the Apocalypse functions as a generic but Christian apocalyptic prophecy concerning an impending and cataclysmic future. For a dedicated audience, one with interest in, familiarity with, and sympathy for the evangelical agenda, Revelation's oddities and enigmas irresistibly lead back to the crucified Christ, detailing his ascension to the highest heavens and his descent into the lowest depths. It is a book that reveals God's suffering servant to be master of the universe.

If Revelation stood alone, it would stand as a house without a foundation, unable to resist the inevitable pressures of incidental misinterpretation and intentional abuse. Thankfully, it was—by a bishop of deep wisdom—firmly attached to the Christian canon as an important if unique New Testament work.[13] Without the contents of the

---

12 "(1) The controlling narratives upon which [Paul] regularly drew included creation and exodus, the foundation stories within any Jewish worldview. Paul employed them, however, to speak of the new creation, and the new exodus, which were accomplished through Jesus' death and new life. He understood the larger story of Israel, from Abraham to the exile and beyond, as coming to a shocking but satisfying completion in Jesus as the crucified and risen Messiah. [paragraph] (2) The different aspects of his apostolic praxis—the Gentile mission, prayer, the vocation to suffering, his collection from Gentile churches to help the impoverished Jewish ones—all grow out of a Jewish, indeed Pharisaic worldview, but have been reordered, turned inside out one might say, by the events of the gospel, particularly the resurrection. It is only because Paul believes that God's new age has arrived that he believes it is time or the Gentiles to hear the good news; and there is no question why he thinks such a dramatic shift in the eschatological timetable has occurred. It can only be because he believes that Jesus has been raised from the dead." N. T. Wright, *The Resurrection of the Son of God* (Minneapolis: Fortress Press, 2003), 275.

Note: Wright's numerical ordering here does not reflect an attempt to arrange Paul's eschatology into dualistic divisions, but his analysis does reflect an eschatological dualism.

13 "Given such a controversial history, why did Athanasius choose to place the Book of Revelation as the capstone of his New Testament canon? Although we have no simple answer, several suggestions emerge from what we know of its history and its use to this day. Many readers of the Christian Bible today say that its placement seems right, since, just as the Book of Genesis, which begins "in the beginning," opens the Hebrew Bible, so John's Book of Revelation closes the Christian Bible with his visions of the end of time, when the "new

New Testament, without the good news it relates, John's Apocalypse would be just another sectarian fiction: fantastical, factitious, and flat. Indeed, many read it precisely as such a book, fundamentally flawed as just another apocalyptic parody of Roman power.[14]

To avoid this pitfall, it is vital to acknowledge John the Revelator not as a mystical, puritan charismatic railing against the Romans, but as a colleague and coworker of the other New Testament evangelists. By the time of Revelation's mass publication, the church had been telling the same story through the same sources for decades, had already developed an arsenal of rhetorical devices and a network of exegetical connections—many of which were tested in the manuscripts of the gospels—all designed to portray Jesus as the Christ in light of Jewish scripture. In delivering his vision to the church, the Revelator followed in the footsteps of pioneers, and built according to their blueprints.

7.3 THE SYNOPTIC CORE

The main narrative body of the three-fold tradition is driven by a three-part structure: baptism, transfiguration, and passion (with the passion including all the events beginning with Judas' betrayal and climaxing in the resurrection).[15] This three-part structure is easiest to detect in Mark, and hinges upon the transfiguration, which is the clutch of the synoptic vehicle, linking and engaging the events of Jesus'

Jerusalem" descends from heaven to inaugurate the long-delayed kingdom." Pagels, *Revelations*, 163, cf 133-170.

14 i.e., "Ultimately, however, if Christian theology is to be intellectually as well as ethically adequate, and as such less luridly anthropomorphic and less patently projectionist, might it not require what Revelation, locked as it is in visions of empires and counter-empires, emperors and counter-emperors, is singularly powerless to provide: a conception of the divine sphere as other than empire writ large?" Stephen D. Moore, *Empire and Apocalypse: Postcolonialism and the New Testament* (Sheffield, England: Sheffield Phoenix Press, 2006), 121.

Note: This seems like the inevitable conclusion of an academy that fails to connect Revelation to the rest of the New Testament, and substitutes Roman culture and history for the missing pieces.

15 Christ's Passion is widely defined as the events of his suffering, beginning with his betrayal and climaxing in the crucifixion, while often his resurrection is counted as a separate event. For the purposes of this discussion, I have chosen to group the resurrection within the passion because that is how Jesus groups the final events of his earthly life in Matthew, Mark, and Luke (Mark 8.31, 9.9-12, 31, 10.33, 14.41, 62, Matt 17.9-12, 22-23, 20.18-19, Luke 9.21, 24.6-8).

baptism and passion.[16] This vital intersection—infrequently receiving the kind of scrutiny it deserves in contemporary scholarship[17]—facilitates a critical transition as the narration shifts gear, and engages the mysteries preceding and following its inexplicable unfolding.

The thematic and linguistic connections between these three flashpoints (baptism-transfiguration-passion) are strong. For example, during his baptism the heavens themselves are torn apart as a spirit from above settles on Jesus, and a voice from heaven identifies him as "my beloved Son;" during the transfiguration, a cloud overshadows the Son as he is changed, and a voice from the cloud identifies Jesus as "my beloved Son" (Mark 1.11, 9.7). The masculine trio beholding Christ's glory during his transfiguration is not quite sure how to react, "for they were terrified;" at his resurrection the feminine trio responds to the empty tomb with familiar fear and trembling (Mark 9.6, Mark 16.8).[18] In dialogue and construction, the transfiguration is an interdependent middle link connected to the opening and closing scenes of the Markan text.

Matthew and Luke do make significant adjustments to certain Markan details. Both eliminate the detail of the disciples' fear during the transfiguration. In the Lukan transfiguration, the heavenly voice identifies Jesus not as the Beloved Son, but as "my chosen Son" (Luke 9.35), which is not identical to the title issued from heaven at his Baptism. But both retain the triptych Markan structure, and even take some steps to reinforce it. Like Mark, Matthew has a single witness meet the women at the tomb, though his radiant appearance corresponds better to the radiantly transfigured Christ (Matt 17.2, 28.3). In Luke, Jesus' resurrection is heralded not by a single witness, but by

---

16 Burton Mack treats the triad of baptism-transfiguration-crucifixion as a set of "mythic transitions" around which the gospel of Mark is chiastically arranged. Mack, *Myth of Innocence*, 333.

17 "While biblical scholarship tends to dismiss the [transfiguration] narrative as ahistorical, its only function being to underline the message of the cross, systematic theology regards it as a peripheral, possessing nothing like the existential import of the incarnation, cross, resurrection or parousia. In either case, the story of the transfiguration—however central to the Gospel narrative—is swallowed up in shadow." Dorothy Lee, "On the Holy Mountain: The Transfiguration in Scripture and Theology." *Colloquium* 36, no. 2 (2004), 149.

18 Mark 9.6, ἔκφοβοι; Mark 16.8, ἐφοβοῦντο

"two men in dazzling clothes" standing beside them, corresponding to the dual presence of Moses and Elijah, "the two men who stood with him" at the transfiguration (Luke 9.30-31, 24.4).[19] Though they develop in their own idiosyncratic ways, the gospels of Matthew and Luke stay very near to the structure that Mark built.

Malachi 3-4, representing a single oracle broken into two chapters in the traditional Christian Bible, seems to have provided Mark with major structural inspiration. His opening subject of reference, right after "the gospel of Jesus Christ" (Mark 1.1-2) and just before "John the Baptizer" (Mark 1.4), is the oracle of Malachi 3,[20] which begins with the promise of a preparatory messenger and the arrival of the Lord:

> "See, I send my messenger to prepare the way before me, and the Lord whom you seek will suddenly come to his temple, and the messenger of the covenant in whom you delight, indeed, he is coming," says the Lord of Armies. "But who can withstand the day of his coming, and who can stand when he appears? For he is like a refiner's fire, and like a launderer's soap" (Mal 3.1-3, cf Mark 1.3).

---

19 Luke 9.30-31a: καὶ ἰδοὺ ἄνδρες δύο συνελάλουν αὐτῷ, οἵτινες ἦσαν Μωϋσῆς καὶ Ἠλίας, οἳ ὀφθέντες ἐν δόξῃ ἔλεγον τὴν ἔξοδον αὐτοῦ ("and behold: two men standing with him, who were Moses and Elijah, who appeared with him in his glory"). Luke 24.4: καὶ ἰδοὺ ἄνδρες δύο ἐπέστησαν αὐταῖς ἐν ἐσθῆτι ἀστραπτούσῃ ("and behold: two men stood near them in gleaming apparel"). The Lukan construction could perhaps represent a symbolic counterpoint to the crucifixion also, as Jesus is placed in between two other condemned men (Luke 23.32). The beginning of the book of Acts contains the early scene of Jesus' Ascension into the heavens, which is likewise witnessed by two men in white robes. Acts 1:10b: καὶ ἰδοὺ ἄνδρες δύο παρειστήκεισαν αὐτοῖς ἐν ἐσθήσεσι λευκαῖς ("and behold: two men stood by them in white robes"); these two witnesses may recall the Transfiguration, and serve as an intertextual link joining the two Lukan books. Therefore, in the construction of Luke-Acts, the dual witness of Moses and Elijah may serve to interrelate the scene of Jesus' Transfiguration, Crucifixion, Resurrection, and Ascension. As witnesses to the major life-events of Christ, they may even symbolize the law and the prophets serving as primary sources of oracular inspiration in, and as the hermeneutical context for, the evangelical preaching and composition of the gospel.

20 Mark 1.3 represents a fusion of both Malachi's oracle and the opening of what is sometimes called Second Isaiah, or the Song of Isaiah (cf Malachi 3.1, Isaiah 40.3). The very early and explicit fusion of these sources in Mark may signal an intentional synthesis of Isaiah's soteriological focus on Israel's redemption through suffering and Malachi's eschatological schema for the day of the Lord.

Malachi's representation of the Lord as a commander of warriors unfolds as a polemic against a corrupt Levitical cult, which must be refined by fire until it presents righteous offerings (Mal 3.3-5). The prophet describes the Levites as rebellious "children of Jacob" who "rob God" by withholding their tithes and offerings (Mal 3.6-8). He condemns those who have abandoned the service and the commandments of God (Mal 3.15). He also describes a book of record kept by the Lord, filled with the names of the righteous who will be spared in the day of judgment (Mal 3.16-18):

> "Look: the day comes, burning as an oven, when all those doing evil will be stubble. The day that comes will burn them up," says the Lord of Armies, "so that it will leave them neither root nor branch. But will rise—to you who fear my name—a sun of righteousness with healing in its rays. You will go out leaping like calves from the stall and trample the wicked, because they will be ashes under the soles of your feet, on the day when I act," says the Lord of Armies.
>
> "Remember the teaching of my servant Moses, the statutes and judgments which I commanded him at Horeb for all Israel. Behold: I will send you the prophet Elijah before the day of the Lord comes, great and terrible. He will turn the hearts of parents toward their children and the hearts of sons to their fathers, so that I will not come and strike the land with destruction" (Mal 4.1-6).

Malachi's final oracle begins with the arrival of a covenantal messenger who will enter into the temple and into Jerusalem to purify the priesthood. It concludes with the arrival of a messenger associated with the laws of Moses and the presence of Elijah, bearing a vital message of reconciliation that must be heeded in order to avert divine disaster.

This sounds like a close synopsis of the events that begin to unfold following the radiant appearance of Moses and Elijah, with Jesus: setting his face toward Jerusalem, attacking the priesthood, triggering his own day of judgment, and the "curse" which it implied for Israel. The centrality of Malachi to Mark's structure is made evident when the oracle is explicitly brought under exegetical scrutiny after the transfiguration:

> Then they asked him, "Why do the scribes say that Elijah must come first?" He said to them, "Elijah indeed is going first to restore all things. How then is it written about the Son of Man, that he must suffer many things and be despised? But I tell you that Elijah has come, and they did to him whatever they desired, as it is written concerning him" (Mark 9.11-13).

Although Jesus' response—as probably intended—generates more questions than it immediately answers, the exchange of dialogue at least acknowledges the reduplicative nature of Mark's reliance on the last oracle of Malachi, which both opens his gospel and molds his depiction of the transfiguration. Malachi 3.3, for example, imagines the Lord as a fiery refiner and a "launderer's soap" (Mal 3.3-4); during the transfiguration Jesus appears with Moses and Elijah, "and his clothes became dazzling white as no launderer on the earth could bleach them" (Mark 9.3, Mal 3.3).[21]

After the event Jesus' apostles are sure that they have witnessed the fulfillment of things anticipated in Malachi (Mark 9.11), which is the beginning of days of "the messenger of the covenant." According to the prophet, this beginning would climax in a day witnessed by God, in which "once more you will see between the righteous and the wicked, between the one serving God and the one who does not serve him" (Mal 3.18). Hereafter, Jesus' road leads to the cross.

A promise of impending revelation—"There are some standing here who will not taste death until they see the kingdom of God having come with power" (Mark 9.1)—introduces the transfiguration account. In the aftermath of the transfiguration the apostles seem to

---

21 Following the Hebrew, rather than the Greek of the LXX, which reads differently. Malachi 3.2, LXX: "He enters as a fiery furnace and as herbs of cleansing" (αὐτὸς εἰσπορεύεται ὡς πῦρ χωνευτηρίου καὶ ὡς πόα πλυνόντων). The Hebrew manuscript translates, "For he is like the fire of a refiner and like the alkali of the launderers." The Markan detail that Jesus' clothes became white "such as a cloth refiner upon the earth is not able thus to whiten," ("οἷα γναφεὺς ἐπὶ τῆς γῆς οὐ δύναται οὕτως λευκᾶναι," Mark 9.3b) is an image-based parallel, rather than an explicit linguistic replication.

believe they have witnessed just such an event, contrary to a prevailing eschatological doctrine of the scribes, derived from the final oracle of Malachi. This is the same oracle that opened Mark's Gospel, and linked the gospel of Christ to the ministry of John the Baptizer (Mark 1.1-4). Relying thus upon the oracle to inform two different scenes and characters creates an exegetical duality, two different chains of connection which seem to overlap and potentially contradict. The Baptizer seems to be the messenger preparing the Lord's way, whereas Jesus seems to be the messenger of the covenant, approaching the Jerusalem temple: two referent personalities, out of one text.[22]

Mark's transfiguration debrief at least acknowledges this exegetical reduplication; Jesus implies that the activities of John the Baptist did indeed reflect the eschatological arrival of Elijah, and that the scribal expectation of his coming had been fulfilled in the person of John (Mark 9.12-13). In Matthew Jesus defuses the Markan exegetical tension by making explicit the parallel fate of the Son of Man and the Baptist as eschatological messengers: so as to one, so also to the other (Matt 17.11-13). Luke handles the duality differently, but elegantly, simply eliminating the debrief altogether and removing any necessary mention of Malachi.[23]

That the apostles believed themselves to have seen, as Jesus' promised, "the kingdom having come with power," is strongly implied by Peter's befuddled reaction during the transfiguration. His offer to build three tents or booths for the three figures of Jesus, Moses, and Elijah is evocative of the wilderness theophanies of Exodus. The Lord often manifested himself in a cloud to speak with Moses, both at Sinai and in the portable tabernacle that led Israel through the wilderness. This era in Israel's history was annually commemorated by a festival of booth-building (Lev 23.33-35, cf Num 29.12-50, Deut 16.13-17).

---

22 Simon S. Lee notes that this creates the parallel implication that the "Way of the Lord" is his approach to Jerusalem and his passion, and asserts that Malachi 4.4-5, with its mention of Moses and Elijah, is a critical influence upon the composition of the Markan transfiguration; Simon S. Lee, *Jesus' Transfiguration and the Believers' Transformation: A Study of the Transfiguration and Its Development in Early Christian Writings* (Tübingen: Mohr Siebeck, 2009), 16-18.

23 Luke incorporates Malachi's oracle elsewhere, cf Luke 1.17, 7.24-27.

Peter seems to believe he is witnessing events of kingdom-founding magnitude which should be likewise commemorated.[24]

Luke's Gospel further teases the Exodus implications of the transfiguration with the additional detail that Moses and Elijah are consulting with Jesus, "speaking of his exodus which he was about to accomplish at Jerusalem" (Luke 9.31). Luke thereby improves the vital connection between the transfiguration and Christ's passion which, in that gospel, is otherwise strained by a prolonged journey to Jerusalem, one markedly lengthier—or at least containing significantly more detail—than Matthew or Mark.[25]

In Matthew Jesus' face itself becomes radiant during his transfiguration, in parallel to the radiance of Moses' own face during the Sinai theophany (Matt 17.3, Ex 34.29-35).[26] This is consistent with Matthew's portrayal of Jesus in parallel to the lawgiver (cf Matt 5-7). But while the synoptic scene of transfiguration is filled with theophanic allusions specific to Sinai and the Exodus,[27] and also to a wide range of generic theophanic conventions that even non-Jews could recognize,[28] the most important connection back to the figure of Moses

24 John Paul Heil's discussion of Peter's three-tent suggestion registers a variety of possible allusions in combination with multiple Old Testament "tent traditions," most of which have roots in the exodus, John Paul Heil, *The Transfiguration of Jesus: Narrative Meaning and Function of Mark 9:2-8, Matt 17:1-8 and Luke 9.28-36* (Rome: Editrice Pontificio Istituto Biblico, 2000), 115-127.

25 "This is not surprising: not only is this the longest section of the Gospel, but it is also the lead-up to events that Luke sees as historically pivotal. So, while there is apocalyptic discourse, intertwined with intertextual, prophetic allusions in the events surrounding John the Baptist and Jesus, as well as during Jesus' Synoptic, Galilean ministry, Luke seems to regard Jesus' approach to Jerusalem and his time there as the rhetorical forum par excellence for apocalyptic discourse." Gregory L. Bloomquist, "The Intertexture of Lukan Apocalyptic Discourse," in *The Intertexture of Apocalyptic Discourse in the New Testament*, ed. Duane F. Watson (Atlanta: Society of Biblical Literature, 2002), 66.

26 In Luke, Jesus' face does not become radiant, but the appearance of his face does "change" (Luke 9.29). This anticipates his hidden appearance to the disciples on the road to Emmaus (Luke 24.15), and also his change of face as he approaches Jerusalem for the last time (Luke 9.25), and may have a relationship with an older tradition (cf Mark 10.32-34).

27 David M. Miller, "Seeing the Glory, Hearing the Son: The Function of the Wilderness Theophany Narrative in Luke 9.28-36," in *The Catholic Biblical Quarterly* 72 (2010), 498; Candida R. Moss, "The Transfiguration: An Exercise in Markan Accomodation," in *Biblical Interpretation* (Brill) 12, no. 1 (2004), 72-74.

28 Moss, "The Transfiguration," 74-89

is probably made in the two-part declaration of the heavenly voice from the "oracular cloud," identifying Jesus as "My Son"—beloved or chosen, as the synoptic case may be—and instructing the apostles to "Hear him" (Mark 9.10, Matt 17.5, Luke 9.35).[29] This core idea of sonship—a role often assigned to Israel and its monarchs in the Old Testament—seems to generate a complex set of exegetical connections throughout the New Testament, and permits the grouping together and synchronization of various Old Testament passages; passages concerning human identity, divine incarnation, messianic mission, and eschatological election cohere in the figure that is the evangelical Son of Man.[30]

---

29 "However, the overshadowing cloud of the transfiguration functions as an *oracular cloud*. As such, it not only interrupts, in an ironic fashion for the audience, Peter's suggestion to make three tents. It also climactically concludes, by providing the oracular mandate of this pivotal mandatory epiphany, the theme of divine or heavenly communication initiated by the conversation that the transfigured Jesus has with Moses and Elijah." John Paul Heil, *The Transfiguration of Jesus*, 131.

30 There is some evidence that such a reading—with the transfiguration as a scene in which the revelation of Jesus as "the Son" discloses a prophetic personification of Israel—existed within the church near the beginning of the third century. Tertullian's treatment of the event is written as a polemic against Marcionite heresies, and is filled with fascinating idiosyncrasies. He identifies Moses and Elijah, for example, not as icons of heavenly manna or as representations of the law and the prophets, but as the two olive trees and branches in Zechariah (*Against Marcion*, 4.22, cf Rev 11). But he is consistent in appealing to a wide array of Jewish sources, dealing with the figure of "the Son" in reference to the utterance of the heavenly voice, associating Jesus with the messianic son of the psalms and the chosen Son of Isaiah. Much like the contemporary exegetes of today, Tertullian is careful to read the transfiguration against a host of Old Testament references, to point out its similarities to the exodus theophanies, to recall the promise of Deuteronomy that God would one day raise up a prophet like as to Moses—but at the heart of Tertullian's exegetical engagement with the synoptic transfiguration is Christ as a personification of Israel. Transitioning from a discussion of Moses' departure during the Lukan transfiguration and moving into the moment of revelatory disclosure, he writes:

> And with this glory [Moses] went away enlightened from Christ, just as he used to do from the Creator; as then to dazzle the eyes of the children of Israel, so now to smite those of the blinded Marcion, who has failed to see how this argument also makes against him. I take on myself the character Israel. Let Marcion's Christ stand forth, and exclaim, "O faithless generation! how long shall I be with you? how long shall I suffer you?" He will immediately have to submit to this remonstrance from me: "Whoever you are, O stranger, first tell us who you are, from whom you come, and what right you have over us" (*Against Marcion*, 4.22-23).

In portraying himself as the authentically transfigured Christ—over-against Marcion's heretical reading of the transfiguration—Tertullian represents the event as a fundamental

While Elijah gets explicit mention following Mark's transfiguration, (Mark 9.11-12, cf Matt 17.10-12), his presence during the event and the subsequent discussion draws our attention to an Old Testament passage that mentions Elijah and Moses in the same breath. Both Moses and Elijah, and not Elijah only, loom large on the eschatological horizon in Malachi. The dynamic of their deference to Christ leads John Paul Heil to emphasize the transfiguration as a "pivotal mandatory epiphany," which demonstrates and asserts the superiority of Jesus as a source of eschatological revelation, over-against both Moses and Elijah.[31]

In addition to identifying Jesus as the Son for the benefit of the apostles, the voice issues the command to "Hear him." This is evocative of "Moses's promise that God would raise up from and for the people of Israel a prophet like Moses, so that "you shall listen to him" in Deuteronomy 18.15-18."[32] This passage famously predicts the eventual appearance of a prophet like Moses from among the people of Israel. It also prefaces explicit instructions for distinguishing between true and false prophets. A prophet's authority is tested against his accuracy: either those who predict things that do not happen should be put to death, or those who predict true things should be heeded and not ignored (Deut 18.19-22). Thus the words of Jesus concerning the Son of Man and his passion—which he begins to deliver just before the account of his transfiguration, and which he revisits immediately thereafter—are emphasized as a test of his prophetic message and identity. The voice on the mountain thunders, "Hear him!" and as Heil writes, "the words of Jesus that the disciples and the audience are

---

affirmation of the Son as a personified Israel. This distinguishes his Christ from Marcion's, which has no substantive, sustaining, or even redemptive connection to the Creator or to the Jewish literature in which that deity is represented, (*Against Marcion*, 4.23). Tertullian's exegesis of the scene rejects the Marcionite impulse to exorcise the presence of the Jewish scriptures out of the gospel(s). His treatment of the transfiguration as a disclosure of Israel in the presence of Moses and Elijah illuminates the event in light of its antecedent sources, condensing a range of complex reference into the single figure of the radiant Christ, the Son, who is Israel embodied—and for Tertullian, it should be no other way. Tertullian, in *The Ante-Nicene Fathers: Latin Christianity: Its Founder, Tertullian*, eds. Alexander Roberts, James Donaldson, and A. Cleveland Coxe (Buffalo: Christian Literature Company, 1885).

31 Heil, *The Transfiguration of Jesus*, 52-73

32 Heil, *The Transfiguration of Jesus*, 166; Tertullian registers the same connection, *Against Marcion* 4.22.

to heed are the words predicting his passion, death, and resurrection, a recurring theme of pivotal significance in each of the Gospel narratives in which the transfiguration occurs."[33]

Following the confession of Peter, Jesus begins to speak about the suffering Son of Man for the first time. Among his disciples, the Son of Man is introduced as a figure that must suffer and die, and then, publically, as a suffering figure who will judge the world "when he comes in the glory of his Father with the holy angels" (Mark 8.31-38). Jesus concludes this two-part doctrinal introduction with a promise that certain someones would soon "see the kingdom of God having come with power" (Mark 9.1). In Matthew and Mark he is careful to reiterate his Son of Man doctrine immediately after Peter, James, and John witness the transfiguration (Mark 9.9-10, Matt 17.9-10).[34]

Christ's betrayal, trial, crucifixion, and resurrection at the end of the gospels confirm, as faithful and true, Jesus' Son-of-Man passion predictions, which lead to and flow out of the transfiguration, sequentially (the Son of Man doctrines begin to appear in conjunction with the transfiguration event, in Mark 8.31, Matt 16.21, Luke 9.21-22) and exegetically (with Jesus consulting the lawgiver and the prophet concerning his own death, as especially in Luke 9.30-31).

Following his resurrection, a review of Jesus' predictions—as mandated in the synoptics (Mark 16.6-8, Matt 28.5-6, Luke 24.5-8)—confirms Christ's passion as the fulfillment of an eschatological schema derived from and fulfilling the law and the prophets. The climactic event of the resurrection confirms the Son-of-Man sayings introduced with the transfiguration, and thereby validates the remaining Son-of-Man assertions. These include declarations of terrestrial and celestial authority (Mark 2.10, cf Matt 9.6, 12.8), as well as oracles of an apocalyptic nature, which seem to predict the destruction of Jerusalem at the hands of the Romans.[35]

---

33 Heil, *The Transfiguration of Jesus*, 73

34 Having removed the post-transfiguration discussion, Luke delays this reiteration until "the next day," after Jesus' subsequent healing of the epileptic boy, Luke 9.37-42, 43-45. Matthew and Mark have parallel sayings in the same sequential placement, Mark 9.30-32, Matthew 17.22-23.

35 "The warnings already mentioned, and those about to be discussed, are manifestly and obviously, within their historical context, warnings about a coming national disaster, involv-

The apocalyptic employment of the Son of Man as an agent of judgment is initially mentioned in Mark just before the transfiguration, and is grounded in the language of crucifixion Jesus first delivered privately to his disciples (Mark 8.31-38). If the formation of the synoptic tradition is influenced in some way by the siege or fall of Jerusalem,[36] the synoptic Son of Man would appear to prefigure the city's impending doom, not only as a divine punishment for the crucifixion of Jesus but as a revelatory confirmation of his Lordship—what his sign predicted has indeed come to pass. This is also consonant with the major synoptic template found in Malachi 3-4, in which the eschatological messenger of the Lord assaults the priesthood and produces a sign of distinction between the righteous and the unrighteous (Mal 4.6). In parallel, the disciples who "heard" Jesus (as emphasized during the transfiguration) are preserved from the judgment that falls so heavily on Jerusalem, by their figurative and literal departure into Galilee (Mark 14.28, 16.7).

As the hub of Mark's Gospel, the middle event of transfiguration sets the stage for Jesus' approach to Jerusalem, his conflict with the temple establishment and Roman authorities, and the events of his passion. Coming immediately after Peter's confession and the formal introduction of the Son of Man, the transfiguration facilitates an evolving exegetical discourse, through which the insight of the audience may develop in tandem with the story, returning—after the resurrection—back to Galilee, where these things first unfolded, where we first saw and heard these things and may now reevaluate them.

But the transfiguration is not only a foreshadowing of the passion and its resurrection, as important as its foreshadowings may be. The transfiguration bears a functional relationship to the first half of the synoptic tradition as well, illuminating not only the death and resurrection of Christ, but also his active ministry, beginning with

ing the destruction by Rome of the nation, the city, and the Temple. The story of judgment and vindication which Jesus told is very much like the story told by the prophet Jeremiah, invoking the categories of cosmic disaster in order to invest the coming socio-political disaster with its full theological significance." Wright, *Jesus and the Victory of God,* 323, cf 354-358, 360-367.

36 Mack, *Myth of Innocence*, 315-316; Joseph B. Tyson, *The New Testament and Early Christianity* (New York: Macmillan Publishing Company, 1984), 158-161.

the event of his baptism, which precipitates a series of enigmatic and unexplained events.[37]

In Mark's Gospel these enigmas begin to unfold immediately, concurrently with Christ's baptism, as Jesus is driven into the wilderness for forty days to contend with the devil, beasts, and angels (Mark 1.12-13). While Matthew and Luke give us vivid accounts of Christ's temptations (Matt 4.1-11, Luke 4.1-13), in Mark the spiritual dynamic his time in the wilderness implies is never made explicit. Instead Jesus simply leaves the wilderness at an appropriate time, though with an unusual message: "And after John was arrested, Jesus went to Galilee, proclaiming the good news of God and saying, "The time is fulfilled and the kingdom of God has come near" (Mark 1.14). Although Jesus attaches to this declaration a call to repent and believe the good news, he does not really explain what he means by the nearness of the kingdom. Neither does he explicate his full meaning when he subsequently identifies himself as the Son of Man, having authority to forgive sins and operate outside normative restrictions (Mark 2.14, 28). These strange sayings leave questions of this identity hanging, pregnant though unspoken, in the air—who exactly is this Son of Man?

Certain actions of Christ before the transfiguration are likewise inexplicable—he displays an unusual impulse toward the type of solitude that marked his time in the wilderness, vanishing from the public eye after prolonged periods of ministerial activity (Mark 1.35-38, 6.45-46, 7.24), and he exhibits an unprecedented level of charismatic power, commanding the weather, walking on water, even raising the dead. At times the audience is tantalized with the implications raised by his many signs. Jesus, for example, chastises his disciples when they receive his spiritual bread literally, even after having twice

37 "In his 1933 article, 'The Transfiguration', J.B. Bernadin made the intriguing suggestion that for Mark the transfiguration was a momentary breakthrough of the pre-existent glory of Christ which was really with him throughout his earthly life, but hidden beneath his outward human form. For Bernadin the transfiguration looks backward in the text, to Jesus' manifestations of power and authoritative teaching, to what Jesus had been and still was, rather than forward to what he would be after the resurrection. Bernadin's argument correctly draws attention to the fact that the transfiguration illuminates the meaning of events earlier, as well as later in the text." Moss, "The Transfiguration," 84.

witnessed his miracles of loaves in the wilderness (Mark 8.14-20). But open confirmation of his messianic secret is withheld until Peter finally identifies his Lord as the Christ (Mark 8.29-30).

While these details may initially seem of tangential connection to the transfiguration, the spectacle upon the mountain is a moment of revelation—not only of divine identity, but of narrative sense—wherein previously perplexing peculiarities in the Markan account are illuminated. In addition to more-fully revealing the Son, the transfiguration confirms the presence of the kingdom of God, "having come with power" before the very eyes of the apostolic trio (Mark 9.1-9), as Jesus declared when he announced at the opening of his ministry that the "kingdom of God is near" (Mark 1.14).[38]

The transfiguration may be further interpreted as a glimpse into the spiritual realm into which Jesus repeatedly retreated, seeking solitude and privacy in his communion with the law and the prophets, elliptically implied when Jesus upbraided his hard-hearted disciples for their obstinate refusal to understand his bread miracles (Mark 8.14-20, cf 6.38-44, 8.1-10). Moses and Elijah are not merely literary symbols artistically representing respective wings of the Jewish canon, though they may serve that function as well; they may also be considered as emblems of manna received out of heaven, as the oracular word that sustains the multitude during its exodus, which is received by the body of Christians through Christ.

Midway through Mark and Matthew—and about a third of the way through Luke—the transfiguration functions as both reveal and twist. The reveal illuminates previously inexplicable behaviors and sayings of Jesus that characterize the preceding portion of the gospel; many of the implications generated by these details are confirmed. At

38 Contra F. F. Bruce: "It cannot be said that the transfiguration was the event which Jesus said would come within the lifetime of some of his hearers; one does not normally use such language to refer to something that is to take place in a week's time." Bruce, *Hard Sayings of the Bible*, 429.

Note: I'm going to go out on a limb here and suggest that the arrival of the kingdom manifested in the transfiguration was an abnormal event justifying an abnormal use of language. Of course Bruce was right to emphasize the fuller arrival of the kingdom after the resurrection, making the kingdom universally accessible, rather than reserved for the inner circle of the apostolic elect, ibid, 429-430.

the same time, the kingdom-founding significance of the transfiguration signals an occasion of exodus-like proportions, injecting new mysteries into the plot, adding to our scope of concern an unexpected eschatological perspective on the fuller identity of the Son of Man. These mysteries, in their turn, receive clarification and confirmation in Jesus' betrayal by Judas, his trial before Israel's leaders, his humiliation before Pilate, his execution by the Romans, his burial by Joseph, his resurrection by God—witnessed to Mary by the Spirit, directing us to Galilee, where first we encountered him.[39]

In Mark, when Judas arrives to betray Jesus into the hands of his rivals, the shame of the moment is illustrated in a most unusual detail: "And a certain young man was following him, being dressed in a linen, and they caught hold of it, but departing he fled naked" (Mark 14.51-52). No explanation is given for this strange snippet. No illumination is offered as to the identity of this young man or the reason for his embarrassment—unless, perhaps, he is the same young man lounging in the tomb during the resurrection, "being dressed in a white robe, sitting on the right."[40] This is the one who first testifies to the resurrection of Jesus, and redirects the memory of his followers to his earlier teachings in Galilee. His identity and presence after the resurrection may be explained in conjunction with Jesus' first Galilean parables, delivered against critics out of Jerusalem (Mark 3.22):

> And having summoned them, in parables he said, "How is Satan able to cast out Satan? And if a kingdom is divided against itself, that kingdom is not able to stand. And if a house is divided against itself, that house will not be able to stand. And if Satan has risen up against himself and has been divided, he is not able to stand, but has come to his end. But no one, having gone into the strong man's house, is able to plunder his property without first binding the strong one—and then he will be able to plunder his house."

39 A very similar circular structure is utilized in John's Gospel, though the middle pivot point of the transfiguration has been removed (cf John 1.35-41, 20.1-2, 11-15).

40 νεανίσκος; Mark 14.51,16.5 are the only times this noun or image is used in Mark's Gospel.

> "Amen, I say to you: All the sins and blasphemies of the sons of men will be forgiven, whatever they may have blasphemed—but whoever blasphemes concerning the holy spirit does not have forgiveness in the age, but is in danger of the judgment." (Because they said, "He has an unclean spirit.") (Mark 3.23-28).

The accusation of the Jerusalem scribes against Jesus at the beginning of Mark's Gospel anticipates, with great irony, the situation of the Jerusalem cult at the end of Mark's Gospel. Having bound and slaughtered the Lord's anointed, and having blasphemed against the Holy Spirit, the temple and its leaders have become a house divided, at war with the one who is actually strong: the Lord. The young man inside the tomb could perhaps be—as some have proposed—the author of the Gospel of Mark appearing as eyewitness to the resurrection in his own story. He could alternatively represent the spirit of holiness which raised Christ from the dead (cf Rom 1.1-6). His shaming at the beginning of Christ's passion—by those who could not recognize him—is the shaming of the very Spirit of God. In Christian estimation, this blasphemy was not forgiven Jerusalem.

7.4 JOHANNINE EXTENSIONS

John's Gospel is a franchise reboot, freely utilizing synoptic content, retooling central characters, shuffling familiar sequences, introducing additional material. There is nothing subtle about this rearrangement of received tradition, and John sends clear, hard-to-miss signals that it is of a different construction than what the evangelists have previously produced. In the synoptics, for example, just before his passion, Jesus confronts the temple establishment during an important religious festival and triggers the final plot against his life (Mark 11.15-18, Matt 21.12-17, Luke 19.45-48). In John, however, this event comes early in the story, and does not lead to his death (John 2.13-25). Instead, his ministry continues for two more years. For an audience familiar with the synoptic trajectory, it should be abundantly clear, very early in John, that this gospel is something a little different.

While the essential shape of the story—with baptism at the beginning and resurrection at the end—remains the same, in John there is no glorious appearing with Moses and Elijah. Yet in its opening passages, there do seem to be definite traces of the transfiguration tradition. In the beginning of John's Gospel is the Word, and the Word is also the Light, and that light comes into this world. The Son thusly incarnated resembles Jesus as he is radiantly changed and clothed in light on the synoptic mountain, together with emblems of manna from heaven, which is God's revelatory word (John 1.1-5, Mark 9.2-8, Deut 8.3). As in 2 Peter 2, Moses and Elijah make no positive appearance with the Lord in the glory he had since the world began, but John includes both eschatological icons in his opening verses just long enough to shove them aside—sure the law came through Moses, but grace and truth come through Jesus Christ (John 1.17); Elijah is similarly reduced (John 1.21).[41]

John is likewise brusque with the synoptic baptismal oracle. Its brief mention feels almost perfunctory and occurs offstage, being vicariously reproduced through the witness of John the Baptist (John 1.32-33). Though the heavenly voice identifying Jesus as "my beloved Son" is not heard in John, the same point is thereby succinctly driven home. There is no ambiguity in the meaning of the event in John: "And I have seen and have testified that this is the Son of God" (John 1.34).[42] But this is not even the primary title thereby given to Christ. In addition to being identified as the Word that is also Light that is also the Son (John 1.1-5, 18), Jesus rapidly accumulates more titles in six additional waves: Lamb of God, Rabbi, Messiah, Jesus (of Joseph) from Nazareth, King of Israel, and last and hardly least, the Son of Man (John 1.29, 38, 41, 45, 49, 51).

Having already reengineered two major evangelical oracles, John adds a third concerning this last, vital identity:

> Nathaniel answered him, "Master, you are the Son of God! You are the king of Israel!" Jesus answered and said to him, "You

41 The role of Elijah and/or Moses as eschatological prophets has been eliminated, or rather, transferred wholly to Jesus (cf John 4.25-26, 6.14-15, 11.25-28).

42 Some Johannine manuscripts read, "the Chosen of God," reflecting the Lukan pronouncement during the transfiguration (John 1.34, Luke 9.35).

> believe because I said to you that I saw you under the fig tree? You will see greater things than these." And he said to him, "Amen, amen, I say to you: you will see heaven opened and the angels of God ascending and descending upon the Son of Man" (John 1.50-51).

The first mystery of Christ in the fourth gospel replicates the experience of Jacob—also known as Israel—when he fell asleep in a peculiar place and saw a vivid vision:

> And he dreamed and—behold!—a stairway resting on earth, the top touching heaven and—behold!—the angels of God going up and going down on it and—behold!—the Lord standing over him.
>
> And he said: "I am the Lord, the God of Abraham your father, and the God of Isaac. The land on which you are lying will I give to you, and to your seed, and your seed will be like the dust of the earth, and you will spread to the west and to the east and to the north and to the south, and in you and in your seed will all the clans of the earth be blessed. And—behold—I am with you and will keep you everywhere you go, and I will bring you again into this land—for I will not leave you until I have finished what I have spoken to you."
>
> And Jacob woke from his sleep and said, "Surely the Lord is in this place, and I did not know." And he was afraid, and said, "This place is dangerous—this is none other but the house of God, and this is the gate of heaven." And Jacob rose up early in the morning, and took the stone that he had put under his head and established it as a memorial stone, and he poured olive oil on top of it (Gen 28.12-18).

Although it has no transfiguration oracle, John's Gospel quickly acknowledges Jesus as the subject of the law and prophets (John 1.41), and even delivers a new saying in which the heavenly spirits of God alight on Jesus the Christ as if he were prototypical Israel. This is,

Christ says, the Son of Man.[43] Early in the gospel, through a conversation with Nathaniel, John explicitly establishes the Son of Man as an icon, title, or referent of more importance in the evangelical telling of Jesus' story than "Rabbi," "Son of God," and "King of Israel" (John 1.49-50). This private apostolic disclosure—this oracle privately delivered by Jesus to the five apostles—helps disciples hermeneutically informed by scripture to identify the Son of Man as a character embodying Israel. Others in John receive no such hermeneutical hint (cf John 12.34).

It seems as if John has disassembled the transfiguration scene, and has reconfigured its major themes and figures so that they perform the same essential function of revelatory disclosure at the opening, rather than the middle, of his gospel. This construction, along with the conscious clustering of so many christological appellatives in its opening episodes, seems to imply that John was produced for an audience that had already been exposed to some form of the synoptic tradition (perhaps Luke, perhaps even Mark or Matthew), or to some similar, early tradition that involved near-identical subjects and topics. It is as if John has seized the reigns of evangelical direction and, in his own gospel vehicle, is steering a disciplined body—such as those we might call disciples—through mainlined synoptic paths, to lead an ever-broadening audience further along.

In comparing John and the synoptics, ties between Luke and John are especially notable. For example, both Luke and John employ the figure of Lazarus so as to illustrate a point about the impending resurrection of Christ (Luke 16.19-31, John 11.1-53, 12.9-11). And there are certain resurrection peculiarities that only Luke and John have in common—particularly, both have two rather than one single heavenly witness at the tomb, and both focus on the wounded hands and feet of the resurrected Lord as a sign of his historical identity (Luke 24.4,

---

43 "The Evangelist adds a saying addressed to all the disciples. Its imagery is complex; Jacob's dream is clearly in the foreground, but there are reminiscences of the baptism of Jesus, possibly of his temptation (see Bammel, 111), and of the eschatological and apocalyptic picture language used of the Son of Man, such as appears in the synoptic Gospels." George Beasley-Murray, *John*, 28.

28-40, John 20.12, 27). But Luke is not the only synoptic gospel with a unique connection to Johannine material.

Mark likewise contains—as does Matthew—the account of Jesus walking on the water (Mark 6.45-52, Matt 14.22-23). This is notably absent in Luke, and yet is present and even structurally central in John (John 6.15-21, cf 4.9-15, 5.2-9). Clearly John is at least aware of traditions Luke did not retain, of which Matthew and Mark were also aware.

Of special note, the solitary witness inside the empty tomb in Matthew and Mark is not simply deleted and replaced—following Luke—by a two-witness construction. Instead, it seems John has protected this anonymous witness by relocating him, while expanding his character profile; the Markan νεανίσκος becomes the Johannine παράκλητος.[44] In Mark he is the first witness inside the tomb, and first affirms the resurrection, and first directs us back to Galilee (Mark 16.6-7, cf Luke 24.4-7). In John he is "the holy spirit whom the Father will send in my name, that one will teach you everything, and remind you of all that I said to you" (John 14.26, cf 15.26). This is the spiritual being that will empower and educate the church, but only after Christ's departure; the story must be finished before it can be told (John 16.7).

There are other various developments. For example, we know that in Mark Jesus chides his disciples for misreading an allegorical warning involving bread despite multiple demonstrations (Mark 8.14-21). This open-ended scolding receives implicit resolution at the transfiguration, where Jesus appears with Moses and Elijah and glows with power from another plane as he prepares to approach his passion—now we know where Jesus gets his fuel from (Mark 9.2-8). Although John has completely reconfigured the transfiguration, he still consciously broaches the same subject of spiritual sustenance when he says, "My food is to do the will of the one sending me, and to finish his work" (John 4.31-34). Similarly, though the Petrine confession of Christ's identity has been eliminated in the Johannine gospel, the Johannine author finds a blunt

44 Mark 14.51, 16.5, translated "young man" or "youth;" John 14.26, 15.26, 16.7, translated variously, "helper," "comforter," "advocate."

way to confirm the same sentiment (Mark 8.27-30, Matt 16.13-20, Luke 9.18-20, John 4.25-26, cf 6.68-69).

An important (and exceedingly obvious) Johannine development is the high styling of its evangelical rhetoric. While mechanically its language is relatively simple and straightforward, metaphor and allegory saturate the fourth gospel beyond the frequently subtle allusions of the synoptics. The presence of this symbolic dynamic in the text is emphasized in its central images. In John, the distinction between those who understand and those who do not is demonstrated in an emphatic, persistent contrast between light and dark. In its opening lines, John associates the Word of God with both life and light, "and the light shines in the darkness, and the darkness did not apprehend it" (John 1.5). In the Johannine beginning, light and darkness allegorically juxtapose opposing states of christological comprehension.

Following its magnificent introduction (John 1.1-18), the Gospel of John contains a steady series of oracular perplexities—the early Son-of-Man oracle is followed by a miracle at a wedding is followed by a symbolic saying about an embodied temple is followed by a riddle about baptism and snakes is followed by a conversation about living water is followed by a miracle at a pool of moving water is followed by a discourse about the Father and the Son is followed by miracles of wilderness-feeding and water-walking is followed by a feast-day revelation is followed by a discussion about true Jewish identity is followed by miraculous restoration of sight is followed by a parable about a good shepherd is followed by a resurrection is followed by the return of the king—and that's just the first third of John.[45]

At every step of the way multiple meanings are intimated, most of which elude the onstage Johannine audience. Jesus, for example, challenges Nicodemus with a basic puzzle straight from scripture, and mocks him as a so-called "master of Israel" when he fails to appreciate the reference (John 3.7-13, Ecc 11.5-6). But the evangelical audience of this exchange may (come to) understand that Jesus has creatively engaged the existentialist Preacher, and has thereby explained the complexities of spiritual inception by way of natural parallel. As an

45 John 1-12; this is an incidental summary, not an exhaustive description.

exegetical puzzle, the oracle functions as an inside reference, creating a bond of privilege between Jesus and the Johannine audience, from which Nicodemus—fixed within the scene—is perpetually excluded.

Inside references are, of course, both acknowledged and employed in the synoptic tradition—the parable of the Sower and the Seed, for example, seems to imply that there are some doctrines that only some, and not all, are meant or able to fully appreciate (Mark 4.3-20).[46] But in the synoptics, many meaningful implications are precisely that: implicit. You do not need to know Psalm 22, for example, to appreciate the Markan crucifixion of Jesus—but it helps. In John, however, the presence of multiple meanings in a given incident or figure or saying is a critical feature that is emphatically acknowledged. Jesus himself explicitly encourages the detection and pursuit of those latent implications that lie beneath the surface of the text (John 7.24, 8.15-16), and John further makes a sharp distinction between those who are and are not able to grasp Jesus' higher truths (cf John 8.40, 18.38).

In John, images of light and darkness function as categories of division between those who have a proper sensitivity to, or understanding of, the gospel of Jesus Christ, and those who do not. This is probably best demonstrated in the notable healing of a Johannine blind man (John 9.1-8). This miracle is a high-caliber irony, taking place right after Jesus reveals himself as the light of the world to the elders and priests of Jerusalem and is rejected (John 7-8, 8.12, cf Isa 9.2). Following the miracle, the blind man who once sat in darkness correctly identifies Jesus as the Son of Man (John 9.24-38, cf 8.12), whereas the Pharisees cannot see or understand just who Jesus really is:

> And Jesus said, "In judgment I came into this world, so that those not seeing might see, and those seeing might become blind." Being with him and having heard this, those of the Pharisees said to him, "Are we blind also?" Jesus said to them,

46 For example, Wright detects certain eschatological dimensions to this parable that only someone familiar with Isaiah's ending would pick up on. Wright, *Jesus and the Victory of God*, 230-231.

"If you were blind you would not have sin—but now that you say, 'We see,' your sin continues" (John 9.39-41).

John juxtaposes the studied ignorance and consequential sin of the Pharisees against the insight of the healed man, and attaches this distinction to an argument about Jesus' identity. Just as the Johannine introduction asserted, the light has come into the world, and the darkness does not understand it. Unlike the Pharisees, however, the audience of John's Gospel has access to privileged information: Jesus is the Word and Beginning and Light and Son (John 1.1-18).[47] These parallels help John's readers in making successful inferences concerning significant implications, which most Johannine figures of authority are not able to do (cf John 7.48). In this way, the fourth gospel teaches Christians to govern the Jewish scriptures through an evangelical set of doctrines revolving around the true identity of Jesus from Nazareth. The essential exegetical function of the synoptics has become an elaborate Johannine art, and John's Revelation is similarly designed to facilitate a deeper uncovering of Christ's identity and mission, through systematic engagement with the Jewish scriptures.[48]

Another important development evidenced in John is summary recapitulation. John 13 introduces the second third of that Gospel, and begins with a poignant description of Jesus' actions right after his

47 This point—that the prologue provides readers with privileged insight—was articulately emphasized by Francis Moloney during a series of lectures which he delivered as a visiting professor at the Dominican School of Theology and Philosophy in the fall of 2012.

48 "Since the nineteenth century, New Testament scholarship has been dominated by approaches that view the text exclusively as text, without reference to the experiences that gave rise to it. Such scholarship emphasizes lexical and grammatical studies, form, redaction, and source criticisms, and historical and sociological analyses of the text. The unspoken assumption is that the New Testament is an artifact of history. Little attempt is made to understand the experience of those who produced it or the influence it continues to exert on those who view it as authoritative… [paragraph] In any age, but especially at its origins, Christianity revolves around the distinctive experience of the person of Jesus Christ, and any study of the New Testament without reference to the experience of Jesus that generated it is inadequate. The New Testament is the early church's considered reflection on the experience of meeting Jesus, the "historical Jesus" of Nazareth and/or the risen Jesus Christ." Bonnie Thurston, "The New Testament in Christian Spirituality" in *The Blackwell Companion to Christian Spirituality* (Oxford: Wiley Blackwell, 2011), 55.

last supper, in language that relates not only the immediate narrative action, but which also summarizes the entire evangelical plot:

> And before the feast of Passover, when Jesus knew that his hour had come, that he should depart out of this world to the Father, having loved his own in the world, he loved them to the end, the devil already putting into the heart of Judas son of Simon Iscariot to betray him.
>
> And during supper, knowing that the Father had given all things into his hands, and that he came from God and was going to God, being raised from supper, removing his garment and having taken a linen cloth, he wrapped himself. Then he poured water into a washbasin and began to wash the disciples' feet, and to wipe them with the towel with which he had been wrapped (John 13.1-5).

Having finished all (but one) of his significant significations, and having withdrawn from public ministry, John's Jesus displays great humbleness in clothing himself and purifying his closest followers as though he were a menial servant. This simple action exemplifies the totality of the incarnation, and it also anticipates the humility of the cross, the way by which Jesus will "depart out of this world to the Father," as has been implied throughout his active ministry (John 1.51, 3.11-13, 14, 6.62, 8.28, 12.23-34, 20.17). The personal agents in the passage, Jesus and Judas, are even carefully associated with opposed spiritual powers, the devil and the Father. This scene, attached to the last supper, marks the beginning of a new section in John's Gospel, and functions as a recapitulative summation of what has already happened, and what is about to happen, and even implies why—God and Satan are at war, and Jesus is the humbly incarnated servant preparing for a covert action intended to overthrow the prevailing powers of the present world order (cf John 12.31, 14.30, 16.11). All this is summarily sketched in a condensed, well-crafted scene.

But the most important development in John is (must be) the increased rhetorical presence of the symbolic Son.

In the synoptic tradition, the Son is a sort of fragmented character with many responsibilities—he is, among many things, a forgiver of sins, Lord of the Sabbath, an apocalyptic judge, the beloved Son, the Davidic Messiah, the Son of God, and also the crucified and resurrected Christ. Many of these roles are illustrated in scenes and pericopes of various structure and function, and may represent distinct layers of early Christian tradition. At the moment of Jesus' transfiguration, all these referents are reduced to the singular, incomparable Son. The transfiguration thus aligns many evangelical Son-of-Man and Son-of-God traditions with a wide range of Jewish scriptures, according to basic principles of rhetorical personification. But this moment of illumination is brief and, for most, blinding, confusing, and disorienting. This mountaintop is too far removed from John's developing audience.

John updates the Son so that he is more accessible; his alternating functions are more-seamlessly integrated into his character profile, so that he appears as a more consistent icon. This is true of the Son of Man specifically—the same Son of Man that appears as Israel is also the manifestation of Israel's judgment, God's apocalyptic guide, Eucharistic food, and crucified Christ (John 1.49-51, 3.13-15, 6.27-62, 8.28, 12.33-34)—and also of the Son generally, as the Son of the Father (John 1.14-18, 3.16-18, 35-36, 5.19-27, 6.40, 8.36, 10.36). Given the explicit nature of the issue in the Johannine text, it seems very likely that one of John's primary goals in writing was to resolve extant synoptic tensions by explicating a rhetorically problematic character, so that an ever-evolving audience might better see his unified, salvific nature (cf John 1.11-14, 1.51, 12.34, 20.30-31).[49]

Probably the most important profile adjustment is the amplification of the Son as divine incarnation. John leaves little room for doubt regarding the full and true identity of Jesus as the human embodiment of God himself. In the synoptics, this conclusion may be implied at certain significant moments, such as when Jesus walks on water, commands the wind and the sea, or is transfigured (Mark

49 This would be true of John's Gospel even if we place its writing after the writing of John's Apocalypse, as some might propose.

4.35-41, 6.45-52, 9.2-8, cf Job 9.1-12, 38.1-18). In John, however, the divine quality of the incarnation is brought into the open for close inspection.

John goes out of his way to emphasize the divine identity of the Son. There are several I AM sayings in John. This too is an originally Markan device (Mark 6.50, 14.62). Often even in the original Greek the meaning of the phrase is ambiguous, and it is further grammatically difficult to render the scene so that most audiences can still appreciate the double entendre; when Jesus asserts that "I AM," the English often reads, "I am he," incidentally suppressing the theological discourse otherwise facilitated through the characters' conversation (cf John 4.25-27). Thankfully, a scene or two makes it hard to miss the wider implications of the phrase. For example, the scene of his arrest demonstrates—almost to the point of caricature—that when Jesus identifies himself thusly, he is presenting a blinding revelation that causes those in darkness to stumble (cf John 1.5, 3.19, 11-9-10, 12.35):

> Having said these things, Jesus went out with his disciples to the other side of the valley of Kedron where was a garden, into which he and his disciples entered. And Judas the Betrayer also knew the place, because many times Jesus was gathered there with his disciples. Then Judas, bringing the cohort and underlings of the high priests and of the Pharisees, came there with lamps and torches and weapons.
>
> Now Jesus, knowing all the things that were coming upon him, went out and said to them, "Whom do you seek?" They answered him, "Jesus of Nazareth." And he said to them, "I AM." And Judas the Betrayer was standing with them. Now when Jesus said to them, "I AM," they went back and fell to the ground. Then he asked them again, "Whom do you seek?" And they said, "Jesus of Nazareth." Jesus answered, I have said to you that I AM (he). If therefore you seek me, let these [my disciples] depart" (John 18.1-8).

In a back-to-back I AM moment, the Greek phrase ἐγω εἰμι (*ego eimi*) is treated in two vividly different ways. When he first utters the expression, it is a declaration of power that forcibly knocks his opponents—led by the Betrayer and representing the conservative Jerusalem establishment—down to the ground. For a moment the Garden of Gethsemane is transformed into an apocalyptic battlefield. Jesus and Judas are agents of eternal light and darkness. I AM is a disclosure of immeasurable weight that crushes the agencies arrayed against the Christ.

But like flipping a switch, Jesus resets the situation, launching his query again. When he gets his answer, he reiterates his reply, but without devastating effect. The force of the disclosure vanishes into the ambiguity of the phrase. In this way, John picks up and expands a critical Markan device, the ambiguous I AM confession of Christ, and also demonstrates the frequent implication of the phrase for those in the audience who might fail to detect its multiple meanings.

Finally, lest there be any doubt left—at all—about the full identity of the one they call Jesus, the conclusion of John includes two sayings in which an assertion of Christ's divinity is difficult to deny. There is, of course, the private resurrection saying delivered to Mary Magdalene, which makes it clear that when the Son talks about his Father, he is talking about the Jewish god (John 20.17). There is also the declaration of the doubtful apostle, when he realizes that the crucified Christ is also the risen Lord: "Thomas answered and said to him, "My Lord and my God!" (John 20.28).

7.5 PAULINE NUTS AND BOLTS

Paul, a prolific rhetorician, was one of the first Christians to carefully portray Christ for a mass audience in a cross-cultural context. The elaborate productions of the four evangelists—Matthew, Mark, Luke, and John—are indebted to his trailblazing work, and are held together by pivotal points therein affirmed:

Paul describes the gospel as a source of a subversive wisdom and power, which confronts the established wisdom and authority of this world.[50]

50 1 Cor 1.20-25, cf Eph 2.1-12; cf Matt 2.1-23, 7.29, 90.6-8, 10.1, 14, 15.1-20, 16.1-11, 21, 17.10, 19.3, 20.18, 21.1-27, 45, 22.15, 34, 41, 23.1-39, 27.1-24, 62-65, 28.1-4, 11-15, Mark 1.22-27, 2.5-11, 3.22-30, 6.14-19, 10.42-43, 12.13-40, 14.53-65, 15.1-5, Luke 5.1-26, 10.25, 11.15, 39-12.6, 13.31, 14.1-6, 23.7-24, 19.45-48, John 1.19-28, 4.1-2, 7.25-26, 47-48, 9.13-

Paul describes the crucified incarnation as humble humiliation for one already equal with God.[51]

Paul describes Christians as heavenly lights shining in this world, and as living sacrifices offered to God.[52]

Paul joins individual believers to the figure of Jesus through the image of the Body of Christ, for the purpose of parallel illustration.[53]

Paul creates a parallel between the prototypical human being and Jesus the Christ, for the same purpose of parallel illustration.[54]

Paul presents the crucified and resurrected Jesus as the eschatological judge over nations and souls.[55]

Paul utilizes images of Israel's exodus to inform the ongoing experience of the church, and—incidentally—portrays the divine agency as destructive influence.[56]

Paul further treats the crucifixion of Christ as the ironic manifestation and fulfillment of the law's inevitable demands.[57]

41, 11.36-57, 12.10, 19, 31, 42, 14.30, 16.11, 17.2, 18.3-14, 19-24, 29-38, 19.6, 15, 21, Rev 1.5-6, 2.26-28, 12.10, 13.2-7, 12, 18.1, 19.16, 20.4-6

51 Php 2.5-11, Eph 1.20-23, 5.8-14, Rom 2.19, 1 Cor 4.5, 2 Cor 4.4; cf Matt 10.32, 11.27, 20.26-28, 27.29, 28.18, Mark 9.12, 10.44-45, Luke 10.22, 22.27, Acts 2.32-36, 8.33, John 1.1-14, 3.35-36, 5.22-29, 10.18, 12.28-32, 13.3-14, 17.1-5, Heb 2.9-18, 5.5-9, 12.2. 1 Pet 2.24, 3.18, 1 John 4.2, 15, Rev 1.4, 3.21, 4.10, 5.12-14, 11.15, 19.16, 20.13

52 Php 2.12-18, Rom 12.1-2, Eph 5.1-2; cf Matt 4.12-17, 5.14-16, Luke 1.76-79, 2.28-32, 8.16-18, 11.33, 16.18, John 1.4-5, 7-9, 3.19-21, 5.35, 8.12, 9.5, 11.9-10, 12.35-36, 46, Acts 13.44-48, 26.15-18, 23, 1 Pet 2.9, 1 John 1.5-7, 2.8-10, Rev 21.23-24, 22.5

53 Rom 7.4-6, 8.10, 12.4-5, Eph 3.6, 4.12, 5.23-33, 1 Cor 10.16-22, 11.23-33, 12.12-31, 2 Cor 4.10, Col 1.15-28; Matt 23.34 26.26, Mark 14.22, Luke 22.19, John 6.35-40, 53-57, Rev 7.4-10, 14-17, 14.1-4, 19.11-16, 20.11-15, 21.9-26

54 Rom 5.12-21, 1 Cor 15.20-22; Matt 17.1-8, Mark 9.2-8, Luke 3.23-38, 9.28-36, Acts 13.38-39, John 1.1-14, 51, 3.16-17, Heb 1.1-14, 12.23, Rev 1.5, 3.14

55 Rom 2.12-16, 14.1-23, 1 Cor 4.3-5, 2 Cor 5.10, 2 Tim 4.1-4, 8; cf Matt 10.15, 11.22-24, 12.41-42, 19.28, Luke 10.14, 31-32, 22.30, John 3.19, 5.22-30, 9.39, 12.31, 47-48, Heb 4.12-16, 12.25-26, Jas 2.12-13, 4.12, 5.9, 1 Pet 2.12, 4.5-6, 17, 2 Pet 2.4, 9, 3.7, 1 John 4.17, Jude 14-15, Rev 17.1, 19.11, 20.4, 12-13

56 1 Cor 3.17, 10.1-12, 15.24-26; cf Matt 10.28, 26.61, 27.40, Mark 1.24, 14.58, 15.29, Luke 4.34, 17.26-30, John 2.19, 3.14-15, Acts 6.14, 13.17-20, 2 Thess 1.9, 2.3, 8, Heb 2.14, 9.22, 10.8, 11.28, Jas 4.12, 1 John 3.8, Jude 5, Rev 9.11-12, 17.8-11

57 Gal 3.10-14, Rom 2.12, 3.19-20, 5.20-21, 6.23, 7.7-25, 1 Cor 15.56; cf John 3.14-15, Heb 9.22, 1 Pet 1.18-201, 3.18, Jas 2.9-11, Rev 9.11-12, 22.3

Paul presents the crucifixion of Christ as the climax of a great, long-developing Mystery which he as an evangelist must deliver to the people.[58]

Paul asserts that there is a coherent, unified spirit animating all of scripture, authoritative over the legalistic letter of the text, being grounded in the superior ministry of Jesus Christ.[59]

Paul notes the removal of the veil that separates God's unmediated revelatory light and the eyes of the people, signifying the full disclosure of his mystery.[60]

Today, Paul is sometimes maligned as a corrupter of an early, pristine, probably preferable, and always hypothetical Christianity. He is, of course, not himself practically perfect in every way—at times, there is a gap between Pauline theory and Pauline practice[61]—but he provides valuable evidence of evangelical continuity, proof that the trends we see developing in the advanced gospel literature of Matthew, Mark, Luke, John, and Revelation are in many ways congruent with the essential traditions of the primitive church.

7.6 THE APOCALYPTIC PORTAL

Within the New Testament canon, apocalypticism is what sets Revelation apart. Other passages, other moments, are of course apocalyptic in tone, oracular in function, mysterious in meaning. But Revelation

58 Rom 10.4-15, 16.25-27, 1 Cor 2.1-16, 4.1-5, 13.2, 14.2, 15.51, Eph 1.8-14, 3.1-13, Col 1.26-27, 2.2, 4.3, 1 Tim 3.9, 16; cf Matt 13.11, 16-17, 35, Mark, 4.11, Luke, 8.10, 10.21-23, 1 Pet 1.10-12, Rev 5.1-5, 10.7

59 2 Cor 3.1-18, 4.3, 13.13, Rom 1.4, 5.5, 9.1, 14.17, 1 Cor 6.19, 12.3, Eph 1.13, 3.5, 4.30, 1 Thess 1.5-6, 2 Tim 1.14, Titus 3.5; cf Matt 3.11, 10.20, 12.32, 28.19, Mark 1.8, 3.29, 13.11, 14.37-39, Luke 3.16, 11.13, 12.10-12, John 1.33, 6.63, 68, 14.26, 15.26, 16.13, 20.22, Acts 1.2, 8, 2.4, 33, 38, 4.31, 11.16, 19.2-6 Heb 9.8, 10.20, 1 Peter 1.12, 3.18, 1 John 2.27, 4.46, Rev 1.4, 10, 2.7, 11, 17, 29, 3.1, 6, 13, 22, 4.2, 5, 5.6, 14.13, 19.10, 22.6, 17

60 2 Cor 3.7-16, Eph 2.13-18; Matt 27.51, Mark 4.22, 15.28, Luke 1.17, 23.45, Acts 9.3, 13.27-29, 26.13, John 1.4-9, 9.39-41, 12.46, 1 Tim 6.16, 2 Tim 1.9-10, Heb 6.19-20, 7.22, 9.3, 10.19-22, 1 John 1.5, Rev 3.7, 4.1, 5.2-9, 11.13-15, 15.5, 20.12, 22.5

61 Cf Rom 1.16, 10.12, 1 Cor 12.13, Gal 3.28, Col 3.11, Phm 4.3, which all mark a radical break from extant social hierarchies, against Eph 5.22-24, 1 Cor 14.34, Col 3.18, 2 Tim 3.6, Acts 16.3, which represent various appeals to existing social hierarchies as a source of relational authority.

is unlike any other canonical New Testament work, being written in an undeniably symbolic or allegorical mode. But at least the consistent method and patterns of John's Revelation suggest that, in many or even most cases, the substantial meaning of each distinct image may be recovered through an appeal to the relevant resources. This is not always the case within the canon but outside of the Apocalypse, wherein the apocalyptic device is otherwise engaged.

Consider again 2 Thessalonians, which addresses some local situation in high apocalyptic style. Unfortunately—because there is no clear appeal to a resource like the Jewish scriptures in its images, and because there is no further record of the historical incident being addressed—it seems impossible to definitively recover the author's specific intentions. And this was perhaps intentional. Sometimes, it is wise to be cautiously ambiguous, even at the risk of being misunderstood. As it stands, the oracle is almost completely closed to outsiders lacking familiarity with the local situation. To lock out those without definite knowledge, and perhaps even to address the situation without perfect knowledge of his own, the author of 2 Thessalonians seems to have relied on intentional, oracular, apocalyptic ambiguity. His deployment of this apocalyptic device represents a clear response to what he perceives as a threat to evangelical, apostolic doctrine (2 Thes 2.1-2, 13-15).

Consider again the apocalyptic tone of 2 Peter, that oracle which contains a transfiguration moment (2 Pet 1.16-19), and also rails hard against false apostles by employing cataclysmic images of primordial judgment extrapolated from Jewish scripture and tradition (2 Pet 1.20-2.22). As with 2 Thessalonians, this polemic is a clear response to a challenge to apostolic doctrine (2 Pet 3.4-18), though in 2 Peter there has been an intentional effort to include relevant Jewish source material (2 Pet 3.1-2). Another important difference between 2 Peter and 2 Thessalonians is that each author is responding to similar but distinct crises. The author of 2 Thessalonians is responding to the claim that the day of the Lord was finished. The author of 2 Peter is responding to the claim that the day of the Lord would never happen (2 Thes 2.2-3, 2 Pet 3.3-4).

Consider now 2 Corinthians 12, wherein Paul—being forced to defend his credentials—alludes to revelations received from the Lord (2 Cor 12.1):

> I know a man in Christ who, fourteen years ago—whether in the body I do not know, or whether out of the body I do not know (God knows)—was caught up to the third heaven. And I know that this man—whether in the body or out of the body I do not know (God knows)—was caught up into paradise and heard things which are not permitted for a man to speak.
>
> On behalf of this man I will boast, but in reference to myself I will not—except in my weaknesses, for if I desire to boast, I would not be a fool, for I would be speaking truth. But I refrain, that no one might ponder more than what he sees in me, or hears from me. And for the greatness of the revelations—so that I should not be exalted—there was given to me a thorn in the flesh, an angel of Satan—so that I should not be exalted (2 Cor 12.1-7a).

Paul's description of secret heavenly revelations sounds very much like what we encounter in Revelation, when the Revelator hears seven secret thunders that he is not yet allowed to openly publish (Rev 10). It is unlikely that Paul is talking about knowledge of John's own charismatic visions, or of some other evangelical Sybil. More likely, he is talking about a particular experience of his own—especially since he goes on to describe a corresponding handicap with which he himself was consequently saddled (2 Cor 12.7-9). But note the ambiguity and surrender of hermeneutical control reflected in Paul's third-person confession. He cannot even confirm the difference between the earthly and heavenly event as he perceived it (2 Cor 12.2-3, cf Acts 9.2-19). All Paul will really let us know—for certain—is that there are truths in heaven that only some have been ordained to receive, and that disclosure of these truths has been expressly forbidden. He has already reluctantly but carefully listed his evangelical credentials (2 Cor 10-11). His visionary admission, filled with careful redundancy, is a further assertion that there are apostolic things indeed undisclosed to his general audience, but known to an elect few. On this point, says Paul, the Corinthian church is simply obligated to trust him, despite his apparent shortcomings (2 Cor 12.10-21). And while he clearly desires their approval and acceptance, Paul elsewhere eschews the verdict of his earthly judges, declares himself responsible to a higher court of authority, and promises that the Lord will "both bring to light the hidden things from darkness, and will manifest the counsels of hearts" (1 Cor 4.2-5, cf 2 Pet 1.19-20, 1 John 1.5-6). Though they may misjudge the evidence, Paul can say no more. Some things will only become clear to his audience over time.

In 2 Corinthians, 2 Peter, and 2 Thessalonians, the respective authors respond to the competing claims of would-be authorities by shifting into apocalyptic rhetoric. In these three moments, contained in what appear to be late or second-wave apostolic works, each writer communicates in multiple rhetorical dimensions, saying some things while carefully leaving out others, in keeping with the common non-disclosure agreements of Hellenistic mystery culture.

This principle of nondisclosure seems to be active in early or first-wave New Testament epistolary literature as well. 1 Peter celebrates the faithfulness of believers who endure hardship without full knowledge of the Lord: "Not having known him, you love him; not seeing him now, you believe in him and rejoice with unfailing and glorious joy" (1 Peter 1.8, cf 9-13). 1 Thessalonians does not want the brethren to be ignorant about those who have "fallen asleep," and paints a picture of Christ's coming in a distinctly oracular mode (1 Thes 4.13, 15). 1 Corinthians defends the evangelical doctrine(s) of resurrection by acknowledging the multiple meanings of important words (like "body"), and then delivers an important "mystery" about what it means to be transformed through resurrection (1 Cor 15.35-51).

Already in the early stages of the evangelical mission, Jewish-Christian writers and preachers were carefully couching sensitive information in oracular, even apocalyptic rhetoric. It is probably important that Paul, in what appears to be his first epistle, is forced to deliver the "Mystery" of the cross for a mystically-minded congregation that is eagerly anticipating the "Revelation of our Lord Jesus Christ" (1 Cor

1.7, 1.17-2.14, cf 2 Pet 1.16-17, 1 John 1.1-2). Christians did not invent religious mysteries. It is precisely because the wider culture is already awash in oracularism that Paul can ask his audience to think of Christian evangelists as "servants of Christ and stewards of God's mysteries" (1 Cor 4.1, cf 2 Pet 1.18, 1 John 1.3-4).[62]

And the New Testament evangelists were not the first Jewish prophets to engage the apocalyptic device, either to reveal or obscure. The book of Daniel stands as the Old Testament prototypical apocalypse, and introduces "one like a son of man," or "one as a son of man," at the height of Daniel's visionary experience (Dan 7.13-14). The precise rendering of the phrase and connotation of the image is still—and perhaps will long remain—the subject of fierce debate, but many have observed that the scene itself bears a strong resemblance to non-Jewish myths involving a younger and an older Canaanite deity, and of gods coming together in victory over primordial disarray, and establishing order in a world of disorder, sometimes represented by the monsters of the deep.[63] The influence of widespread, archetypal combat myths can be seen also in other Old Testament works that celebrate the ascension of God over the chaotic and unpredictable forces of nature.[64] In this way, ancient Jewish writers often laid claim to the stories of their non-Jewish contemporaries, and baptized the

62 Consider the words of Socrates via Plato centuries before the advent of Christianity: "Perhaps the people who direct the religious initiations are not so far from the mark, and all the time there has been an allegorical meaning beneath their doctrine that he who enters the next world uninitiated and unenlightened shall lie in the mire, but he who arrives there purified and enlightened shall dwell among the gods. You know how the initiation practitioners say, 'Many bear the emblems, but the devotees are few'? Well, in my opinion these devotees are simply those who have lived the philosophical life in the right way—a company which, all through my life, I have done my best in every way to join, leaving nothing undone which I could do to attain this end. Whether I was right in this ambition, and whether we have achieved anything, we shall know for certain, if God wills, when we reach the other world, and that, I imagine, will be fairly soon." Plato, *Phaedrus*, 69c-d, in *The Collected Dialogues of Plato Including the Letters*, eds. Edith Hamilton and Huntington Cairns (Princeton: Princeton University Press, 1961), 59.

63 Collins, *Daniel*, 98-104; cf Boyarin, *The Jewish Gospels*, 45-46

64 Gen 1.1-3, 2 Sam 21.1-16, Job 38.1-18, Ps 18.1-18, 29.1-11, 74.12-16, 77.6-20, 104.1-30, 135.1-6, 147.12-20, Pr 8.22-31, Isa 26.20-27.1, 28.1-2, 40.12-23. Not an exhaustive list.

best of their imaginative and artistic traditions into the monotheism championed by the Hebrew canon.[65] [66]

Apocalypticism is vivid in Daniel. But Daniel is not the first visionary to use symbolic stories to change the way his audience perceived reality—this is an old trick of the earlier prophets, those bold seers who stood up to even those kings who claimed divine rights.[67] Such is the case of Nathan the prophet, who—once upon a time in Israel—spun a tale for good King David, about a stolen sheep:[68]

> And the thing was bad, which David did in the eyes of the Lord, and the Lord sent Nathan to David. And he came to him, and said to him, "There were two men in a certain city—one rich, and one poor. And the rich man had very much livestock and cattle, but the poor man had nothing, but for one small lamb that he had purchased. He let her live, and she matured along with him and with his children, and she used to eat from his portion, and drink from his cup, and lie in his lap, for she was like a daughter to him. And a visitor came to the rich man, and

65 Someone will surely say, "But do the Hebrew scriptures always champion monotheism? Are there not passages that imply the existence or presence of multiple gods (cf Ps 82.1), over whom the Jewish god is often supreme? Isn't that henotheism, or even polytheism, rather than monotheism?" Yes, verily. But by the time the Hebrew canon is complete, polytheism and henotheism hath receded, and monotheism hath prevailed. Therefore, be ye silent..

66 For more on the presence and influence of ancient combat myths and motifs in the book of Revelation, see Adela Yarbro Collins, *The Combat Myth in the Book of Revelation* (Missoula: Scholars Press, 1976).

67 "The prophets of Israel and Judah are one of the most amazing groups of individuals in all history. In the midst of the moral desert in which they found themselves, they spoke words the world has never been able to forget. ... The prophets come from all classes. Some are sophisticated, others as plain and natural as the hillsides from which they come. Some hear God roaring like a lion; others hear the divine decree in the ghostly stillness that follows the storm. [paragraph] Yet one thing is common to them all: the conviction that every human being, simply by virtue of his or her humanity, is a child of God and therefore in possession of rights that even kings must respect. The prophets enter the stage of history like a strange, elemental, explosive force. They live in a vaster world than their compatriots, a world in which pomp and ceremony, wealth and splendor count for nothing, where kings seem small and the power of the mighty is as nothing compared with purity, justice, and mercy." Smith, *The World's Religions,* 6054-6064/8303.

68 Huston Smith also examines this incident, with a somewhat different focus, Smith, *The World's Religions*, 5999/8303.

> he was reluctant to take of his own flock or herd and prepare for the traveller who had come to him—so he took the poor man's lamb, and prepared that for the man who had come to him."
>
> And David got really angry with the man, and he said to Nathan, "As the Lord lives, the guy who has done this deserves to die. He will restore the lamb fourfold, because he did this thing, and because he had no pity."
>
> And Nathan said to David, "You are that guy" (2 Sam 11.27b-12.7a).

Of course there is nothing apocalyptic about the story the prophet tells to the king. It is parabolic in nature, but delivered as the recitation of a legal matter, as if Nathan is dutifully reporting the simple, insensitive theft of livestock by some corrupt elitist. David's response reads like a legal verdict of guilt, given in his kingly capacity as judge. When Nathan pulls back the curtain, exposing the symbolic nature of the story and the true situation (2 Sam 12.7b-15), the king's indictment stands as a statement of self-condemnation, foreshadowing God's own eternal judgment against his royal house (2 Sam 12.10). In this way, an early Hebrew prophet uses a symbolic narrative to allegorize concrete events, thereby elevating the perspective of his audience, so that David can understand his past and future in the light of God's revelatory judgment, which Nathan himself received from the Lord. Later prophets—Daniel, of course, and also the evangelist we call John—amplified this parabolic technique by expanding it to cosmological proportions through the apocalyptic genre, allegorizing stories of much greater complexity, and reserving the prophetic reveal for the offstage rather than onstage audience.

While it was by no means alien to the wider culture, the apocalyptic rhetoric employed by the Christian evangelists of the New Testament is developed out of, and grounded in, the Jewish prophetic tradition. While Old Testament systems of oracular delivery of course evolved over time, the function of early parabolic rhetoric and late apocalyptic rhetoric is much the same. The prophets seek to produce fundamental changes in perspective, to reverse dispositions, to adjust inclinations, to bring audiences to a new understanding of themselves, and of the world around them. To do this, they sometimes disclosed or acknowledged—in full or in part—special revelation received from the highest authority. This, too, is a function of John's Revelation, which serves as an apocalyptic portal through which the willing and able may be wholly transported to the celestial sphere.

7.7 THE REVELATION OF JESUS

The Revelator, ostensibly exiled to Patmos for his Christian preaching, tells us that his revelatory experience occurred while he was "in the spirit on the Lord's Day" (Rev 1.9). This could mean, I suppose, that John was in a contemplative mood on a Sunday, and thereupon entered into a mystical trance wherein he saw with some third eye transcendent visions of a catastrophic future. Or, perhaps, it means that what he relates thereafter is an apocalyptic vision of those events which he believes constitute the Day of the Lord—or perhaps it is a little bit of both. But whatever the calendar date, it is upon this occasion that he first hears and sees "one like the Son of Man," standing among seven lamps (Rev 1.12-13).

These seven lamps seem to reference to the menorah, a special type of candle with seven branches associated with the Jerusalem temple (Ex 24.9-10, 1 Kgs 7.23-26, 2 Chr 4.2-6). In the opening sequence of Revelation the lamps function as a symbol of the seven churches and their angels, which are addressed in the subsequent oracles (Rev 1.20, cf Rev 2-3). The Son of Man explains the appearance of these candles as a "mystery," immediately alerting the audience to the symbolic or allegorical nature of the images with which they are soon to be barraged, and further correlating the seven angels of the Asian churches with the seven "spirits of God" before the heavenly throne, and the seven angels of judgment that frequently appear throughout the remainder of the book (Revelation 4.5, 5.6, 8.2, 6, 15.1-8, 16.1, 17.1, 21.9):

> And turning, I saw seven golden lampstands, and in the middle of the lampstands, one like the Son of Man, being clothed in a full robe, and being girded around the chest with a golden belt,

> and his head and hair white as white wool, as snow, and his eyes as a flame of fire, and his feet like finished bronze, as refined in a furnace, and his voice was like the voice of many waters, and in his right hand holding seven stars, and from his mouth was coming a sharp, double-edged sword, and his face was as the sun shining in its strength.
>
> And when I saw him, I fell at his feet like a dead man. And he placed his right hand upon me, saying, "Fear not—I am the first and the last, and the living one. And I was dead, and—behold—I am alive in the ages of the ages, and have the keys of Death and of Hades" (Rev 1.12b-18).

Most of these details are a mash-up of Danielic descriptions. The "one like a Son of Man" makes a famous appearance at the height of Daniel's first major vision; an angelic being dressed in a white robe and golden belt, with a look of lightning, flickering eyes, finely bronzed feet, and a roaring voice shows up a few chapters later; the Revelator's overawed collapse to the ground is very similar to Daniel's own reaction; the Son's comforting words to John are likewise similar to the angel's treatment of Daniel (Dan 7.13, 10.5-12). But not every detail is from Daniel—the seven stars in the Son's hand are unique to the Revelator's experience, being pertinent to his own mysteries; the double-edged sword proceeding from his mouth is evocative of the Servant in Isaiah (Rev 1.20, Isa 49.2, cf Heb 4.12, Rev 2.12, 16, 19.15).

John qualifies his entire revelation by declaring that it was delivered to him by "the angel" or messenger of Jesus (Rev 1.1), and then introduces us to the Son of Man (1.12-18). The only other time one like the Son of Man again clearly manifests in the Apocalypse is at the beginning of an important harvest (Rev 14.14), but the relationship established between the Son of Man and his seven angels in the Mystery of the lamps may be intended to imply the Son's presence and agency throughout Revelation (cf Rev 17.1, 21.9). This incarnated being initiates John into the heavenly mysteries, and holds keys of power, which open and shut the gates of the spiritual realms through which John subsequently passes (Rev 1.17, 20, 3.7-8, 4.1, 9.1, 20.1).

This is similar to what we find in John's Gospel, where the Son of Man serves as apocalyptic revelator, being the heavenly Word descended to the earthly plane, distributing oracular sayings among many that only a few—those willing to accept his claims of authority—are capable of accurately parsing (John 1.1-4, 14, 3.11-15, 6.60-63). A key difference is that, in Revelation, the heavenly Son does not simply manifest within the earthly sphere with important information; he precipitates a spiritual journey, and opens the way of discovery, so that John may ascend to the heavens and see with his own eyes the unveiling of God's Mystery.

Method

A vivid feature of the Apocalypse is the way it incorporates and adapts the works of former Jewish seers, rearranging them according to evangelical sensibilities. Revelation takes freely from primary works like Genesis, Exodus, Leviticus, Numbers, and Deuteronomy, Isaiah, Jeremiah, Lamentations, Ezekiel, Daniel, a host of lesser prophets, and additional books of various types—Job, Psalms, Chronicles, Kings, and so on. This strongly suggests that the Revelator saw his own project as a continuation of the narratives and objectives of the First Testament, that covenant focused on the history and destiny of God's people, Israel. At the same time, it seems abundantly clear that the Revelator's careful work does not rely solely on the ancient Jewish prophets. The story he himself is telling should, of course, be grouped together with the stories of the Old Testament. But it is a story to end all stories, bringing Israel's national expectations to a climax and—in a sense—to a close, while inaugurating a Second Testament, the beginning of a new covenant covering a wider range of peoples.

Another notable aspect of Revelation is its tendency toward subversion and renovation. Few things are entirely original to John's Apocalypse. Cosmic battles, heavenly beings, and cataclysmic portents are oracular tropes that were part and parcel of ancient Mediterranean culture. Many of the Revelator's literary creations look and feel like what we find in so-called "pagan" art and architecture. As master of a demonic horde of locust-like monsters, for example,

Apollyon is a figure that is consonant with Apollo, a Hellenistic deity already associated with locusts.[69] And, as Elisabeth Schüssler Fiorenza notes, the image of a heavenly woman and a baby retreating from a dragon can likewise be found in sources that predate John's Apocalypse;[70] yet the Revelator "reinterprets this international ancient myth in terms of Jewish expectation. His emphasis on the travail of the woman does not derive from the ancient pagan myth but takes inspiration from the Hebrew Bible's image of Israel-Zion in messianic times."[71]

This penchant for taking internationally common images and giving them a Jewish-Christian backstory or connotation is something evidenced also in the Gospel of John. Consider again its notable snake-on-a-stick (John 3.14-15). Many contemporary readers must have originally associated this serpentine symbol with an immensely popular god of healing and medicine called Asclepius—but the author of John represents Christ himself as adopting this sign in order to symbolize his own crucifixion, and attaches this representation to Mosaic tradition. As anyone who has ever decorated a Christmas tree or hidden an Easter egg must know, Christians have been laying claim to the religious traditions of other peoples for a very long time. Perhaps the many close parallels between John's Revelation and its pagan antecedents is one reason that many interpreters have gone far astray in exegeting this very difficult book. For those who fail to detect the scriptural referents buried in the details, the Revelation of Jesus looks like just another apocalypse.

Structure

Further compounding its difficulty, Revelation is the most structurally complex book of the New Testament. It relies upon intratextual

69 cf Barr, *Tales of the End*, 2920/6687; Fiorenza, *Revelation*, 1108/2255

70 "The myth of the queen of heaven with the divine child was internationally known at the time of John. Variations appear in Babylonia, Egypt, Greece, Asia Minor, and especially in the texts about astral religion. Elements of this myth are: the goddess and the divine child, the great red dragon and his enmity to mother and child, and the motif of the protection of mother and child." Fiorenza, *Revelation*, 1243/2255.

71 Fiorenza, *Revelation*, 1250/2255

linguistic and numerical cues to link disjointed sequences, and to unite dispersed narrative groupings. It seems likely that the majority of Revelation's popular audience experienced its distinctive segments as performance pieces, through a scribal rhetorician trained and practiced in the reading and delivery of oracular texts.[72] In such a setting, the detection of these discrete, notable cues would have been vital in reconstructing both sequence and meaning.[73]

Revelation Major (Rev 4-22) is notoriously difficult to break apart into neat sections, precisely because the Revelator has been so careful to intertwine them. But three major sequences may be thusly outlined:

The Heavenly Temple (Revelation 4-9)
The Heavenly War (Revelation 11-20)
The Heavenly City (Revelation 21-22)

It is possible to arrange these three sections in a linear chronology, so that the war in heaven follows the breaking of the seven seals, and so that the arrival of the heavenly city follows the conclusion of the heavenly war:

Heavenly Temple → Heavenly War → Heavenly City

It is also possible to group these three sections as parallel narratives, so that the breaking of the seals is concurrent with stages of the heavenly

72 "Silent reading was virtually unknown in the Greco-Roman world, and written documents were so expensive—and libraries, so rare—that public readings were fairly common. So most people could be expected to be familiar with the scene set by [John's] opening: a rhetor enacts these words in front of an audience already familiar with the major characters." Barr, *Tales of the End*, 1043/6687.

73 "There have been many divergent attempts to discern the structure of Revelation by identifying its major divisions. The difficulty that has been experienced in these attempts results partly from the fact, as Barr puts it, that 'whereas our concern is to divide the book, John's concern was to bind it together'. As we shall see, John has taken considerable care to integrate the various parts of his work into a literary whole. But he has also indicated a clear structure of the kind that is necessary for hearers or readers to find their way through his vision. This structure is intimately connected with the meaning his work conveys, but we must expect it to be signaled by linguistic markers. John, it is important to remember, was writing in the first place for *hearers* (1:3), even though he must also have expected some readers who would study his work at leisure. In a text intended for oral performance the structure must be indicated by clear linguistic markers." Bauckham, *The Climax of Prophecy*, 1-2.

war, and so that the arrival of the heavenly city represents an important moment during the battle. In this reading, the parts concurrently inform one another.[74]

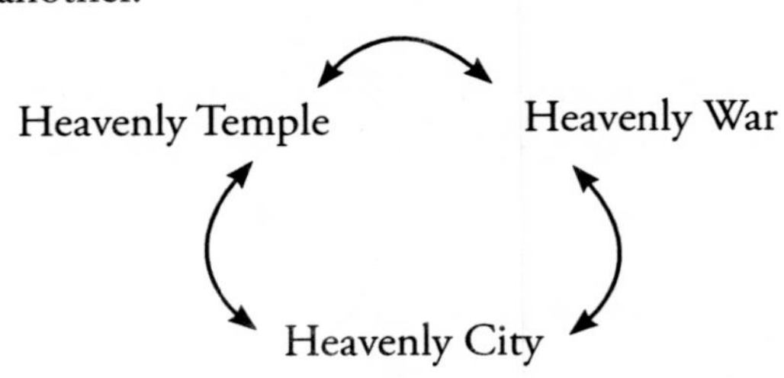

Because the Apocalypse relies upon an implicit christological vision, and places the living audience (the church) inside this active revelation, into the middle of the action, the story is simultaneously ongoing and yet resolved—the thousand years are unfolding, and are leading inevitably to a predetermined end. In this reading, the arrival of the heavenly kingdom on earth is an event that occurs midway through the story, but is not made manifestly obvious until the end.

Audience

Revelation Minor (Rev 1-3) brings specific churches facing specific trials into the ongoing archetypal narrative that unfolds in Revelation Major (Rev 4-22). Its synagogues of Satan, prophets of Balaam, and its Jezebel represent figures or groups known among the churches. While these are typologically sympathetic to the antagonistic forces that confront the heroes and saints of the lamb, they are not the primary subjects of reference in the major archetypal visions which follow. Except for—perhaps—the opening appearance of the Son of Man,[75] the introductory chapters of Revelation Minor could be deleted from the book, and the integrity of Revelation Major would be unharmed. Nevertheless, the opening chapters of the Apocalypse ingeniously draw a wide audience into a higher plane, intensifying

74 Concurrent alignment: Revelation 7.4-11, 11.1-2, 14.1-4, 21.15-17

75 Revelation 1.1-19. This, too, could be deleted, though John's induction into heaven (Revelation 4.1) would thus be more abrupt, a quite dramatic beginning for a three-part mystery performance. In a completely hypothetical reconstruction, Revelation 10 could function as an introduction to some primitive configuration of Revelation Major.

mundane, terrestrial experiences of social conflict through a corresponding reflection of their spiritual realities:

<u>Revelation Minor</u>
Earthly Church
=
<u>Revelation Major</u>
Heavenly Temple
Heavenly Army
Heavenly City

By attaching the experiences of major churches in Asia Minor to the Johannine Apocalypse, the author of Revelation encourages each congregation to see itself as part of a sacred temple, creating an allegorical parallel in which the suffering of the saints is the means by which God's holy house is sanctified. And by placing those saints in parallel with the heavenly armies led by Christ, the Revelator teaches the church to see itself as engaged in spiritual combat, in heavenly warfare fraught with cosmological and eschatological significance. Likewise, in describing the arrival of a city founded on twelve apostles and a lamb, the Revelator teaches the church to see its social hierarchy as a divinely ordered institution.

The final draft of Revelation—the book as we now have it—is clearly intended for mass distribution throughout the churches of Asia Minor. But the church is a big place. Not every Christian is fascinated by symbolic puzzles of indefinite value. Revelation is not for everyone.[76] You do not need to understand its convolutions to be a better person, or even a good saint. The book is designed to appeal to those who are already attracted to the apocalyptic venue, and will not be pleasing to all.

Among those who are indeed willing to engage obscure allegories of uncertain meaning, Revelation is an inexhaustible resource, which may be visited and revisited, discovered and rediscovered from generation to generation, as the customs of the church develop, mature, ossify, decay, and fall away, to be renewed again by those ambitious

---

76 Contra Wright, *Revelation for Everyone.*

leaders and saints who are willing to tackle the hardest sayings of the Good Book.

But of these, only some are adequately equipped. The effective study of Revelation takes determined, consistent, long-term preparation. A reader must thoroughly know the Jewish scriptures if she or he hopes to successfully penetrate the interpretive maze so carefully constructed by the Revelator according to his Christian sensibilities. Today, the Bible is a commonplace staple. Time and technology have granted us lightning-fast access to a canonical library of works that was assembled over thousands of years. In the beginning this was not so. Complete or extensive collections of the Jewish oracles of God were rare by comparison, and costly. It seems unlikely that many such collections would have been accessible beyond the circles of the synagogues, save for what was preserved in the great libraries of the Gentiles and—of course—by Christian saints convinced of their revelatory value. The level of scriptural mastery necessary to adequately handle Revelation represents a lifetime of disciplined study, such as is common in devout households both then and now, which may be alternatively attained—I suppose—through an intense program of studious research.

And of those adequately equipped, some are simply unprepared, being hindered by a natural aggregation of prejudices: methodological partiality, denominational preference, doctrinal preconception. To fully enter into the Revelator's vision, many readers of necessity must set aside traditional eschatologies, christologies, or theologies which they themselves have already inherited, consciously or unconsciously, from their own contexts. It takes a certain determination—or, perhaps, desperation—to launch out into the uncharted waters of the hermeneutical abyss with no clear direction, and no promise of safe passage. It is true that many souls have thus been lost.

But for the willing, equipped, and prepared, there is a way forward, uncertain though it may seem. Much of what was written prior to Revelation—books like Matthew, Mark, and Luke, epistles associated with Peter, Paul, and John—carefully and systematically engage the Jewish scriptures, comparing the events of Jesus' life against the expectations of the Jewish saints, in celebration of the good news confirmed in these ancients. Applying the same basic set of assumptions, methods, and goals of earlier Christian evangelists to the Revelator's work yields abundant fruit. The Apocalypse brings together the archetypal myths of the ancient world, the theological assertions of the Jewish scriptures, and the evangelical declaration of the Christians, producing a vision of multicultural monotheism that, to this very day, remains open to a range of eschatological and theological interpretation and application, being perpetually relevant to the revolutions of this final age.

Author

> I John, your brother and partner in the suffering and the kingdom and the endurance in Jesus, was on the island called Patmos because of the word of God and the witness of Jesus (Rev 1.9).

That is all the explicit information given to the audience regarding the author, the visionary narrator throughout the Apocalypse. Early Christians knew him as John the Apostle. Our first record of this identification is found in the writings of Justin Martyr, writing roughly seventy years after Revelation was first published in Asia Minor.[77] Many scholars today are skeptical of this connection, and have taken to calling the author of Revelation "John of Patmos." Perhaps the truth lies somewhere in the middle.[78]

---

77 Justin Martyr, *Dialogue with Trypho*, 81. Cf Pagels, who seems to imply that this connection was novel or fictitious based on the prior silence of the historical record, Pagels, *Revelations*, 106.

78 "Western Asia Minor (modern Turkey) was a hub of early Christian social and literary activity... Paul himself spent considerable time in the region (esp. at Ephesus), perhaps several years, and a circle of his followers actively wrote from there to "congregations" or "assemblies" (*ekklesiai;* commonly translated "churches") in the same vicinity, producing the writings we know as the Pastoral Epistles, (1-2 Timothy, Titus), Ephesians, and Colossians. ... Writings attributed to Peter likewise find their home here, in the form of 1 Peter, a "diaspora" (dispersion) letter written to Christians living in Asia, Bithynia, and other provinces of Asia Minor. John, the Jewish prophet of the Apocalypse, communicated his visions regarding the destinies of God's people and Satan's people to congregations in the seven cities of Asia, Ephesus among them. There are also strong traditions that place the Johannine

In reading Revelation, certain characteristics of its primary author(s) are evident:

1. A strong background in oracular Jewish literature, as evidenced by the prolific presence of the scriptures within Revelation.
2. A deeply-committed Christian perspective, as evidenced by his evangelical disposition and his free rearrangement of both Jewish and Gentile material around the gospel of his Lord.
3. Familiarity with some form of what we now call the synoptic gospel, as evidenced by his arrangement of the Apocalypse around three climactic "woes" that correspond to the central narrative pivots of that tradition (Rev 9.11-12, Mark 1.9-13; Rev 11.1-14, Mark 9.1-8; Rev 11.15-18, Mark 15.22-39).
4. Familiarity with the Johannine gospel, as evidenced by close parallel chains of exegetical reference shared between Revelation and John—such as the Destroyer and the serpentine snake that must be uplifted, or the battle of Armageddon and the appearing of one whom they pierced (John 3.14-15, Rev 9.11-12, Num 21.1-9; John 18.30-37, Rev 16.17-18, Zec 12.7-10).

In attempting to identify the authorial origins of Revelation, these factors should be taken into consideration, and narrow the range of candidates considerably. They suggest an apostolic disposition, considerable pastoral and theological experience, and an immense sense of authority. The oldest traditions associating John the Apostle with both John's Gospel and Revelation may indeed be true. But it is doubtful that he worked alone and in a void; no man is an island. It seems likely that the final edition of Revelation is the result of collaborative effort. The sharp difference in language between John's Gospel and John's Apocalypse may suggest that different scribes were involved in each respective production, and that the drafting and revision process was not uniform between the two projects. It could further suggest that John's Gospel, carefully written in common, straightforward Greek, is a work meant for popular access, whereas the idiosyncratic, Hebraic Greek of Revelation could indicate that John's Apocalypse was meant

---

communities—as represented in the Gospel of John and the epistles (1-3 John)—in western Asia Minor." Harland, *Associations, Synagogues, and Congregations*, 1.

for a more specialized, niche consumption, or was crafted to preserve and convey a uniquely Jewish perspective on the universal gospel.

Both major Johannine works show signs of second-wave adaptation: John's Gospel has an epilogical section that addresses the inevitable death of the apostle, rectifying a rumor that Jesus had promised him total immortality (John 21, cf 21.21-24, Mark 9.1); John's Apocalypse has a major prological section that is functionally dependent on what follows (Rev 1-3). These additions may represent updates to original Johannine work, undertaken by scribes, students, or colleagues of John the Apostle, perhaps even previously associated with the production of the original literature under his long-term supervision and instruction. Perhaps they believed that the best way to honor their overseer and guide after his passing was to preserve, update, and circulate his creative, powerful material beyond a privileged Johannine circle. Alternatively, it seems possible that these additions could represent the work of the original author, as he himself prepared to follow his Master into an eternal life in the heavens. In this scenario, Revelation would seem to be his last, great work, released to the church in the final years of his life.[79]

Purpose

The Christian Apocalypse is, obviously, the easiest book of the New Testament to abuse. Its images of bloodshed and its destructive tone have contributed to centuries of church warfare against heathens and infighting with heretics. Multiple readings abound. Never in the history of the church or academy has there been a definite consensus about what the book really means. Great men and women have doubted its value. Its strangeness has left several saints puzzled about its purpose and even its very presence in the canon. Because Revelation is framed as a work of prophecy, many conclude that John the Revelator expected the heavenly warriors of God to sunder the heavens at any moment, achieving absolute victory over the armies of earth through unstoppable divine force.

---

79 The traditional date for John's Revelation is 95 CE. The traditional date for John's death is ca. 100 CE.

This could have been his vision, but if so, it is not without its own irony. It seems likely that God's militant conquering of the unbelievers was a fantasy that many of the earliest Christians were themselves forced to abandon, on the very day that they watched Roman soldiers nail their messiah to a piece of wood. Yet still, militant eschatology persisted in Israel, and—as synoptic Jesus predicted—this culture of resistance against the imperial powers ordained by God led to the catastrophic destruction of Jerusalem. Revelation is written, in large part, as a reaction to that event, and explains the destruction of Israel's great city as the consequence of Zion's great sin against her great king.

Revelation is a conservatory project, showcasing the Jewish temple, priesthood, scriptures, culture, and identity within a definitively Christian frame, for the benefit of a culturally diverse, ideologically sympathetic readership. Like the prophet Ezekiel, John the Revelator extends the legacy of the law and the prophets to a changing audience in changing circumstances. He does not abandon the theological principles which sustained him before the fall of his beloved city, but he does accept the changes which Rome has wrought upon Zion's landscape—old Jerusalem is gone, but New Jerusalem abideth forever.

Revelation is also an evangelical project, making room for both Jews and Gentiles in the kingdom of God, while carefully walling out those unwilling to accept the terms and conditions of the Christian covenant. In some ways, Jerusalem's destruction was a catalyst for this development, speeding the inevitable separation of the young Christian cult from its Jewish progenitor. As Israel's leaders and teachers began to fortify their surviving native culture in the aftermath of the cataclysm of 70 CE, the radical nature of the apostolic proclamation must have been an increasingly vivid contrast against a retrenching Jewish orthodoxy.

The Apocalypse was written as the church was becoming increasingly international, as more and more Gentiles were entering into the Christian social sphere in numbers that threatened to overwhelm the Jewish platform from which the apostles had launched their gospel. Like the later epistle of Peter, the Apocalypse of John draws a border of distinction around the Christian institution—the Jewish saints gathered out of Israel with the lamb in the heavenly temple are the same Jewish saints which boundary and define the sacred city (Rev 7.4, 21.17), which is inhabited by an international body (Rev 7.9, 21.24). Though it houses a Gentile majority, the Christian establishment is, in the Revelator's presentation, undeniably and irreversibly Jewish in structure, presciently anticipating the anti-Semitic impulse of hostile converts who would attempt to detach the good news of the Christian gospel from its Hebrew roots. Even while advancing the evangelical mission through a popular spiritual medium, the Apocalypse is deeply anchored in Jewish scripture, Jewish history, and Jewish identity. In this way, the Revelator strikes a balance between the traditional devotion of a more-orthodox Judaism and the charismatic mysticism of Hellenistic culture, permitting theological innovation for the sake of Christian evangelization while preempting Gnostic excess and Marcionite hostility.

Finally, as puzzle literature, Revelation is an encrypted vault of core Christian theology, functioning as a complex eschatological support network derived from the Jewish scriptures and sustained by the evangelical spirit. It simultaneously conceals and discloses valuable insight into the hard sayings of the scriptures, New and Old. These answers may be retrieved by those who ask, seek, and knock persistently, those striving to grow in grace and in the knowledge of our Lord Jesus Christ. To facilitate this necessary growth, John the Revelator has presented to the church a Mystery of the highest order.

CONCLUSION

John's Revelation is an allegory of the New Testament, a metaphor for the gospel. It is an extensive series of parable-like episodes. These episodes depict the spiritual reality which generated the earliest Christian movement. Through typologically sympathetic Old Testament symbols and referents, the book of Revelation systematically represents the experiences of Israel, Jesus, and the church as the experiences of a conjoined body, united in God across space and time. This heavenly vision of the gospel is framed as an apocalyptic prophecy, and is presented to the church as a template or guide by which it may understand its history, present situation, and ultimate destiny.

John the Revelator shared a kindred spirit with those Christian preachers who sought to instill in their various audiences a sense of cosmological relevance while relating the astounding story of Jesus' life, death, and resurrection. As with the gospels, the Revelation of John accomplishes this by fundamentally relying upon the sacred scriptures, appealing to Moses, to the prophets, to the historians, to the poets and their psalms.

In this way, the book of Revelation is an Apocalyptic Gospel, utilizing the oracles of God to illuminate the life of Christ.

AFTERWARD

In what has preceded, I have briefly proposed many things that I hope others wiser and more sage-like than myself will take up for further examination. Admittedly, I remain perplexed—and a little unsettled—that I should have to name the obvious: that John's Revelation is a revelation of Christ. Someone, for the love of God, improve upon what I have done, for surely ye may do greater things than these.

Therefore, as ye think on these things, prove everything, hold fast to that which is good, and discard the rest. There is much more which I would like to declare unto you—but the saying is hard, and you cannot bear it now. Already I have said too much, and I have left too much unsaid. In this, I ask you, my brothers and sisters in the academy, to forgive my faults, my most grievous faults, and the sins which I have committed, in what I have herein written, and in what I have herein failed to write.

Brothers and sisters in Christ, do not abandon what you have previously believed for new theories, cleverly devised. This short volume is just a sketch, one I hope may help those who are stuck in rocky or thorny or shallow soil, and are struggling to thrive. It is my sincere prayer that you may herein find what you need for growth, or that you find it elsewhere. But remain in the Lord. As for me and my house, I suppose we shall have to go back to church.

May the grace of our Lord Jesus be with you all.

Amen.

BIBLIOGRAPHY

Aland, Kurt, Matthew Black, Carlo M. Martini, Bruce M. Metzger, Maurice Robinson, and Allen Wikgren. *The Greek New Testament, Fourth Revised Edition (with Morphology).* Logos Edition. Stuttgart: Deutsche Bibelgessellschaft, 1993; 2006.

Aune, David E. *The Influence of Roman Imperial Court Ceremonial on the Apocalypse of John.* Chicago: Chicago Society of Biblical Research, 1983.

—. *The Word Biblical Commentary: Revelation 6-16.* Nashville: Thomas Nelson Publishers, 1998.

Barr, David L., ed. *Reading the Book of Revelation: A Resource for Students.* Vol. 44. Atlanta: Society of Biblical Literature, 2003.

—. *Tales of the End: A Narrative Commentary on the Book of Revelation.* 2nd Kindle Edition. Salem: Polebridge Press, 2012.

—. ed. *The Reality of Apocalypse: Rhetoric and Politics in the Book of Revelation.* Atlanta: Society of Biblical Literature, 2006.

Bauckham, Richard. *The Climax of Prophecy: Studies on the Book of Revelation.* London: T&T Clark: A Continuum Imprint, 1993.

—. *The Theology of the Book of Revelation.* New York: Cambridge University Press, 1993.

Beale, G. K. *The Book of Revelation: A Commentary on the Greek Text.* Logos Edition. Grand Rapids: W.B. Eerdmans; Paternoster Press, 1999.

Beasley-Murray, George. *John.* A Word Biblical Commentary, Vol. 36. Nashville: Thomas Nelson, 2000.

Bloomquist, L. Gregory. *The Intertexture of Apocalyptic Discourse in the New Testament.* Edited by Duane F. Watson. Atlanta: Society of Biblical Literature, 2002.

Blount, Brian K. "The Witness of Active Resistance: The Ethics of Revelation in African American Perspective." In *From Every People and Nation: The Book of Revelation in Intercultural Perspec-*

tive, edited by David M. Rhoads, 471-743/4278. Minneapolis: Fortress Press, 2005.

Borg, Marcus J. *Jesus: Uncovering the Life, Teachings, and Relevance of a Religious Revolutionary.* New York: HarperOne, 2006.

—. *Reading the Bible Again for the First Time: Taking the Bible Seriously but Not Literally.* New York: HarperCollins, 2001.

Boxall, Ian. *The Revelation of Saint John.* London: Continuum, 2006.

Boyarin, Daniel. *The Jewish Gospels: The Story of the Jewish Christ.* New York: The New Press, 2012.

Brenneman, James E. "Debating Ahab: Characterization in Biblical Theology." In *Reading the Hebrew Bible for a New Millennium: Form, Concept, and Theological Perspective*, edited by Kim Wonil et all, 89-107. Harrisburg: Trinity Press International, 2000.

Brown, Francis, Samuel Rolles Driver, and Charles Augustus Briggs. *Enhanced Brown-Driver-Briggs Hebrew and English Lexicon.* Oak Harbor: Logos Research Systems, 2000.

Brown, Raymond E. *The Birth of the Messiah: A Commentary on the Infancy Narratives in the Gospels of Matthew and Luke.* New Haven and London: Yale University Press, 1993.

—. *The Community of the Beloved Disciple.* New York: Paulist Press, 1979.

Caird, G.B. *The Language and Imagery of the Bible.* Philadelphia: The Westminster Press, 1980.

—. *The Revelation of St. John the Divine.* New York and Evanston: Harper & Row, 1966.

Campbell, Stan and James S. Bell Jr. *The Complete Idiot's Guide to the Book of Revelation.* Kindle Edition. Indianapolis: Alpha Books, 2002.

Canty, Aaron. *Light & Glory: The Transfiguration of Christ in Early Francisan and Dominican Theology.* Dexter: The Catholic University of America Press, 2011.

Charles, R. H. "The Letter of Aristeas." In *Apocrypha and Pseudipgrapha of the Old Testament in English*, by R. H. Charles. Oxford: The Clarendon Press, 1913.

Cohn, Norman. *Cosmos, Chaos & the World to Come: The Ancient Roots of Apocalyptic Faith.* Second Edition. New Haven and London: Yale University Press, 1993.

Collins, Adela Yarbro. *Cosmology and Eschatology in Jewish and Christian Apocalypticism.* Leiden: E. J. Brill, 1996.

—. *The Combat Myth in the Book of Revelation.* Missoula: Harvard Theological Review, 1976.

Collins, John J. *Daniel: With an Introduction to Apocalyptic Literature.* Kindle Edition. Edited by Rolf Knierim and Gene M. Tucker. Grand Rapids: William B. Eerdmans Publishing Company, 1984.

—. *Introduction to the Hebrew Bible.* Minneapolis: Fortress Press, 2004.

—. *The Apocalyptic Imagination: An Introduction to Jewish Apocalyptic Literature.* 2nd Kindle Edition. Grand Rapids, Michigan: William B. Eerdmans Publishing Company, 1998.

Crossan, John Dominic. *The Historical Jesus: The Life of a Mediterranean Jewish Peasant.* San Francisco: HarperCollins, 1991.

Daly, Robert J., ed. *Apocalyptic Thought in Early Christianity.* Grand Rapids: Baker Academic, 2009.

Danker, Frederick W. *Jesus and the New Age: A Commentary on St. Luke's Gospel.* Philadelphia: Fortress Press, 1988.

Dodd, Charles H. *According to the Scriptures: The Substructure of New Testament Theology.* Nisbet & Co. LTD, 1952.

—. *Christ and the New Humanity.* Philadelphia: Fortress Press, 1965.

—. *The Apostolic Preaching.* Edinburgh: R & R Clark, LTD, 1951.

—. *The Authority of the Bible.* Fontana Books, 1960.

Edersheim, Alfred. *The Temple, Its Ministry and Services as They Were at the Time of Jesus Christ.* Bellingham: Logos Bible Software, 2003.

Elwell, Walter A., and Barry J. Beitzel. *Baker Encyclopedia of the Bible.* Logos Edition. Grand Rapids: Baker Book House, 1988.

Fiorenza, Elisabeth Schüssler. "Babylon the Great." In *The Reality of Apocalypse: Rhetoric and Politics in the Book of Revelation*, edited by David L. Barr, 243-269. Atlanta: The Society of Biblical Literature, 2006.

—. *Revelation: Vision of a Just World.* Kindle Edition. Edited by Gerhard Krodel. Minneapolis: Fortress Press, 1991.

Frankfurter, David. "The Revelation to John." In *The Jewish Annotated New Testament*, edited by Amy-Jill Levine and Marc Zvi Brettler, 463-498. New York: Oxford University Press, 2011.

Freedman, David Noel, Allen C. Myers, and Astrid B. Beck, ed. *Eerdman's Dictionary of the Bible.* Grand Rapids: W.B. Eerdmans, 2000.

Friedman, Richard Elliot. *The Bible with Sources Revealed: A New View Into the Five Books of Moses.* San Francisco: HarperSanFrancisco, 2003.

Fuller, Reginald H. *The Formation of the Resurrection Narratives.* Tübingen: Fortress Press, 1980.

Gregg, Steve. *Revelation, Four Views: A Parallel Commentary.* Nashville: Thomas Nelson, 1997.

Gruen, Eric S. *Heritage and Hellenism: The Reinvention of Jewish Tradition.* Berkeley and Los Angeles: University of California Press, 1998.

Hadas, Moses. *Aristeas to Philocrates (Letter of Aristeas).* New York: Harper & Brothers, 1951.

Hamilton, Edith and Huntington Cairns. *The Collected Dialogues of Plato Including the Letters.* Princeton: Princeton University Press, 1961.

Hanegraaff, Hank. *The Apocalypse Code.* Nashville: Thomas Nelson, 2007.

Harland, Philip A. *Associations, Synagogues, and Congregations: Claiming a Place in Ancient Mediterranean Society.* Kindle Edition. Minneapolis: Fortress Press, 2003.

Heil, John Paul. *The Transfiguration of Jesus: Narrative Meaning and Function of Mark 9:2-8, Matt 17:1-8 and Luke 9.28-36.* Rome: Editrice Pontificio Istitutio Biblico, 2000.

Hendriksen, William, and Simon J. Kistemaker. *Exposition of the Gospel According to Mark.* New Testament Commentary. Logos Edition. Vol. 10. Grand Rapids: Baker Book House, 1953-2001.

Herrmann, John, and Annewies van den Hoek. "Apocalyptic Themes in the Monumental and Minor Art of Early Christianity." In *Apocalyptic Thought in Early Christianity*, edited by Robert J. Daly, 33-80. Grand Rapids: Baker Academic, 2009.

Hoffman, Matthias Reinhard. *The Destroyer and the Lamb: The Relationship between Angelomorphic Lamb Christology in the Book of Revelation.* Tubingen: Mohr Siebeck, 2005.

Horsley, Richard A. "The Kingdom of God and the Renewal of Israel: Synoptic Gospels, Jesus Movements, and Apocalypticism." In *The Encyclopedia of Apocalypticism: The Origins of Apocalypticism and Judaism in Christianity*, edited by John J. Collins. New York: Continuum, 2000. 303-344.

Josephus, Flavius and William Whiston. *The Works of Josephus: Complete and Unabridged.* Peabody: Hendrickson, 1987.

Juergensmeyer, Mark. *Terror in the Mind of God: The Global Rise of Religious Violence.* Berkeley and Los Angeles; London: University of California Press, 2001.

Kaiser, Walter C. Jr. et all. *Hard Sayings of the Bible.* Downers Grove: InverVarsity Press, 1996.

Kistemaker, Simon J., and William Hendriksen. *Exposition of the Actions of the Apostles.* Grand Rapids: Baker Book House, 1953-2001.

Kraybill, J. Nelson. *Apocalypse and Allegiance: Worship, Politics, and Devotion in the Book of Revelation.* Kindle Edition. Grand Rapids, Michigan: Brazos Press, 2010.

Kromholtz, Bryan. *On the Last Day: The Time of the Resurrection of the Dead According to Thomas Aquinas.* Fribourg: Academic Press Fribourg, 2008.

Kugel, James. *How to Read the Bible: A Guide to Scripture, Then and Now.* Kindle Edition. New York, London, Toronto, Sydney: Free Press, 2007.

LaHaye, Tim, and Jerry B. Jenkins. *Left Behind: A Novel of the Earth's Last Days.* Carol Stream, Illinois: Tyndale, 1995.

Lee, Dorothy. "On the Holy Mountain: The Transfiguration in Scripture and Theology." *Colloquium* 36, no. 2 (2004): 143-159.

—. *Transfiguration.* London: Continuum, 2004.

Lee, Simon S. *Jesus' Transfiguration and the Believers' Transformation: A Study of the Transfiguration and Its Development in Early Christian Writings.* Tübingen: Mohr Siebeck, 2009.

Lindsey, Hal and C.C. Carlson. *The Late Great Planet Earth.* Grand Rapids: Zondervan Publishing House, 1970.

Mack, Burton L. *A Myth of Innocence.* Philedelphia: Fortress Press, 1988.

Mackie, Scott D. "Seeing God in Philo of Alexandria: Means, Methods, and Mysticism." *Journal for the Study of Judaism*, no. 43 (2012): 147-179.

McGinn, Bernard. "Turning Points in Early Christian Apocalypse Exegesis." In *Apocalyptic Thought in Early Christianity*, edited by Robert J. Daly, 81-107. Grand Rapids: Baker Academic, 2009.

McGuckin, John Anthony. *The Transfiguration of Christ in Scripture and Tradition.* Lewiston/Queenston: The Edwin Mellen Press , 1986.

Metzger, Bruce M. *A Textual Commentary on the Greek New Testament, Second Edition, a Companion Volume to the United Bible Societies' Greek New Testament.* London, New York: United Bible Societies, 1994.

—. *Breaking the Code: Understanding the Book of Revelation.* Nashville: Abingdon Press, 1993.

Miller, David M. "Seeing the Glory, Hearing the Son: The Function of the Wilderness Theophany Narrative in Luke 9.28-36." *The Catholic Biblical Quarterly* 72 (2010): 498-517.

Moloney, Francis J. *Sacra Pagina: The Gospel of John.* Edited by Daniel J. Harrington. Vol. 4. Collegeville: The Liturgical Press, 1998.

Moore, Stephen D. *Empire and Apocalypse: Postcolonialism and the New Testament.* Sheffield: Sheffield Phoenix Press, 2006.

Moro, Pamela A., James E. Myers and Artuher C. Lehman, ed. *Magic, Witchcraft, and Religion: An Anthropological Study of the Supernatural.* New York: McGraw-Hill, 2008.

Moss, Candida R. "The Transfiguration: An Exercise in Markan Accomodation." *Biblical Interpretation* (Brill) 12, no. 1 (2004): 69-89.

Moyise, Steve. *The Old Testament in the New: An Introduction.* London and New York: Continuum, 2001.

Nilsson, Martin P. *Greek Folk Religion.* Philadelphia: University of Pennsylvania Press, 1941.

O'Callaghan, Paul. *The Christological Assimilation of the Apocalypse: An Essay on Fundamental Eschatology.* Dublin: Four Courts Press, 2004.

Oropeza, B. J. "Echoes of Isaiah in the Rhetoric of Paul: New Exodus, Wisdom, and the Humility of the Cross in Utopian-Apocalyptic Expecations." In *The Intertexture of Apocalyptic Discourse*, by

Duane F. Watson, 113-136. Atlanta: Society of Biblical Literature, 2002.

Pagels, Elaine. *Revelations: Visions, Prophecy, & Politics in the Book of Revelation.* New York: Viking, 2012.

Pantel, Louise Bruit Zaidman and Pauline Schmitt. *Religion in the Ancient Greek City.* Translated by Paul Cartledge. Cambridge: Cambridge University Press, 1989.

Pippin, Tina. "The Heroine and the Whore: The Apocalypse of John in Feminist Perspective." In *From Every People and Nation: The Book of Revelation in Intercultural Perspective*, edited by David Rhoads. Minneapolis: Fortress Press, 2005.

Plato. *The Collected Dialogues of Plato.* Edited by Edith Hamilton and Huntington Cairns. Princeton: Princeton University Press, 1961-82.

Robbins, Vernon K. "The Intertexture of Apocalyptic Discourse in the Gospel of Mark." In *The Intertexture of Apocalyptic Discourse in the New Testament*, by Duane F. Watson, edited by Christopher R. Matthews, 11-44. Atlanta: Society of Biblical Literature, 2002.

Roberts, Alexander, James Donaldson, and A. Cleveland Coxe. *The Ante-Nicene Fathers: Latin Christianity: Its Founder, Tertullian.* Buffalo: Christian Literature Company, 1885.

—. *The Ante-Nicene Fathers: The Apostolic Fathers with Justin Martyr and Irenaeus.* Logos Edition. Vol. 1. Buffalo: Christian Literature Company, 1885.

Robertson, David. *Word and Meaning in Ancient Alexandria: Theories of Language from Philo to Plotinus.* Hampshire: Ashgate Publishing Company, 2008.

Roetzel, Calvin J. *The World that Shaped the New Testament.* Atlanta: John Knox Press, 1985.

Rowland, Christopher. *The Open Heaven: The Study of Apocalyptic in Judaism and Early Christianity.* London: The Camelot Press Ltd, Southampton, 1982.

Sanders, E. P. and M. Davies. *Studying the Synoptic Gospels.* London: Trinity Press International, 1989.

Satlow, Michael L. "Philo on Human Perfection." *Journal of Theological Studies* (Oxford University Press) 59, no. 2 (October 2008): 500-519.

Sava, A. F. "The Wound in the Side of Christ." *Catholic Biblical Quarterly*, 1960: 343-46.

Schaff, Philip. *A Select Library of the Nicene and Post-Nicene Fathers of the Christian Church, First Series: St. Augustine's City of God and Christian Doctrine.* Edited by Philip Schaff. Vol. 2. Buffalo, New York: Christian Literature Company, 1887.

Scott, Bernard Brandon. *Hear Then the Parable.* Minneapolis: Fortress Press, 1989.

Shipley, Graham. *The Greek World After Alexander: 323-30 BC.* Edited by Fergus Millar. London and New York: Routledge, 2000.

Smith, F. G. *The Revelation Explained: An Exposition, Text by Text, of the Apocalypse of St. John.* Kindle Edition. Edited by Joel Erickson et all. Grand Junction, Michigan, 1906.

Smith, Huston. *The World's Religions, Revised and Updated.* EBook: HarperCollins, 2003.

Smith, Jonathan Z. *Drudgery Divine: On the Comparison of Early Christianities and the Religions of Late Antiquity.* Chicago: The University of Chicago Press, 1990.

Smith, Jonathan Z. "Wisdom and Apocalyptic." In *Visionaries and Their Apocalypses*, edited by Paul D. Hanson, 101-120. London and Philadelphia: Fortress Press, 1983.

Smith, Mark S. *God in Translation: Deities in Cross-Cultural Discourse in the World.* Grand Rapids: Wm. B. Eerdmans Publishing Co., 2010.

Society of Biblical Literature. "Apocalypse: The Morphology of a Genre." Edited by J. J. Collins. *Semeia: An Experimental Journal for Biblical Criticism* (Scholars Press), 1979.

Spence-Jones, H. D. M., ed. *Zechariah: The Pulpit Commentary.* Logos Edition. London; New York: Funk & Wagnalls Company, 1909.

Strong, James. *A Concise Dictionary of the Words in the Greek Testament and the Hebrew Bible.* Logos Edition. Bellingham, WA: Logos Bible Software, 2009.

Swedenborg, Emanuel. *Heaven and Its Wonders and Hell: From Things Heard and Seen.* First published in Latin, London, 1758. Kotch Edition, 1907. Kindle Edition 2012. Ebook: Webber, Theodore D., 1907-2012.

—. *The Apocalypse Revealed: Wherein are Disclosed the Arcana There Foretold, Which Have Hitherto Remained Concealed.* Latin Edition 1766. Kotch Edition 1907. Kindle Edition 2012. Translated by L.H. Tafel and John Whitehead. Vols. 1-3. EBook: Webber, Theodore D., 2012.

Swete, Henry Barclay, ed. *The Apocalypse of John.* 2nd ed. Classic Commentaries on the Greek New Testament. Logos Edition. New York: The Macmillan Company, 1906.

Tarnas, Richard. *The Passion of the Western Mind: Understanding the Ideas That Have Shaped Our World View.* New York: The Random House Publishing Group, 1991.

Tenney, Merril C. *New Testament Survey.* Revised. Edited by Walter M. Dunnett. Grand Rapids: InterVarsity Press, 1953-1961.

Thomas Nelson Publishers. *The Holy Bible: New Revised Standard Version.* Nashville, 1989.

Thurston, Bonnie. "Christian Spirituality in the New Testament." In *The Blackwell Companion to Christian Spirituality*, edited by Arthur Holder. Oxford: Wiley Blackwell, 2011.

Tripolitis, Antonia. *Religions of the Hellenistic-Roman Age.* Kindle Edition. Cambridge: William B. Eerdmans Publishing Company, 2002.

Tyson, Joseph B. *The New Testament and Early Christianity.* New York: Macmillan Publishing Company, 1984.

Van der Merwe, Christo. *The Lexham Hebrew-English Interlinear Bible.* Bellingham: Lexham Press, 2004.

Wainwright, Arthur W. *Mysterious Apocalypse: Interpreting the Book of Revelation.* Nashville: Abingdon Press, 1993.

Wallis, Faith. *Bede: Commentary on Revelation.* Liverpool: Liverpool University Press, 2013.

Walvoord, John F., and Roy B. Zuck, Dallas Theological Seminary. *The Bible Knowledge Commentary: An Exposition of the Scriptures.* Logos Edition. Wheaton: Victor Books, 1985.

Weinrich, William C. *Ancient Christian Commentaries on Scripture: Revelation.* Downers Grove: Intervarsity Press, 2005.

—. *Ancient Christian Texts: Greek Commentaries on Revelation.* Downers Grove: InterVarsity Press, 2011.

—. *Ancient Christian Texts: Latin Commentaries on Revelation.* Downers Grove: InterVarsity Press, 2011.

Wiersbe, Warren W. *The Bible Exposition.* Logos Edition. Wheaton: Victor Books, 1996.

Wood, D. R. W., and I. Howard Marshall, eds. *New Bible Dictionary.* Logos Edition. Leicester, England; Downers Grove, IL: InterVarsity Press, 1996.

Wright, N.T. *Jesus and the Victory of God.* Minneapolis: Fortress Press, 1996.

—. *Revelation for Everyone.* Kindle Edition. Louisville: Westminster John Knox Press, 2011.

—. *The Resurrection of the Son of God.* Minneapolis: Fortress Press, 2003.

Yonge, Charles Duke. *The Works of Philo: Complete and Unabridged.* Peabody: Hendrickson, 1995.

CPSIA information can be obtained
at www.ICGtesting.com
Printed in the USA
FSOW01n1728110516
20213FS